The Complete Zojirushi Rice Cooker Cookbook

250 Classic Recipes Made Easy With Zojirushi Rice Cooker And Modern Techniques For An Unrivaled Cuisine

Amy M. Noel

Introductions

The ideal rice cooker is one that makes the entire procedure so simple that there isn't much time between your desire for a bowl of plump, aromatic grains and lunch. You're halfway to garlicky fried rice, crispy pilaf, or sushi casserole whenever the mood hits. Do you want to prepare delicious rice without a rice cooker, in the oven or on the stove, salty with your own tears? A rice cooker is required for excellent rice. And the greatest rice cooker is the Zojirushi Micom Rice Cooker and Warmer, which our food editors use on a daily basis at Bon Appètit.

Why are Zojirushi rice cookers so good?

Although it isn't the cheapest model on the market, the Zojirushi Micom Rice Cooker and Warmer with a 5.5 cup (cups of uncooked rice) capacity is one of our top selections for a reason. Not only does this Japanese-designed model dependably cook immaculate, ultra fluffy rice, but it also costs less than the brand's higher-end induction model, which is adored by rice connoisseurs everywhere.

So, why do some cookers cost $40 and others cost over $400? The short answer is that less expensive models can only tell you when there is no more water in the cooking pot, whereas higher-end "smart" cookers, such as this one, are equipped with a microcomputer that uses "fuzzy logic" to compensate for human error (for example, if you accidentally added too much liquid to the pot, it can sense that and adjust so your grains don't become mushy).

The simple LCD control screen has a clock and programmable cook settings for each type of rice, such as white or long grain, brown, porridge, and mixed grains, eliminating any guesswork. The broad inner pot effectively distributes heat, guaranteeing that each batch of rice is cooked to perfection. A countdown timer tells you when your rice is done, a delay timer keeps an eye on you in the future, and an automated "keep warm" function keeps your grains warm until you're ready.

The versatility of this rice cooker, however, is what really shines out to us. This isn't a one-time use device: Steam your vegetables in large quantities. Pour the cake batter into the oiled inner pot and use the cake menu option to watch it rise to perfection. Then relax and enjoy how simple it is to clean your rice cooker: wipe off the stainless steel outside, remove and hand wash the inner lid, then toss the dishwasher-safe inner pot into your machine.

TABLE OF CONTENTS

RECIPES

1.CATERPILLAR ROLL

Ingredients (makes 1 roll):

- 1 full sheet nori (seaweed)
- 1-1/4 cup cooked sushi rice
- 1/2 tsp. roasted white sesame seeds
- Cooked eel (defrosted or canned), cut into 3/4" W x 8" L
- 2 cucumber sticks, 1/4" W x 8" L
- 2 imitation crab sticks, about 4" L
- 1/2 avocado

Water for hands:

- 1 cup water
- 1 Tbsp. rice vinegar

Topping (optional):

- 2 stalks chives
- Mayonnaise
- Chili sauce
- For Dipping and Condiments:
- Soy sauce
- Wasabi
- Gari (pickled ginger)

Instructions

1. A bamboo mat is required (makisu).
2. Make sure the bamboo mat is ready. Wrap plastic wrap around the bamboo mat thoroughly on both sides. To wet hands, combine water and rice vinegar in a small basin.
3. Place a nori sheet, shiny side down, horizontally on a cutting board. Step 1: Using the vinegar water from step 1, wet your hands. On top of the nori sheet, equally distribute the sushi rice. Ensure that the entire sheet is covered.
4. Sprinkle the rice with roasted white sesame seeds. Place the nori on the bamboo mat near the bottom edge, sesame side down, with sushi rice and sesame side down.
5. Fill with fillings. Place the eel, cucumber, and imitation crab in the center of the nori, lengthwise.
6. To make sushi into a cylinder, roll up the bamboo mat and press forward. Roll forward after pressing down once at the midway point to ensure all ingredients are in place.
7. Remove the bamboo mat from the roll by pressing it firmly. Remove it from the equation.

8. Cut the avocado into pieces. Remove the avocado's stone and peel it, then arrange the flat side down. Using a thin knife, cut a short way across. Spread avocado slices by gently tapping on the top and elongating the avocado with the side of the knife as a guide. Make sure there's enough avocado on the top of the roll to cover it.
9. Using the side of a knife, transfer avocado slices. Place slices on top of the roll with care.
10. Wrap plastic wrap around the roll. Then cover with the bamboo mat and gently press to cuddle the avocado slices to the roll.
11. Remove the bamboo mat from the plastic wrap and cut it into 8-10 pieces.
12. Transfer to a serving plate after removing the plastic wrap. To complete the caterpillar effect, add an optional topping. Between the first and second portions, add chives as antennae. Make eyes with mayonnaise and chili sauce on the first slice, and color accents on the rest.
13. Soy sauce, wasabi, and gari are served on the side. Enjoy!

2.SHRIMP TEMPURA ROLL

Ingredients (makes 1 roll):

- 1 full sheet nori (seaweed)
- 1-1/4 cup cooked sushi rice
- 3 Tbsp. tenkasu or agedama (crunchy tempura bits)
- 2 tempura shrimps
- 2 cucumber sticks, 1/4" W x 8" L size
- 2 imitation crab sticks, about 4" L
- 1 yamagobo (pickled mountain burdock), about 8" L and 1/4" thick or thinner

Water for hands:

- 1 cup water
- 1 Tbsp. rice vinegar

Topping:

- Eel sauce or teriyaki sauce
- For Dipping and Condiments:
- Soy sauce
- Wasabi
- Gari (pickled ginger)

Instructions

1. A bamboo mat is required (makisu).
2. Make sure the bamboo mat is ready. Wrap plastic wrap around the bamboo mat thoroughly on both sides. To wet hands, combine water and rice vinegar in a small basin.

3. Prepare the nori and rice as directed. Place the nori sheet on a cutting board horizontally, with the shiny side facing down. Step 1: Using the vinegar water from step 1, wet your hands. On top of the nori sheet, equally distribute the sushi rice. Ensure that the entire sheet is covered.

4. Cover the sushi rice with tenkasu and the bamboo mat you created in step 1. To press tenkasu onto the sushi rice, lightly push on the mat.

5. Lay the bamboo mat flat after removing it. Place the nori on the bamboo mat with the tenkasu side facing down and the sushi rice side facing up.

6. Fill with fillings. Place the tempura shrimps lengthwise in the center of the nori, tails protruding from the left and right edges. Place the cucumber, imitation crab, yamagobo, and shrimps in a bowl.

7. To make sushi into a cylinder, roll up the bamboo mat and press forward. Roll forward after pressing down once at the midway point to ensure all ingredients are in place.

8. Remove the bamboo mat from the roll by pressing it firmly. Wrap in plastic wrap and cut into little pieces (usually 8-10 pieces).

9. Transfer to a serving plate after removing the plastic wrap. Eel sauce should be drizzled over the roll.

10. Soy sauce, wasabi, and gari are served on the side. Enjoy!

3. BROWN RICE

Ingredients:

- Short grain brown rice
- Water

Instructions

1. Add the rice to the inner cooking pan using the plastic measuring cup that came with your Zojirushi rice cooker.
2. Fill the pan halfway with cold water and rinse the rice once more to eliminate any debris before draining.
3. If your rice cooker does not have a "BROWN" setting, use the plastic measuring cup used to measure the rice and add 1-1/2 times the amount of water to the rice. (If using a rice cooker without the "BROWN" mode, keep the amount of brown rice to 2/3 of the capacity of the rice cooker to avoid it overflowing.) If you want a softer texture, gradually increase the amount of water.) To guarantee consistent cooking, the rice should be completely soaked and leveled.
4. Place the inner cooking pan in the rice cooker after wiping off any excess water on the outside. Securely close the lid and turn on the rice cooker. If your rice cooker has a "BROWN" setting, select it and hit START. (If you're using a rice cooker that doesn't have a "BROWN" mode, soak the brown rice for 30 minutes before hitting START.)
5. When the brown rice is done cooking, remove the lid and fluff with the nonstick rice spatula before serving.

4.WHITE RICE

Ingredients:

- Short- or medium-grain white rice
- Water

Instructions

1. Using the measuring cup that came with the rice cooker, accurately measure your rice. Fill the cup to the brim with rice, then level it off. Pour the rice into the inner frying pan that has been left empty.
2. Rinse the rice until the water runs clear. Drain the rice grains by gently rubbing them between your palms.
3. Add water to the "WHITE RICE" water level that corresponds to the amount of rice you're cooking (for example, if you're cooking 3 cups of rice, use water level 3 for "WHITE RICE"). To ensure equal cooking, make sure that all of the rice grains are submerged and that the surface of the rice is flat and level.
4. Place the inner cooking pan in the rice cooker after wiping off any excess water from the outside. Press START after selecting the "WHITE RICE" menu choice.
5. Allow 15 minutes for the cooked rice to'rest' once it has finished cooking. You won't have to wait if you use a Micom rice cooker because this is done automatically. To fluff and serve your rice, open the rice cooker and use the special nonstick rice spatula.

5. ARTICHOKE MIXED BROWN RICE

Ingredients (serves 4-6):

- To Cook in the Rice Cooker:
- 2 cups (rice measuring cup) short or medium grain brown rice
- Water to fill to water level 2 for "BROWN RICE," or 3 cups (rice measuring cup)

To Prepare Separately:

- 2 Tbsp. olive oil
- 1/2 medium onion, minced
- 2 (14 oz.) canned artichoke hearts in water, drained and chopped
- 1 tsp. salt
- 1/4 tsp. pepper
- 1 lemon zest
- 2 Tbsp. fresh dill, chopped

Instructions

1. Use the measuring cup that came with your rice cooker to correctly measure the rice. Once the rice has been rinsed, drain it and set it in the inner frying pan. Skip to step 3 if using leftover rice.
2. Water should be added to the "BROWN RICE" water level, or as directed in the ingredients. Use the "BROWN" setting to cook the rice.
3. When the rice cooker's timer goes off, heat a large frying pan over medium high heat, add the olive oil, and sauté until the onion is tender, about 5 minutes.
4. Add the artichokes and cook for another 3 minutes.
5. Mix in the cooked brown rice, salt, pepper, and lemon zest until everything is well combined and heated.
6. Remove the pan from the heat and stir in the dill.
7. Serve and savor at any time of day!

6. ASPARAGUS RICE WITH SEARED SCALLOPS

Ingredients (serves 4-6):

- To Cook in the Rice Cooker:
- 1 cup (rice measuring cup) long grain white rice
- Water to fill to water level 1 for "LONG GRAIN WHITE," or 1-1/4 cups (rice measuring cup)

For Blanching Asparagus:

- 2 quarts water
- 1 Tbsp. salt for blanching water
- 12 oz. fresh asparagus
- 1 clove garlic, peeled
- 1 whole fresh shallot, peeled
- 2 quarts ice water to chill

To Add to Blender:

- 2 Tbsp. whole butter at room temperature
- 1/2 tsp. salt
- Blanching water as needed

To Garnish:

- 1/2 lb. large sea scallops
- 1/2 tsp. salt
- 2 tsp. canola or other neutral flavored vegetable oil

Instructions

1. Use the measuring cup that came with your rice cooker to correctly measure the rice. Once the rice has been rinsed, drain it and set it in the inner frying pan. Fill the container halfway with water for "LONG GRAIN WHITE," or as directed in the ingredients. If available, cook the rice on the "LONG GRAIN WHITE" or "MIXED" option.
2. Blanch the asparagus while the rice is cooking. In a saucepan, bring the water to a boil and add 1 tbsp of salt. Prepare 2 quarts of ice water as well. Remove and discard the hard ends of the asparagus. Remove the asparagus tips, about 2 inches long, and set aside. Remove the remaining stalks off the stalks and chop them into small, even pieces.
3. Blanch the asparagus stalks (but not the tips), garlic, and shallot for 1 minute in boiling water. Remove from the boiling water and immerse in ice water to cool completely.
4. Remove the cold asparagus from the ice water and combine it with salt and softened butter in a blender. Puree until smooth; if necessary, add a tiny bit of the blanching water to aid smooth mixing.
5. With asparagus tips, repeat the blanching and chilling method; keep tips separate for garnishing.

6. In a small sauté pan (6-8" diameter), heat the oil until it is very hot, almost smoking. Season scallops with salt and cook until they are gently browned. Remove the scallops from the pan when they are done.
7. Toss the asparagus tips briskly in the hot pan to cook through.
8. When the rice is done, mix in the asparagus puree carefully.
9. Serve in dishes with scallops and asparagus tips on top of each serving.

7. AVOCADO BOWL WITH YOGURT SAUCE

Ingredients (serves 4):

To Cook in the Rice Cooker:

- 2 cups (rice measuring cup) long grain white rice
- Water to fill to water level 2 for "LONG GRAIN WHITE," or 2-1/2 cups (rice measuring cup)

To Prepare Separately:

- 1-1/2 cups Greek yogurt
- 1/2 tsp. salt
- 1 tsp. honey
- 1 Tbsp. parsley, minced
- 3 ripe avocados, pitted and peeled
- 1 cup heirloom tomatoes, diced

Instructions

1. Use the measuring cup that came with your rice cooker to correctly measure the rice. Once the rice has been rinsed, drain it and set it in the inner frying pan.
2. Fill the container halfway with water for "LONG GRAIN WHITE," or as directed in the ingredients. If available, cook the rice on the "LONG GRAIN WHITE" or "MIXED" option.
3. To make the sauce, combine yogurt, salt, honey, and parsley in a small basin.
4. Avocados should be cut into bite-size pieces.
5. When the rice is done cooking, fluff it lightly with the rice spatula. Top with yogurt sauce, tomatoes, and avocados in individual bowls.
6. Enjoy!

8. BAKED "MAC AND CHEESE" STYLE BROWN RICE

Ingredients (serves 4-6):

To Cook in the Rice Cooker:

- 2 cups (rice measuring cup) short grain brown rice
- Water to fill to water level 2 for "BROWN RICE"

To Prepare Separately:

- 1 cup whole or skim milk
- 1 Tbsp. of corn starch, dissolved in 2 Tbsp. cold milk
- 1/2 cup each grated cheddar, Monterey jack, mozzarella and ricotta cheeses
- 1 tsp. Worcestershire sauce
- 1 pinch ground nutmeg
- 1 pinch ground cayenne or other hot chili powder
- Salt to taste
- 1 cup crushed tomatoes in puree
- 1/2 cup parmesan cheese; grated

Instructions

1. Add the rice to the inner cooking pan using the plastic measuring cup that came with your Zojirushi rice cooker. Fill the pan halfway with cold water and rinse the rice once more to eliminate any debris before draining.
2. Fill the corresponding water level for "BROWN RICE" with water. Use the "BROWN" setting to cook the rice.
3. While the rice is cooking, bring the milk to a boil and thicken it by whisking the starch mixture into the milk while it simmers. Remove the thickened milk from the heat and mix in the cheeses to melt while they are still hot. Season with Worcestershire sauce, nutmeg, cayenne powder, and salt once smooth.
4. When the rice is done, combine it with the heated cheese mixture and pour into a heatproof baking dish.
5. Make small holes in the rice/cheese mixture with a soup spoon at irregular intervals, fill with crushed tomatoes, and smooth over to cover tomatoes. On top, grate some parmesan cheese.
6. Preheat the oven to 425°F and bake until the top is golden brown and bubbling.
7. Serve with a side of green salad.

9. BAKED RICE CASSEROLE WITH ARTICHOKES AND MUSHROOMS

Ingredients (serves 3-4)

To Cook in the Rice Cooker:

- 1-1/2 cups (rice measuring cup) long grain white rice
- Water to fill to water level 1-1/2 for "LONG GRAIN WHITE," or 1-3/4 cups (rice measuring cup)
- 1/2 tsp. salt

To Prepare Separately:

- 1/8 cup olive oil
- 4 oz. fresh white mushrooms, quartered
- 3-4 canned or fresh small artichoke hearts, quartered
- 16 oz. prepared mushroom soup, not condensed
- 1/2 tsp. Worcestershire sauce
- 1/2 cup grated parmesan cheese
- 1/4 cup parsley, chopped
- Ingredients (serves 6-8)

To Cook in the Rice Cooker :

- 3 cups (rice measuring cup) long grain white rice
- Water to fill to water level 3 for "LONG GRAIN WHITE," or 3-3/4 cups (rice measuring cup) water
- 1 tsp. salt

To Prepare Separately :

- 1/4 cup olive oil
- 8 oz. fresh white mushrooms, quartered
- 7-8 canned or fresh small artichoke hearts, quartered
- 32 oz. prepared mushroom soup, not condensed
- 1 tsp. Worcestershire sauce
- 1 cup grated parmesan cheese
- 1/2 cup parsley, chopped

Instructions

1.
    Use the measuring cup that came with your rice cooker to correctly measure the rice. Once the rice has been rinsed, drain it and set it in the inner frying pan.
2. In the inner cooking pan, combine the water and salt, and stir thoroughly with the rice spatula. If available, cook the rice on the "LONG GRAIN WHITE" or "MIXED" option.
3. Prepare the mushroom and artichoke mixture while the rice is cooking. Heat olive oil in a heavy frying pan until it begins to smoke. Add the quartered mushrooms and cook, stirring occasionally to avoid burning, until golden brown and slightly crisp on all sides. Keep heated in a dish.
4. In the same frying pan, cook artichoke hearts until golden brown and crisp. With the mushroom, set aside.
5. Preheat the oven to 425°F when the rice cooker starts counting down to completion.
6. Heat mushroom soup and Worcestershire sauce in a small sauce saucepan over low heat. Take care not to overcook. When it gets too hot, turn it off and keep it warm.
7. Combine parmesan cheese and parsley in a separate bowl.
8. When the rice has done cooking, fluff it lightly using a rice spatula. In a large mixing bowl, combine the mushroom soup and the cream of mushroom soup. Toss the rice with 1/2 of the parmesan cheese and parsley combination, as well as all of the sauteed mushrooms and artichokes. Stir gently to mix and distribute evenly. Fill a big oven-safe casserole or ceramic basin halfway with mixed rice.
9. On top of the prepared casserole, sprinkle the remaining parmesan cheese and parsley mixture. Bake for 15–20 minutes, or until the top of the casserole is golden brown and the mushroom soup is boiling around the edges, in a preheated oven.
10. Remove the dish from the oven and set aside to cool for 5 minutes. Serve the baked casserole right away on heated plates.
11. Enjoy!

10. BAKED RICE "GRATIN"

Ingredients (serves 4-6):

To Cook in the Rice Cooker:

- 3 cups (rice measuring cup) short grain white rice
- Water to fill to water level 3 for "WHITE RICE"
- 1 tsp. salt

To Prepare Separately:

- 1 (24 oz.) can mild flavored cream soup (such as potato, leek or celery), not condensed
- 12 oz. milk
- 1/2 cup parmesan cheese, grated
- 1 Tbsp. extra virgin olive oil
- 1 tsp. salt
- To Top Rice Before Baking:
- 1/4 cup plain breadcrumbs
- 1/4 cup parmesan cheese, grated

Instructions

1. Use the measuring cup that came with your rice cooker to correctly measure the rice. Drain the rice and set it in the inner cooking pan after rinsing it until the water runs clean.
2. In the inner cooking pan, add water to the proper water level for "WHITE RICE," as well as salt, and stir thoroughly with the rice spatula. Use the "WHITE RICE" setting to cook the rice.
3. In a small bowl, combine cream soup, milk, and 1/2 cup parmesan cheese while the rice is cooking.
4. Using a small amount of olive oil, lightly coat the inside of each ovenproof dish. Save the rest for a later date.
5. Preheat the oven to 450°F when the rice cooker starts counting down to completion.
6. Add the cream soup mixture and salt to the cooked rice once it has finished cooking. Using the rice spatula, thoroughly combine the ingredients.
7. Fill each greased dish halfway with the rice mixture. Drizzle the remaining olive oil over the breadcrumbs and parmesan cheese.
8. Preheat the oven to 350°F and bake the plates for 20-30 minutes.
9. Remove each dish from the oven with care. Serve right away and enjoy!

11. BAKED RISOTTO LASAGNA STYLE

Ingredients (serves 4-6)
To Cook in the Rice Cooker:

- 3 cups (rice measuring cup) short grain white rice
- Water to fill to water level 3 for "WHITE RICE"
- 1 tsp. salt

To Prepare Separately:

- 1/2 cup Mozzarella cheese, shredded
- 1/4 cup Parmesan cheese, grated
- 3 Tbsp. plain or Italian style breadcrumbs
- 1 Tbsp. extra virgin olive oil
- 1 (15 oz.) jar Italian style "Four Cheese Sauce"
- 1 (15 oz.) jar Italian style marinara or meat sauce

Instructions

1. Use the measuring cup that came with your rice cooker to correctly measure the rice. Drain the rice and set it in the inner cooking pan after rinsing it until the water runs clean.
2. Using the rice spatula, add water to the proper water level for "WHITE RICE," and stir thoroughly with rice. Use the "WHITE RICE" setting to cook the rice.
3. In a mixing dish, combine Mozzarella cheese, Parmesan cheese, and breadcrumbs.
4. Using a small amount of olive oil, lightly coat the inside of an oven-safe dish. Save the rest for a later date.
5. When the rice is done cooking, add the Italian style "Four Cheese Sauce" to the cooked rice and mix it in evenly with the rice spatula.
6. Preheat the oven to 450 ° Fahrenheit. 1/3 of the mixed rice should be evenly distributed in the greased dish, then 1/3 of the marinara sauce or meat sauce should be evenly distributed over the first layer of rice. Continue until all of the rice and sauce has been consumed. Finally, a coating of marinara or meat sauce should be applied.
7. Drizzle remaining olive oil evenly over the cheese mixture and sprinkle with cheese and breadcrumb mixture from step 3.
8. Bake for 10 to 20 minutes in a preheated oven.
9. When the baking is done, divide the mixture into dishes and serve right away. Enjoy!

12. BEAN ONIGIRI TRIO

Ingredients (makes 6 onigiri):
To Cook in the Rice Cooker:

- 2 cups (rice measuring cup) short or medium grain white rice
- Water to fill to water level 2 for "WHITE RICE"

For Mixing:

- 1/4 cup green peas, frozen
- 1/4 cup edamame, shelled frozen
- 1/4 cup red beans or kidney beans (canned) drain and rinse

For Seasoning Rice:

- 1/2 tsp. salt

For Finishing Touch:

- 1/2 tsp. roasted white sesame seeds

Instructions

1. Use the items mentioned under "To Cook in the Rice Cooker" to make white rice.
2. Prepare the beans while the rice cooks. Boil one cup of water with 1/2 tsp salt in a small saucepan (not in the ingredients). Boil for 3 minutes with frozen green peas. Place green peas in a basin with boiling water and put aside to cool. Boil edamame for 3 minutes and red beans for 30 seconds using the same manner.
3. When the rice is done cooking, move it to a separate bowl, season with 1/2 tsp salt, and fluff gently with a rice spatula. Divide the servings evenly among three bowls, then gently combine the drained green peas, edamame, and red beans in each.
4. Cut a 7 to 8-inch-long piece of plastic wrap and set it in a small basin. Cover the plastic wrap with half of the green pea rice mixture. By lightly squeezing your hands together, gather the plastic wrap over the rice and form a triangle rice ball. The rice ball should be hard enough not to fall apart, yet fluffy enough not to be smashed.
5. Make two of each type of onigiri by repeating step 4.
6. Remove the plastic wrap from the dish. On the red bean onigiri, sprinkle roasted white sesame seeds. Enjoy!

13. BIBIMBAP (KOREAN RICE BOWL)

Ingredients (serves 4):

To Cook in the Rice Cooker:

- 2 cups (rice measuring cup) short or medium grain white rice
- Water to fill to water level 2 for "WHITE RICE"

To Prepare Separately:

- 1 cup daikon radish, julienned
- 1/2 bunch spinach
- 2 cups bean sprouts
- 1 cup carrots, julienned
- 1 tsp. sugar
- 1 Tbsp. vinegar
- 1 tsp. soy sauce
- 2 tsp. dark sesame oil
- 1 tsp. salt
- 2 tsp. vegetable oil
- 8 oz. ground beef

Sauce:

- 1 clove garlic, minced
- 2 tsp. sugar
- 2 tsp. soy sauce
- 2 tsp. dark sesame oil

Toppings:

- 4 eggs
- A handful crushed Korean dry seaweed
- 2 tsp. sesame seeds
- Gochuchang (seasoned red pepper paste) to taste

Instructions

1. Use the measuring cup that came with your rice cooker to correctly measure the rice. Drain the rice and set it in the inner cooking pan after rinsing it until the water runs clean.
2. For "WHITE RICE," add water to the appropriate water level. Use the "REGULAR" (if available) or "WHITE RICE" setting to cook the rice.
3. Prepare the toppings while the rice is cooking. Set aside 1/4 tsp salt, sugar, and vinegar in daikon radish.

4. Prepare the spinach by blanching it. Drain and rinse with cold water before squeezing off excess moisture. Dress with 1/4 tsp. salt, soy sauce, and 1 tsp. sesame oil after cutting into 3 inch long segments.
5. Toss the bean sprouts in boiling water for a few minutes to blanch them. Drain and toss with 1 tsp sesame oil and 1/4 tsp salt.
6. Heat vegetable oil in a frying pan over medium heat and sauté carrots for one minute before seasoning with 1/4 tsp salt. Remove from the equation.
7. Combine all sauce ingredients in a small bowl. Heat a frying pan and saute the ground beef for 3 minutes before adding the sauce and cooking until all of the liquid has been absorbed.
8. Cook four eggs sunny side up in a skillet.
9. When the rice is done cooking, divide it into individual serving bowls. Squeeze the daikon radish to remove any extra liquid. Arrange all of the prepped vegetables and beef on the rice in a radial pattern.
10. On top of each bowl, place one sunny side up egg in the center. Crushed seaweed and sesame seeds are sprinkled on top. Serve with a side of gochuchang.

14. BLACK SESAME CAKE

Ingredients (for NS-VGC05):

- 1/2 cup all purpose flour (sifted)
- 2 large eggs (separate white from yolk)
- 1/4 cup sugar
- 4 Tbsp. ground black sesame seeds
- 2 Tbsp. soy milk
- 1 tsp. sesame oil
- Vanilla extract to taste
- Butter (to coat the inner cooking pan)

Ingredients (for NS-TGC10/NS-TSC10):

- 1 cup all purpose flour (sifted)
- 4 large eggs (separate white from yolk)
- 1/2 cup sugar
- 1/3 cup ground black sesame seeds
- 4 Tbsp. soy milk
- 1/2 Tbsp. sesame oil
- Vanilla extract to taste
- Butter (to coat the inner cooking pan)

Ingredients (for NS-TGC18/NS-TSC18):

- 1-1/3 cups all purpose flour (sifted)

- 6 large eggs (separate white from yolk)
- 3/4 cup sugar
- 2/3 cup ground black sesame seeds
- 1/3 cup soy milk
- 1 Tbsp. sesame oil
- Vanilla extract to taste
- Butter (to coat the inner cooking pan)
- *Ground black sesame seeds may be sold in Asian grocery stores.
- *May substitute black sesame seeds with white sesame seeds.

Instructions

1. Lightly and evenly grease the interior of the inner frying pan with butter.
2. In a mixing basin, beat egg whites until stiff but not separated, gradually adding sugar. Beat in the egg yolks and vanilla essence until thick.
3. With a rubber spatula, combine flour, ground black sesame seeds, and soy milk. Mix in the sesame oil quickly and thoroughly without over-mixing.
4. Pour the batter from step 3 into the greased inner frying pan and tap the pan on the counter to remove any trapped air. Place the pan in the rice cooker and set the setting to "CAKE." The bake time for NS-VGC05 and NS-TGC/TSC10 is 45 minutes, and 65 minutes for NS-TGC/TSC18.
5. When the cake is done baking, remove it from the pan and set it aside to cool.

15. BROWN RICE & BLACK BEAN CRISPS

Ingredients (serves 3-4):
To Cook in the Rice Cooker:

- 1-1/2 cups (rice measuring cup) brown rice
- Water to fill to water level 1.5 for "BROWN RICE"
- 1/2 tsp. salt

To Prepare Separately:

- 1/2 (15 oz.) can black beans, rinsed and drained
- 3 strips cooked bacon, finely chopped
- 1/4 cup gluten free Mexican style tomato salsa
- 1/4 cup green onion, finely chopped
- 1/2 tsp. dried thyme
- Salt, to taste
- 1/2 Tbsp. gluten free canola oil or other neutral flavored oil

Topping (Optional):

- 1 whole egg per cake
- Gluten free ketchup or chili sauce, to taste
- 1/2-1 Tbsp. cilantro, chopped

Ingredients (serves 6-8):
To Cook in the Rice Cooker:

- 3 cups (rice measuring cup) brown rice
- Water to fill to water level 3 for "BROWN RICE"
- 1 tsp. salt

To Prepare Separately:

- 1 (15 oz.) can black beans, rinsed and drained
- 6 strips cooked bacon, finely chopped
- 1/2 cup gluten free Mexican style tomato salsa
- 1/2 cup green onion, finely chopped
- 1 tsp. dried thyme
- Salt, to taste
- 1 Tbsp. gluten free canola oil or other neutral flavored oil

Topping (optional):

- 1 whole egg per cake

- Gluten free ketchup or chili sauce, to taste
- 1-2 Tbsp. cilantro, chopped

Instructions

1. Use the measuring cup that came with your rice cooker to correctly measure the rice. Once the rice has been rinsed, drain it and set it in the inner frying pan. To the inner cooking pan, add water to the proper water level for "BROWN RICE," as well as salt. Then, using the rice spatula, thoroughly mix in the rice. Use the "BROWN" setting to cook the rice.
2. Prepare the other ingredients while the rice is cooking. Combine black beans, bacon, salsa, green onion, thyme, and salt in a large mixing basin.
3. When the rice is done cooking, fluff it lightly with a rice spatula and spread it out on a big platter.
4. When the rice is cool enough to handle, add it to the salsa mixture and knead until all of the ingredients are well incorporated.
5. Make rice cakes with wet hands, about 3 inches wide and 1/2 inch thick, and lay on a big platter. Rice cakes can be produced and stored in the refrigerator for up to 2 days.
6. Heat the oil in a skillet over medium-high heat. When the oil is very hot, gently set the rice cakes in the skillet and turn the heat down to medium. Fry the cakes until they are crisp and heated in the center on both sides. Serve right away.

Optional:

Keep the cakes warm while you prepare the eggs. Place one fried egg on top of each cake, drizzle with ketchup or chili sauce, and top with cilantro.

Enjoy!

16. BROWN RICE AND CHICKPEA SALAD WITH ORANGE AND RED ONION

Ingredients (serves 4-6):
To Cook in the Rice Cooker:

- 1 cup (rice measuring cup) short or medium grain brown rice
- Water to fill to water level 1 for "BROWN RICE"
- 1/4 tsp. salt

To Prepare Separately:

- 1/2 small red onion, thinly sliced
- 1 (7 oz.) canned chickpeas, drained and rinsed
- 8 to 10 oil cured black olives, pitted and chopped
- 2 Tbsp. extra virgin olive oil
- 2 large oranges, sectioned, cut into bite-size pieces
- 2 to 3 Tbsp. squeezed orange juice from sectioned oranges listed above
- 1 tsp. lime juice
- 1/4 cup parsley, chopped
- 1/4 tsp. ground cumin
- 1/8 tsp. ground cayenne pepper
- 1/8 tsp. ground cinnamon

For Garnish:

- Several leaves of tender lettuce such as Bibb or Butter lettuce

Instructions

1. Use the measuring cup that came with your rice cooker to correctly measure the rice. Once the rice has been rinsed, drain it and set it in the inner frying pan.
2. To the inner cooking pan, add water to the proper water level for "BROWN RICE" and salt. Then, using the rice spatula, thoroughly mix in the rice. Use the "BROWN" setting to cook the rice.
3. In a large mixing bowl, combine the remaining ingredients while the rice is cooking. This can be completed several hours ahead of time.
4. When the rice is done cooking, fluff it with a rice spatula and spread it out on a big platter. This can be prepared ahead of time and stored in the refrigerator for up to a day.
5. When the rice has cooled, add the orange and onion combination and gently stir. If you mix the rice too much, it will become gluey.
6. Serve immediately with lettuce leaves as a garnish.

17. BROWN RICE AND TURKEY SLOPPY JOES

Ingredients (serves 6):

To Cook in the Rice Cooker:

- 1 cup (rice measuring cup) short grain brown rice
- Water to fill to water level 1 for "BROWN RICE"

To Prepare Separately:

- 1 Tbsp. olive oil
- 1 medium onion, diced
- 12 oz. lean ground turkey
- Sea salt and freshly ground pepper to taste
- 1 cup ketchup
- 2 Tbsp. yellow mustard
- 1/8 tsp. cayenne pepper
- 2 tsp. brown sugar
- 1 Tbsp. tomato paste
- 1-1/2 tsp. red wine vinegar
- 6 soft sandwich rolls

Instructions

1. Add the rice to the inner cooking pan using the plastic measuring cup that came with your Zojirushi rice cooker. Fill the pan halfway with cold water and rinse the rice once more to eliminate any debris before draining.
2. Fill the corresponding water level for "BROWN RICE" with water. Use the "BROWN" setting to cook the rice.
3. While the rice is cooking, heat olive oil in a heavy-bottomed sauté pan over medium-high heat and sauté onions until transparent, about 2-3 minutes.
4. Season the ground turkey with salt and pepper, then brown it thoroughly, breaking it up with a wooden spoon – about 7-10 minutes.
5. Combine the ketchup, mustard, cayenne pepper, brown sugar, and tomato paste in a mixing bowl. Reduce heat to low and continue to cook for another 10-12 minutes, or until the mixture is thick but not dry.
6. When the brown rice is done cooking, add it to the sauté pan with the turkey mixture and toss to blend. Serve on buns with red wine vinegar and seasonings to taste.

18. BROWN RICE TABBOULEH

Ingredients (serves 3-4):

To Cook in the Rice Cooker:

- 1.5 cups (rice measuring cup) short or medium grain brown rice
- Water to fill to water level 1.5 for "BROWN RICE"
- 1/2 tsp. salt

To Prepare Separately:

- 2 small tomatoes, ripe, cut into small cubes
- 1-1/2 cup European cucumber, cut into small cubes
- 1/8 cup green onion, minced
- 3/4 cup parsley, minced
- 1/8 cup mint leaves, chopped
- 1/8 cup extra virgin olive oil
- 1 Tbsp. lemon juice
- 1 pinch paprika or cayenne powder
- Salt and black pepper to taste

Ingredients (serves 6-8):

To Cook in the Rice Cooker:

- 3 cups (rice measuring cup) short or medium grain brown rice
- Water to fill to water level 3 for "BROWN RICE"
- 1 tsp. salt

To Prepare Separately:

- 3 medium tomatoes, ripe, cut into small cubes
- 3 cups European cucumber, cut into small cubes
- 1/4 cup green onion, minced
- 1-1/2 cups parsley, minced
- 1/4 cup mint leaves, chopped
- 1/4 cup extra virgin olive oil
- 2 Tbsp. lemon juice
- 1 pinch paprika or cayenne powder
- Salt and black pepper to taste

Instructions

1. Use the measuring cup that came with your rice cooker to correctly measure the rice. Once the rice has been rinsed, drain it and set it in the inner frying pan.
2. In the inner cooking pan, add water to the proper water level for "BROWN RICE" and salt. Then, using the rice spatula, thoroughly mix in the rice. Use the "BROWN" setting to cook the rice.
3. When the rice is done cooking, fluff it lightly with a rice spatula and spread it out on a big platter to cool for 30 minutes.
4. In a large mixing bowl, combine the remaining ingredients (except salt and pepper) as the rice cools.
5. When the rice has cooled, add the remaining ingredients and gently stir. If you mix the rice too much, it will become gluey. Season to taste with salt and pepper. Serve right away. Enjoy!

19. BUTTERED LOBSTER RICE

Ingredients (serves 2-3):

To Cook in the Rice Cooker:

- 1 cup (rice measuring cup) long grain white rice
- 1-1/4 cups water
- 1/4 tsp. salt
- 1/2 Tbsp. melted butter
- 1/8 tsp. cayenne pepper

To Prepare Separately:

- 6-8 oz. Maine lobster meat, cooked and removed from shell
- 1 Tbsp. butter
- 1/2 fresh lemon, juiced
- 1/4 cup chopped parsley, loosely packed (reserve 1 Tbsp. for lobster)

Ingredients (serves 4-6):
To Cook in the Rice Cooker:

- 3 cups (rice measuring cup) long grain white rice
- 3-3/4 cups water
- 1/2 tsp. salt
- 1 Tbsp. melted butter
- 1/2 tsp. cayenne pepper
- To Prepare Separately:
- 12-16 oz. Maine lobster meat, cooked and removed from shell

- 2 Tbsp. butter
- 1 fresh lemon, juiced
- 1/2 cup chopped parsley, loosely packed (reserve 2 Tbsp. for lobster)

1. ### *Instructions*

   Use the measuring cup that came with your rice cooker to correctly measure the rice. Once the rice has been rinsed, drain it and set it in the inner frying pan.
2. Using the rice spatula, combine water, salt, melted butter, and cayenne pepper in the inner cooking pan. Use the "MIXED" setting to cook the rice.
3. While the rice is cooking, chop the lobster meat into large bite-sized pieces, place on a microwave-safe plate, and keep at room temperature until the rice is finished. Cook for 15 minutes in boiling water with 2 tbsps of salt if using raw lobster (not included in ingredients list). Transfer the lobster to a microwaveable plate with tongs, remove the shell, and chop into large bite-size pieces.
4. When the rice cooker's timer goes off, melt butter in a sauce pan until just browned, then add lemon juice, stir well, and remove from heat. Set aside 1 tbsp for step 6 for 2-3 servings. Set aside 2 tbsps for step 6 if serving 4-6 people.
5. When the rice has done cooking, fluff it lightly using a rice spatula. Toss in the lemon butter and the remainder of the parsley gently. With salt, adjust the flavor to your liking (not included in the ingredients list).
6. Microwave the lobster meat on high for 30 seconds to warm it up. Using the remaining lemon butter and parsley, coat the lobster meat.
7. Warm rice and heated lobster are served on warm plates.
8. Serve when still hot. Enjoy!

20. CAPRESE RICE SALAD

Ingredients (serves 4-6):
To Cook in the Rice Cooker:

- 2 cups (rice measuring cup) long grain white rice
- 2-1/2 cups (rice measuring cup) water
- 2 fresh basil leaves, whole
- 1 dry bay leaf, whole
- 2 sprigs of fresh thyme leaves, remove from stem
- 1/2 tsp. salt
- 1/8 tsp. black pepper, coarse ground

To Add to Cooked, Cooled Rice:

- 6-8 oz. fresh mozzarella, cut into large bite sized pieces
- 1 cup fresh tomato, chopped
- 1/2 cup pine nuts, slightly toasted
- 1/2 cup kalamata olives, pitted
- 1/4 cup fresh basil leaves, roughly chopped
- 1 Tbsp. extra virgin olive oil
- 1/4 tsp. salt

Instructions

1. Use the measuring cup that came with your rice cooker to correctly measure the rice. Once the rice has been rinsed, drain it and set it in the inner frying pan.
2. Salt and pepper the water in a separate bowl, then pour it into the inner frying pan. On top of the rice, scatter the herbs.
3. Use the "MIXED" setting to cook the rice.
4. In a large mixing bowl, combine the remaining ingredients while the rice is cooking. Allow the mixture to marinate in the refrigerator.
5. Remove the basil and bay leaf when the rice has finished cooking. With a rice spatula, fluff the rice and spread it out on a big plate. Refrigerate for 30 minutes to cool.
6. When the rice is cool enough to handle, combine it gently with the marinated tomato/mozzarella combination.
7. Serve right away.

21. CAULIFLOWER CREAMED RICE WITH SEARED SALMON

Ingredients (serves 4-6):

To Cook in the Rice Cooker:

- 2 cups (rice measuring cup) long grain white rice
- Water to fill to water level 2 for "LONG GRAIN WHITE," or 2-1/2 cups (rice measuring cup)
- 1/2 tsp. salt

To Prepare Separately:

- 1 medium head cauliflower, cut into florets
- 4 fresh garlic cloves, peeled
- 2 large shallots, peeled
- 1 Tbsp. whole butter
- 1/2 tsp. salt
- 1 Tbsp. fresh thyme leaves
- 1/2 tsp. ground black pepper
- 1 lb. (4-6 slices) fresh salmon fillets, sliced 1/2" thick
- 1 tsp. fresh lemon zest
- 1/2 tsp. fresh thyme
- Salt and pepper to taste
- 1 Tbsp. olive oil to sear salmon

Instructions

1. Allow salmon to come to room temperature while the other ingredients are prepared by sprinkling lemon zest, thyme, salt, and pepper over it.
2. Use the measuring cup that came with your rice cooker to correctly measure the rice. Once the rice has been rinsed, drain it and set it in the inner frying pan. Add water to the "LONG GRAIN WHITE" water level, or as directed in the ingredients, along with salt. If available, cook the rice on the "LONG GRAIN WHITE" or "MIXED" option.
3. Cook the cauliflower, shallots, and garlic until soft in a large saucepan of salted water while the rice is cooking. Place them in a blender with the butter and purée until thick and smooth while still hot.
4. Using a wooden spoon or plastic spatula, whisk in the thyme and black pepper to the cauliflower puree in a large mixing basin. Keep the bowl warm by covering it with plastic wrap or aluminum foil until the rice is done.
5. When the rice is done, fold it into the cauliflower mixture, cover, and keep warm until the salmon is done.
6. In a sauté pan large enough to accommodate the salmon comfortably, heat the olive oil and sear the salmon for about 1 minute on each side, or until the salmon is cooked through and has a golden brown crust on the outside.

7. When the fish is done, divide the rice-cauliflower mixture among separate serving dishes and top with salmon filets. Finish the platter by dusting lemon zest threads over the salmon. Serve immediately, while the food is still hot.

8. On the side of the platter, serve your favorite vegetable, such as steamed and browned cauliflower, as seen below.

22. CHAKIN-SUSHI

Ingredients (makes 14 pieces):
For Sushi Rice:

- 1 cup cooked sushi rice
- 1-1/2 Tbsp. rice vinegar
- 1 Tbsp. sugar
- 1/4 tsp. salt

To Add to Sushi Rice:

- 2 medium dried shiitake mushrooms
- 1/2 cup water to soak shiitake (reserve)
- 2 tsp. sake (rice wine)
- 2 tsp. shoyu (soy sauce)
- 2 tsp. mirin (Japanese sweet rice wine)
- 1/3 tsp. sugar
- 3 oz. crab meat, precooked
- 2 tsp. white sesame seeds, roasted
- a handfull momi-nori (hand crushed small pieces of nori seaweed)

For Egg Crêpe:

- 9 eggs
- 2 tsp. corn starch, mixed with 2 tsp. water
- 2 tsp. sugar
- 2 tsp. sake (rice wine)
- 1/4 tsp. salt

To Tie:

- 7 green onions
- 1 cup raw rice, about 12 oz. cooked rice

Instructions

1. Sushi rice can be made with the items provided. Prepare the materials to be added to the sushi rice in order to make sushi rice. To rehydrate the shiitake mushroom, soak it in water for 30 minutes to an hour. The shares will be held in reserve.
2. Slice the shiitake mushroom and simmer for 5 minutes, or until most of the liquid has evaporated, in the saved stock, sake, shoyu, mirin, and sugar. Remove the pan from the heat and set it aside.
3. If there is any cartilage in the crab meat, find it and remove it.
4. When the cooked shiitake mushroom has cooled to room temperature, combine it with crab meat, sesame seeds, and momi-nori in a sushi rice bowl and set aside.
5. Make the crêpes with the eggs. Combine the eggs, corn starch solution, sugar, sake, and salt in a large mixing basin. Preheat a nonstick frying pan over medium heat, then pour in the egg mixture and make 14 7-inch egg crêpes. Stack the crêpes on a dish with parchment paper between them.
6. Each green onion should be cut in half lengthwise strips and blanched before being placed in cold water.
7. Place a bite-sized scoop of mixed sushi rice in the center of one crêpe sheet on a cutting board.
8. Wrap the crêpe around the filling and tie with green onion. To adjust the length of the onion, cut away any extra.
9. To produce thirteen additional chakin-sushi pieces, repeat steps 8 and 9.
10. Serve and have fun!

23. CHEESE CAKE

<For NS-VGC05>

- Butter for coating the inner cooking pan
- 3.5 oz. cream cheese
- 3 Tbsp. sugar
- 1-1/2 eggs, separate white from yolk
- 2 Tbsp. all purpose flour, sifted
- 1/2 Tbsp. fresh cream
- 2 tsp. lemon juice
- 0.4 oz. butter, melted
- Vanilla extract, to taste
- 1-1/2 Tbsp. sugar (for beating egg whites)

For Garnish (optional):

- Whipped cream
- Fruits

<For NS-TGC10 / NS-TSC10>

- Butter for coating the inner cooking pan
- 7.1 oz. cream cheese
- 1.8 oz. sugar
- eggs, separate white from yolk
- 1.1oz all purpose flour
- 1.7 oz. fresh cream
- 4 tsp. lemon juice
- 0.7 oz. butter, melted
- Vanilla extract, to taste
- oz. sugar (for beating egg whites)

For Garnish (optional):

- Whipped cream
- Fruits

<For NS-TGC18 / NS-TSC18>

- Butter for coating the inner cooking pan
- 10.6 oz. cream cheese
- 2.5 oz. sugar
- 5 eggs, separate white from yolk
- 1.8 oz. all purpose flour, sifted
- 2.0 oz. fresh cream
- 2 Tbsp. lemon juice
- oz. butter, melted
- Vanilla extract, to taste
- 1.8 oz. sugar (for beating egg whites)

For Garnish (optional):

- Whipped cream
- Fruits

Instructions

1. Lightly and evenly grease the interior of the inner frying pan with butter.
2. Soften cream cheese at room temperature or in the microwave for 30 seconds at 500 watts.
3. In a mixing bowl, beat softened cream cheese with a spatula until smooth. Blend in the sugar.
4. One at a time, add the yolks to the cream cheese mixture. Blend together the sifted all-purpose flour, fresh cream, lemon juice, melted butter, and optional vanilla extract.
5. Prepare the meringue. With a whisk, whip egg whites until frothy in a separate bowl. Don't overwhisk the mixture. Add sugar gradually until the egg whites start to maintain their shape.
6. With a spatula, gently fold the meringue into the cream cheese mixture. Don't overmix the ingredients.

7. Fill the oiled inner cooking pan halfway with the meringue and cream cheese mixture and lightly tap the bottom of the pan to remove any trapped air. Close the lid on the rice cooker and place the pan inside.
8. Choose the "CAKE" option. Press START/REHEAT after setting the cooking duration to 70 minutes for NS-VGC05, 60 minutes for NS-TGC10 / NS-TSC10, and 80 minutes for NS-TGC18 / NS-TSC18.
9. When the cake is done baking, carefully remove it from the pan and set it aside to cool.
10. Place the cake in the refrigerator to chill. Remove from the oven and top with whipped cream and fruits, if desired.
11. Variations in flavor: Soak raisins in rum to soften them. After step 6, lightly coat with flour and add. (For NS-VGC05, use 2 tbsps; for NS-TGC10 / NS-TSC10, use 1.1 oz.; and for NS-TGC18 / NS-TSC18, use 1.8 oz.)

24. CHEESE SENBEI (RICE CRACKERS)

Ingredients (serves 4):

- 1 cup cooked short or medium grain brown rice
- 2 Tbsp. grated Parmesan cheese
- 2 tsp. Italian parsley, chopped
- 1 tsp. white sesame seeds

Instructions

1. Combine all materials in a gallon plastic bag with a 10" x 14" opening and mix well.
2. Roll out the mixture with a rolling pin on a flat surface over the bag.
3. To produce a square shape, fold the edges of the mixture together.
4. With the rolling pin, thin out the square as much as possible.
5. Cut parchment paper to a size of 10" x 14". Remove the rice square from the plastic bag and place it on parchment paper. Continue to place the plastic sheet on top.
6. If the rice square is too delicate, transfer it between two cutting boards. Place one cutting board beneath the plastic bag containing the rice square and cover it with parchment paper. Place the other cutting board on top of the parchment paper, then flip the boards over so the plastic bag and rice square are on top. It's also possible to do this with two baking sheets.
7. With a butter knife, cut the plastic sheet into bite-sized squares. To separate squares without cutting through the plastic, gently press with the edge of a butter knife.
8. Remove the plastic wrap, lay the rice squares on the parchment in the microwave, and cook for 7 minutes on high (at 1200W) or until the rice has dried and hardened.
9. When the crackers are cold enough to touch, serve them.
10. Enjoy!

25. CHESAPEAKE CRAB CARROT RICE

Ingredients (serves 4-6):

To Cook in the Rice Cooker:

- 2 cups (rice measuring cup) Jasmine rice
- 16 oz. carrot juice
- 1 tsp. Maryland style crab boil seasoning
- 1/2 tsp. salt

To Add to Cooked Rice:

- 1 Tbsp. grated lemon zest
- 1/2 cup parsley, chopped
- 8 oz. crab meat

Ingredients (serves 2-3):

To Cook in the Rice Cooker:

- 1 cup (rice measuring cup) Jasmine rice
- 8 oz. carrot juice
- 1/2 tsp. Maryland style crab boil seasoning
- 1/4 tsp. salt

To Add to Cooked Rice:

- 1/2 Tbsp. grated lemon zest
- 1/4 cup parsley, chopped
- 4 oz. crab meat
    1. ### Instructions
       Place the rice in the inner cooking pan after correctly measuring it with the measuring cup that came with your rice cooker.
    2. Using the rice spatula, combine the carrot juice, crab boil seasoning, and salt in the inner frying pan. Use the "MIXED" setting to cook the rice.
    3. When the rice has done cooking, fluff it lightly using a rice spatula.
    4. Toss in the grated lemon zest, minced parsley, and crab meat carefully.
    5. Serve right away. Enjoy!

26. CHICKEN VINDALOO (INDIAN CHICKEN CURRY)

Ingredients (serves 4-6):

To Cook in the Rice Cooker:

- 2 cups (rice measuring cup) basmati rice
- 3 cups (rice measuring cup) water

For Marinade:

- 1-1/2 lbs. boneless, skinless chicken thighs, cut into thirds
- 1 Tbsp. garam masala
- 2 Tbsp. kashmiri chili powder (may substitute with Hungarian paprika)
- 1/8 tsp. red chili powder, adjust amount for preferred hotness
- 3 Tbsp. coconut vinegar (may substitute with wine vinegar)
- 1 tsp. palm sugar (may substitute with light brown sugar)
- 2 Tbsp. garlic, crushed
- 1 Tbsp. ginger, crushed
- 2 tsp. salt

For sauce

- 2 Tbsp. ghee (may substitute with vegetable oil)
- 1 tsp. mustard seeds, whole
- 1 large onion, finely chopped
- 1 lb. baby potatoes, whole or cut into halves
- 1 (14.5 oz.) can diced tomatoes
- 1/2 cup water
- 1 tsp. lime juice

Topping:

- 1/4 cup fresh coriander leaves, chopped

Instructions

1. Use the measuring cup that came with your rice cooker to correctly measure the rice. Drain and place in the inner cooking pan after a brief rinse.
2. Using the "WHITE RICE" preset, add water and cook the rice.
3. Place the chicken thighs in a large plastic bag with all of the marinade ingredients and toss to combine. Allow 15 to 1 hour to marinate.

4. In a large pan over medium heat, heat the oil, then add the mustard seeds and fry for 30 seconds, or until they start to pop. Keep an eye out for the bursting seeds.
5. Sauté the onions in the pan for 5 minutes.
6. Cook for another 5 minutes after adding the chicken and potatoes.
7. Bring the tomatoes, water, and salt to a boil, then reduce to a low heat and cook for about 30 minutes, or until the sauce thickens and the chicken and potatoes are done. Stir occasionally.
8. Toss in the lime juice and season with salt to taste (not included in the ingredients list). Remove the pan from the heat.
9. When the rice is done cooking, fluff it gently with a rice spatula and serve on individual dishes.
10. Into individual bowls, spoon the curry and top with chopped coriander.
11. Serve with rice and eat while it's still hot!

27. CHILI CHEESE RICE AND HOT DOGS

Ingredients (serves 2-3):

To Cook in the Rice Cooker:

- 1 cup (rice measuring cup) long grain white rice
- 4 oz. low sodium beef broth
- 4 oz. water

To Prepare Separately:

- 1/2 cup chili sauce
- 1/2 cup canned red kidney beans
- 1/2 Tbsp. olive oil
- 1 medium onion, sliced
- 2-3 hot dogs
- 1/2 cup cheddar cheese, shredded
- 1/4 cup scallions, thinly sliced
- 2-6 sprigs cilantro

Ingredients (serves 4-6):

To Cook in the Rice Cooker:

- 2 cups (rice measuring cup) long grain white rice
- 8 oz. low sodium beef broth
- 8 oz. water

To Prepare Separately:

- 1 cup chili sauce
- 1 cup red kidney beans, canned
- 1 Tbsp. olive oil
- 2 medium onions, sliced
- 4-6 hot dogs
- 1 cup cheddar cheese, shredded
- 1/2 cup scallions, thinly sliced
- 4-12 sprigs cilantro

Instructions

1. Use the measuring cup that came with your rice cooker to correctly measure the rice. Once the rice has been rinsed, drain it and set it in the inner frying pan.
2. Using the rice spatula, combine the beef broth and water with the rice. Use the "MIXED" setting to cook the rice.
3. While the rice is cooking, put the chili sauce and kidney beans in a small sauce pan and heat on low for about 10 minutes, turning occasionally to avoid burning. Keep warm.
4. In a medium sauté pan, heat the oil, then add the onions and cook over medium heat. Reduce heat to low and cook, stirring occasionally, until the onions are tender and golden brown.
5. Boil, microwave, or grill hot dogs according to your preference. Cut each one into eight pieces and keep them warm.
6. When the rice is done, remove it from the inner pan and pour it into the warmed chili sauce mixture.
7. Warm plates are ideal for serving. Sprinkle shredded cheese on top of the caramelized onions, allowing the cheese to melt slightly.
8. Cooked hot dogs should be placed next to the rice, and chopped onions and cilantro should be garnished on the plate. If desired, serve with warm tortillas or bread.

28. CLASSICALLY BUILT ONIGIRI

Ingredients (makes 4 onigiri):
To Cook in the Rice Cooker:

- 2 cups (rice measuring cup) short or medium grain white rice
- Water to fill to water level 2 for "WHITE RICE"

For Seasoning Recipes

- 1/2 tsp. salt
- For Filling:
- 2 oz. salmon filet
- 1/4 tsp. sea salt
- 2 umeboshi (pickled Japanese plum)

For Wrap (optional):

- 4 sheets nori seaweed, cut into 4" x 2" each
    1. **Instructions**
       Use the items mentioned under "To Cook in the Rice Cooker" to make white rice. To learn how to make "white rice," go here.
    2. When the rice is done cooking, move it to a separate bowl, season with 1/2 tsp salt, and fluff gently with a rice spatula. Remove from the equation.
    3. Preheat the oven or broiler to 450 ° Fahrenheit. Place the salmon filet on a paper towel and season with sea salt. Allow for a 5-minute rest period.
    4. 5 minutes under the broiler or in the oven until fish is cooked through. Remove any bones and skin from the cooked salmon and place it in a basin. Set aside after breaking into bite-sized pieces.
    5. Set aside the umeboshi pits, which can be removed with a knife or your fingers. When using a knife, be cautious.
    6. Cut a 7 to 8-inch-long piece of plastic wrap and set it in a small basin. Cover the plastic wrap with a quarter cup of cooked rice. In the center of the rice, place half of the salmon from step 4. By lightly squeezing your hands together, gather the plastic wrap over the rice and form a triangle rice ball. The rice ball should be hard enough not to fall apart, yet fluffy enough not to be smashed.
    7. Remove the plastic wrap from the dish. Wrap the bottom of the onigiri in a nori sheet. To prepare another salmon onigiri, repeat steps 6 and 7.
    8. Umeboshi can be used to make two extra onigiri.
    9. Enjoy!

29. CRANBERRY & RICE CONFETTI MIX

Ingredients (serves 4):

To Cook in the Rice Cooker:

- 1 cup (rice measuring cup) long grain white rice
- Water to fill to water level 1 for "LONG GRAIN WHITE," or 1-1/4 cups (rice measuring cup)
- 1/4 tsp. salt

To Add to Cooked, Cooled Rice:

- 1 cup dried cranberries
- 1/4 cup slivered almonds, toasted
- 2 green onions, finely sliced
- 1/2 cup cilantro leaves, finely chopped
- 1/2 tsp. grated ginger
- 1 orange
- 1 Tbsp. extra virgin olive oil

Instructions

1. Use the measuring cup that came with your rice cooker to correctly measure the rice. Once the rice has been rinsed, drain it and set it in the inner frying pan.
2. Fill the container halfway with water for "LONG GRAIN WHITE," or as directed in the ingredients. Mix in the salt thoroughly. If available, cook the rice on the "LONG GRAIN WHITE" or "MIXED" option.
3. When the rice is done cooking, fluff it with a rice spatula and spread it out on a big platter. Refrigerate for 30 minutes to cool.
4. The orange should be peeled and segmented. Keep the juice aside.
5. When the rice has cooled, combine gently with the cranberries, almonds, green onions, cilantro, ginger, orange segments, orange juice, and olive oil.
6. Refrigerate for a further 20-30 minutes to allow flavors to meld. If you mix the rice too much, it will become gluey.
7. Serve and have fun!

30. CREAMY OATMEAL BRÛLÉE

Ingredients (serves 4):

- 1 cup (rice measuring cup) steel cut oats
- Water to fill to water level 1 for "STEEL CUT OATMEAL," or 2-1/2 cups (rice measuring cup)
- 1 cup (rice measuring cup) half & half
- To Garnish:
- 3-4 Tbsp. light brown sugar
- Fruits of your choice
- Mint leaves
- You will need 4 small heat resistant soup bowls.

Instructions

1. Please use the measuring cup that came with your rice cooker to measure the rice.
2. Using the measuring cup that came with your rice cooker, correctly measure steel cut oats. Steel-cut oats should be placed in the inner frying pan. Fill the cup halfway with water for "STEEL CUT OATMEAL," or as directed in the ingredients.
3. Place the inner cooking pan in the rice cooker's main body and turn it on. Use the "STEEL CUT OATMEAL" (if available) or "PORRIDGE" setting to cook the steel cut oats.
4. When the steel cut oats are done cooking, remove the lid and stir in the half-and-half with the rice spatula.
5. Fill heat-resistant soup cups halfway with oatmeal.
6. Light brown sugar should be divided. Spread the topping evenly over the oats with a spoon. Melt the sugar with a torch or an oven broiler to create a crispy top.
7. Fruits and mint leaves can be garnished.
8. Enjoy!

31. CRISP GRILLED YAKI-ONIGIRI

Ingredients (makes 4 onigiri):
To Cook in the Rice Cooker:

- 2 cups (rice measuring cup) short or medium grain white rice
- Water to fill to water level 2 for "WHITE RICE"

For Rice Balls:

- 1 Tbsp. shoyu (soy sauce)
- 2 tsp. toasted white sesame seeds (optional)

For Shoyu Based Basting Sauce:

- 2 tsp. shoyu (soy sauce)
- 2 tsp. sugar
- 2 tsp. mirin (Japanese sweet rice wine)

For Miso Based Basting Sauce:

- 2 tsp. red miso paste
- 2 tsp. sugar
- 1 Tbsp. mirin (Japanese sweet rice wine)

Instructions

1. Use the items mentioned under "To Cook in the Rice Cooker" to make white rice. To learn how to cook white rice, go here.
2. When the rice is done cooking, move it to a separate bowl, drizzle with shoyu, and fold in the optional sesame seeds gently using a rice spatula.
3. Cut a 7 to 8-inch-long piece of plastic wrap and set it in a small basin. Cover the plastic wrap with a quarter cup of cooked rice. By lightly squeezing your hands together, gather the plastic wrap over the rice and form a triangle rice ball. The rice ball should be hard enough not to fall apart, yet fluffy enough not to be smashed. Make three more onigiri by repeating the previous method.
4. Make the basting sauces ahead of time. In separate bowls, combine the ingredients for each sauce.
5. Use an electric grill or a frying pan to cook the onigiri. Preheat the Indoor Electric Grill (EB-CC15/EB-DLC10) for 6 minutes on "HI" or until the operation light turns off. Heat 1 tsp vegetable oil (not listed in the ingredient list) in a frying pan over medium heat.
6. Place the onigiri on the grill after removing the plastic wrap. Please be cautious when using a hot grill or pan.
7. Reduce the heat setting to "MEDIUM." Baste the tops of the onigiri with sauce, flip, and bake for another minute or until crispy brown. Grill the other side in the same manner.

8. Serve immediately.
9. Enjoy!

32. DECONSTRUCTED CALIFORNIA ROLL

Ingredients (serves 4-6):
For Sushi Rice:

- 3 cups (rice measuring sup) short or medium grain white rice
- Water to fill to water level 3 for "SUSHI RICE"
- 4 Tbsp. rice vinegar
- 3 Tbsp. sugar
- 1 tsp. salt

To Prepare Separately:

- 12 oz. king crab leg meat, removed from shell, slice into bite size pieces
- 1/2 European cucumber, thinly sliced
- 1-2 ripe but firm avocados, peeled, stoned and thinly sliced
- 1 sheet nori (dried seaweed), cut into thin strips

Condiments (Optional):

- Soy sauce
- Wasabi

Instructions

1. Sushi rice can be made with the items provided. To learn how to make sushi rice, click here.
2. Sushi rice is portioned into bowls, and crab meat, cucumber, and avocado are arranged on top of the rice. Serve at room temperature with nori strips on top.
3. Optional: Serve with wasabi and soy sauce.

33. EASTERN MEDITERRANEAN VEGETABLES AND BROWN RICE

Ingredients (serves 2-3):

To Cook in the Rice Cooker:

- 1.5 cup (rice measuring cup) short grain brown rice
- 12 oz. vegetable broth
- 1/2 clove garlic, minced
- 1/4 tsp. celery seed
- 1/4 tsp. salt
- Water to reach water level 1.5 for "BROWN RICE"

To Prepare Separately:

- 1/2 cup cooked spinach, roughly chopped
- 1/2 cup cooked artichoke hearts, quartered
- 1/8 cup sun dried tomatoes, drained of oil and chopped
- 1/8 cup pistachio nuts, shelled and toasted
- 1/2 Tbsp. extra virgin olive oil
- 1/2 tsp. red wine vinegar
- 1/8 cup fresh parsley, coarsely chopped
- 1/4 cup ricotta salata cheese, crumbledIngredients (serves 4-6):

To Cook in the Rice Cooker:

- 3 cups (rice measuring cup) short grain brown rice
- 24 oz. vegetable broth
- 1 clove garlic, minced
- 1/2 tsp. celery seed
- 1/2 tsp. salt
- Water to reach water level 3 for "BROWN RICE"

To Prepare Separately:

- 1 cup cooked spinach, roughly chopped
- 1 cup cooked artichoke hearts, quartered
- 1/4 cup sun dried tomatoes, drained of oil and chopped
- 1/4 cup pistachio nuts, shelled and toasted
- 1 Tbsp. extra virgin olive oil
- 1 tsp. red wine vinegar
- 1/4 cup fresh parsley, coarsely chopped
- 1/2 cup ricotta salata cheese, crumbled

Instructions

1. Use the measuring cup that came with your rice cooker to correctly measure the rice. Once the rice has been rinsed, drain it and set it in the inner frying pan.
2. In the inner cooking pan, combine the vegetable broth, garlic, celery seed, and salt.
3. If necessary, add water to the proper water level for "BROWN RICE" (do not add water if vegetable broth has reached or exceeded the water scale).
4. Using the rice spatula, thoroughly combine the ingredients and cook the rice on the "BROWN" setting.
5. In a microwaveable bowl, add spinach, artichokes, sun dried tomatoes, and pistachios while the rice cooks.
6. Microwave the spinach mixture for 1 minute once the rice has done cooking.
7. In a separate container, add olive oil, red wine vinegar, chopped parsley, and crumbled ricotta salata cheese while the spinach mixture warms.
8. Remove the rice from the rice cooker and place it in a warm bowl. With a fork, fold in the spinach mixture. Then gently stir in the parsley and cheese combination.
9. Immediately serve in heated bowls.

34. FLUFFY RICE ALFREDO

Ingredients (serves 4-6):

To Cook in the Rice Cooker:

- 3 cups (rice measuring cup) long grain white rice
- Water to fill to water level 3 for "LONG GRAIN WHITE," or 3-3/4 cups (rice measuring cup)
- 1 tsp. salt

To Prepare Separately:

- 1 (15 oz.) jar prepared Alfredo sauce
- 1 cup green peas, frozen
- 1 tsp. freshly ground pepper
- 1 cup Parmesan cheese, finely grated
- 3 oz. prosciutto, thinly sliced strips (about 6 slices)

Instructions

1. Using the measuring cup that came with your rice cooker, accurately measure the rice. Drain and place in the inner cooking pan after a brief rinse.

2. Fill the container halfway with water for "LONG GRAIN WHITE," or as directed in the ingredients. Use the rice spatula to mix the salt into the inner cooking pan with the rice. If available, cook the rice on the "LONG GRAIN WHITE" or "MIXED" option.
3. Prepare the other ingredients and keep them separate while the rice cooks.
4. When the rice has done cooking, fluff it lightly using a rice spatula. Microwave Alfredo sauce and green peas separately in microwave-safe vessels for 30 to 60 seconds or until warm.
5. Toss the rice with the warmed sauce, peas, and black pepper.
6. Fill warm bowls halfway with mixed rice. Top with prosciutto pieces and a generous amount of grated Parmesan cheese. Serve right away.
7. Enjoy!

35. FRUITY RICE CUSTARD PUDDING

Ingredients (serves 6-8):

- 2 cups (rice measuring cup) long grain white rice
- Water to fill to water level 2 for "LONG GRAIN WHITE," or 2-1/2 cups (rice measuring cup)
- 2 egg yolks
- 3 cups whole milk
- 1/3 cup sugar
- 1/4 tsp. salt
- 2 tsp. vanilla extract

For Topping:

- 2 kiwi fruits
- 1/2 mango
- 6 strawberries
- 1 Tbsp. honey or maple syrup
- 1 tsp. cinnamon powder
- 6-8 Tbsp. whipped cream

Instructions

1. Use the measuring cup that came with your rice cooker to correctly measure the rice. Once the rice has been rinsed, drain it and set it in the inner frying pan. Fill the container halfway with water for "LONG GRAIN WHITE," or as directed in the ingredients. If available, cook the rice on the "LONG GRAIN WHITE" or "MIXED" option.
2. Transfer cooked rice to a large sauce pan once it has finished cooking. Simmer for 15 minutes, or until thickened, over low heat, stirring frequently. Remove the pan from the heat.
3. Combine egg yolks, sugar, and salt in a small bowl. Mix thoroughly.
4. In a separate bowl, whisk together the egg yolk mixture from step 3 and the rice from step 2.

5. Place the saucepan back on the stovetop. Cook for one minute over medium heat, stirring constantly.

6. Remove the pan from the heat and stir in the vanilla extract. Fill dessert dishes halfway with pudding. Refrigerate for at least 2 hours and up to 2 days after wrapping each bowl in plastic wrap.

7. All fruits should be diced into 1/3-inch cubes. Set aside after dressing with honey.

8. Remove the plastic wrap from the cold rice pudding and sprinkle cinnamon powder over the rice. Add a dollop of whipped cream on top, along with the diced fruits from step 7.

9. Enjoy!

36. FURIKAKE (RICE SPRINKLES)

Ingredients (serves 4):
To Cook in the Rice Cooker:

- 2 cups (rice measuring cup) short or medium grain white rice
- Water to fill to water level 2 for "WHITE RICE"

For Basic Furikake:

- 1 oz. (28g) bonito flakes
- 1 Tbsp. soy sauce
- 1-1/2 Tbsp. mirin (Japanese sweet rice wine)
- 1 Tbsp. white toasted sesame seeds

Additional Flavors:

- Kombu:
  2" x 2" kombu seaweed, reconstituted with 2 tbsps water for 10 minutes then cut into 1/4" square pieces
- Spicy:
  1/4 tsp. crushed red pepper
- Crunchy:
  3 large potato chips, crushed
- Ginger:
  1 tsp. fresh ginger, minced
- Nori:
  7" x 4" nori seaweed, cut into 1/4" square pieces
- Citrusy:
  1 tsp. lime peel, grated

Instructions

1. To cook white rice in the rice cooker, use the ingredients given under "To Cook in the Rice Cooker."
2. Prepare the furikake while the rice is cooking. Crush the bonito flakes with your hands if they're bigger than a half inch. In a frying pan, combine bonito flakes, soy sauce, and mirin, and simmer over low heat.
3. Add one of the above "Additional Flavors" to the pan, or combine various ingredients to make your own.
4. Cook, stirring constantly, until the majority of the liquid has been absorbed, about 3 minutes. Cook for another minute after adding the white toasted sesame seeds.
5. Furikake is served on top of freshly cooked rice. Furikake can be stored in the fridge for up to 7 days.

37. GARLIC FLAVORED BEEF YAKIMESHI, STIR-FRIED RICE

Ingredients (4 to 6 servings):
To Cook in the Rice Cooker:

- 3 cups (rice measuring cup) short or medium grain white or brown rice
- Water to fill to water level 3 for "WHITE RICE" or "BROWN RICE"

To Prepare Separately:

- 2 Tbsp. butter
- 5 large garlic cloves, cut into thin slices
- 10 oz. beef sirloin cut into 1/3 inch cubes
- ½ tsp. sea salt
- 2 to 3 tsp. shoyu (soy sauce)
- 1 Tbsp. mirin (Japanese sweet rice wine)
- 2 oz. Swiss chard, cut into thin strips crosswise with white stem
- 1 to 2 tsp. freshly ground black peppercorn

Instructions

1. Use the measuring cup that came with your rice cooker to correctly measure the rice. Place white rice in the inner cooking pan after rinsing until water clears, or brown rice in the inner cooking pan after a fast rinse.
2. Depending on whether you're using "WHITE RICE" or "BROWN RICE," add water to the appropriate water level. White rice should be cooked on the "HARDER," "REGULAR" (if available), or "WHITE RICE" setting, whereas brown rice should be cooked on the "BROWN" setting.

3. When the rice is done cooking, strain it and rinse it under cold tap water to chill it down and eliminate any excess starch. Before stir-frying the rice, drain it and let it aside for 20 minutes. If you're using rice that's already been cooked and stored in the fridge, skip this step.

4. Melt butter in a wok or large skillet over high heat. When the pan is hot, add the garlic slices and cook over medium-low heat until they are gently yellow, flipping them over occasionally. Remove the garlic cloves and set them aside in a small cup.

5. Season beef cubes with salt and pepper, then add to a wok and cook over medium heat until the outside is faintly brown. Cook beef over moderately high heat, stirring constantly with a spatula, until all juices have been absorbed.

6. Cook, stirring constantly with a spatula, until the rinsed or cooled rice is heated through. Cook until the greens wilt, then add the swiss chard. Cooked garlic and freshly ground black peppercorns are added.

7. While still hot, divide and serve in 4 to 6 bowls.

38. GOMOKU SUSHI

Ingredients (serves 5-6):
To Cook in the Rice Cooker:

- 3 cups (rice measuring cup) short or medium grain white rice
- Water to fill to water level 3 for "SUSHI RICE"

To Prepare Separately:

- 0.5 oz. chopped carrots
- Small piece Gobo (burdock)
- 1 oz. bamboo shoot
- 1 oz. lotus root
- 2 raw shiitake mushrooms
- 1 chikuwa or fish cake

Vinegar mix:

- 4 Tbsp. rice vinegar
- 3 Tbsp. sugar
- 1 tsp. salt
- (A)
- 120mL dashi
- 2 Tbsp. sugar
- 1 Tbsp. soy sauce
- 1 Tbsp. mirin (or sake)

- 1 tsp. salt
- (B)
- 2 large eggs
- 1 tsp. mirin
- Pinch of salt

To top:

- Nori (seaweed)
- Boiled shrimp
- Boiled field peas
- Pickled ginger to taste

Instructions

1. Use the measuring cup that came with your rice cooker to correctly measure the rice. Place rice in inner cooking pan after rinsing until water is clear.
2. For "SUSHI RICE," add water to the appropriate water level. Use the "SUSHI" option to cook the rice.
3. Shred gobo and finely chop carrots, lotus roots, bamboo shoots, raw shiitake mushrooms, and chikuwa. Cook these ingredients in dashi (A) until all of the dashi has been used up. In a separate bowl, combine the ingredients from (B) and pour half of the mixture into a hot, greased crepe pan to produce a thin crepe. Remove the crepe from the pan and repeat with the remaining batter. Egg crepes should be cut into small, thin strips.
4. When the rice is done cooking, transfer it to a big, shallow dish and loosen it with a rice spatula. (Avoid using metal because it may react with the vinegar.) Pour the vinegar mixture over the rice and fold it in with a spatula. While the rice is still hot, combine the vinegar seasoning.
5. Fan the rice with a hand or electric fan as you fold in the vinegar mixture. Continue to fan and mix the rice until it has reached room temperature and is glossy.
6. Mix together the cooked ingredients from Step 3 and top with thinly sliced crepes.
7. Top with red ginger, nori (seaweed), boiling shrimp, and cooked field peas.

39. GREEN PEAS AND ASPARAGUS DORIA

Ingredients (Serves 2):

To Cook in the Rice Cooker:

- 1 cup (rice measuring cup) short or medium grain white rice
- Water to fill to water level 1 for "WHITE RICE"

For Blanching Green Peas and Asparagus:

- 2 quarts water
- 1 Tbsp. salt
- 1/2 bunch asparagus
- 1/2 cup green peas, fresh or frozen
- 2 quarts ice water to chill

For Buttered Rice:

- 1 Tbsp. butter
- 1 tsp. garlic, minced
- 1/4 tsp. salt
- 1/8 freshly ground black pepper

For Béchamel Sauce (White Sauce):

- 2 Tbsp. butter
- 1/2 small onion, minced
- 1/2 cup beef broth
- 3 Tbsp. all purpose flour
- 1-1/2 cup half and half
- 1/4 tsp. salt
- Pinch of ground white pepper

For Topping:

- Grated Parmesan cheese, according to taste

Instructions

1. 2 individual (12 oz.) gratin pans or a casserole dish that holds more than 24 oz.
2. Use the measuring cup that came with your rice cooker to correctly measure the rice. Drain the rice and set it in the inner cooking pan after rinsing it until the water is clear.
3. For "WHITE RICE," add water to the appropriate water level. Use the "WHITE RICE" setting to cook the rice. When the rice has done cooking, fluff it lightly using a rice spatula.
4. Blanch asparagus and green peas while the rice is cooking. In a pot, bring the water to a boil and add 1 tbsp of salt. Prepare 2 quarts of ice water as well. Remove the hard ends of the

asparagus and discard them. Cut into little pieces to make it easier to eat. Cook for 2 minutes in boiling water with chopped asparagus and green peas. Strain and immediately immerse in freezing water. Remove from the equation.

5. Make the buttered rice after the rice has finished cooking. In a sauté pan over medium heat, melt 1 tbsp butter, then add the garlic and cook for 5 seconds. Cook for 3 minutes after adding the cooked rice, salt, and pepper to the pan. Remove the pan from the heat and spoon buttered rice into each gratin dish.

6. Preheat the oven to 475 ° Fahrenheit.

7. To make the Béchamel sauce, combine all of the ingredients in a mixing bowl. In a sauté pan over medium heat, melt 2 tbsps butter, then add the onion and cook for 2 minutes. Pour the beef broth into the pan and heat for 3-5 minutes, or until almost all of the liquid has evaporated. 2 minutes after adding the flour to the pan, whisk until smooth and the mixture gets a light golden color. Make sure you don't go too dark. Stir in the half-and-half until it starts to simmer and has a creamy texture, about 5 minutes.

8. Remove the pan from the heat, season with salt and white pepper, then stir in the drained asparagus and green peas.

9. In each gratin dish, pour the sauce over the rice. Sprinkle Parmesan cheese evenly over the top and bake for 10 minutes, or until golden brown.

10. Serve with a side of Parmesan cheese while it's still hot.

40. GREEN TEA RICE

Ingredients (serves 4):
To Cook in the Rice Cooker:

- 2 cups (rice measuring cup) short or medium grain white or brown rice
- Water to fill to water level 2 for "WHITE RICE" or "BROWN RICE"

To Prepare Separately:

- 1 Tbsp. green tea leaves
- 1-1/2 cups cold water
- 1/2 tsp. salt
- 1/2 tsp. sugar
- 1 Tbsp. sesame seeds, roasted

Instructions

1. Steep tea leaves for about an hour in 1-1/2 cups cold water, then filter. The steeping water can be used to make cold tea.

2. Use the measuring cup that came with your rice cooker to correctly measure the rice. Place white rice in the inner cooking pan after rinsing until water clears, or brown rice in the inner cooking pan after a fast rinse.
3. Depending on whether you're using "WHITE RICE" or "BROWN RICE," add water to the appropriate water level. White rice should be cooked on the "HARDER," "REGULAR" (if available), or "WHITE RICE" setting, whereas brown rice should be cooked on the "BROWN" setting.
4. When the rice is done, add the filtered tealeaves, salt, sugar, and sesame seeds.
5. Serve right away.

41. GREEN VEGETABLE SUSHI

Ingredients (serves 4-6):
To Cook in the Rice Cooker:

- 3 cups (rice measuring cup) short or medium grain white or brown rice
- Water to fill to water level 3 for "SUSHI RICE" (for white rice) or "BROWN RICE"

To Prepare Separately:

- 5 Tbsp. rice vinegar
- 2 Tbsp. sugar
- 2 tsp. and additional pinches sea salt
- 1 Tbsp. olive oil or vegetable oil
- 1 cup fresh or frozen peas, cooked in salted boiling water for 1 to 2 minutes, drained and cooled in cold water with ice cubes, then drained
- 1 cup shelled fresh or frozen edamame soybeans, cooked in salted boiling water for 4 to 5 minutes, cooled in cold water with ice cubes, then drained
- 6 stalks asparagus, tough end removed and brown scale removed (becomes 3 ounce), cut into thin slices diagonally
- 1 small ripe but firm avocado, peeled and stoned – about 5 ounces, cut into 1/3-inch cubes
- 1/4 cup raisin, chopped
- 1/3 cup walnuts, toasted and roughly chopped
- 3 Tbsp. finely minced pickled ginger (see step 6 for recipe)
- 1/4 cup finely minced parsley or coriander

Instructions

1. Use the measuring cup that came with your rice cooker to correctly measure the rice. Place white rice in the inner cooking pan after rinsing until water clears, or brown rice in the inner cooking pan after a fast rinse.

2. If using white rice, add water to the "SUSHI RICE" water level; if using brown rice, add water to the "BROWN RICE" water level. For white rice, use the "SUSHI" option, and for brown rice, use the "BROWN" setting.
3. Combine the rice vinegar, sugar, and 2 tsps salt in a small glass container with a lid. Shake the container with the lid on until the sugar and salt have dissolved.
4. Transfer the rice to a wooden sushi tub or a porcelain bowl once it has finished cooking (do not use metal). Toss the rice with the vinegar dressing in an equal layer. Allow 30 minutes for the rice to cool while covered with a clean wet cloth.
5. Gently fold in all of the additional ingredients into the rice.
6. Divide into 4 to 6 bowls and serve.

Pickled Ginger

- Prepare a day in advance for better flavor
- 2.5 ounce ginger, sliced paper thin
- 3 Tbsp. rice vinegar
- 1 tsp. sugar
- 1/4 tsp. sea salt

Bring the vinegar, 1 tbsp water, sugar, and salt to a simmer in a small saucepan. Bring water to a boil in a separate saucepan. Cook for 40 seconds after adding the ginger. Drain the ginger and place it in the marinade with the vinegar. Allow it to sit for at least 3 hours. Drain the ginger before using it, gently pressing off any leftover pickling juice, and then cut it.

42. GRILLED YAKI-ONIGIRI

Ingredients (makes 6 yaki-onigiri):

To Cook in the Rice Cooker:

- 2 cups (rice measuring cup) short or medium grain white rice
- Water to fill to water level 2 for "WHITE RICE"

For Kimchi Yaki-onigiri:

- 1/3 cup kimchi, chopped
- 1 tsp. sesame oil
- 3 Korean style seaweed sheets (optional)
- Salt, to taste

For Cheese Yaki-onigiri:

- 1/2 cup shredded cheddar cheese
- 1/2 Tbsp. red miso paste
- 2 tsp. honey

Instructions

1.
   Use the items mentioned under "To Cook in the Rice Cooker" to make white rice. To learn how to cook white rice, go here.
2. When the rice is done cooking, divide it in half and place it in two separate dishes. Toss the kimchi into one of the bowls and fold it in gently with the rice spatula. Season with salt to taste. With the rice spatula, carefully mix the cheese into the other bowl.
3. Cut a 7 to 8-inch-long piece of plastic wrap and set it in a small basin. Cover the plastic wrap with 1/3 of the kimchi rice. By lightly squeezing your hands together, gather the plastic wrap over the rice and form a triangle rice ball. The rice ball should be hard enough not to fall apart, yet fluffy enough not to be smashed. Make three of each of these onigiri in this manner for a total of six onigiri.
4. Prepare the cheese yaki-onigiri basting sauce. Combine miso and honey in a small bowl.
5. Use an electric grill or a frying pan to cook the onigiri. Preheat the Indoor Electric Grill (EB-CC15/EB-DLC10) for 6 minutes on "HI" or until the operation light turns off.
6. Remove the onigiri from the plastic wrap. Brush sesame oil onto the surface of the kimchi yaki-onigiri. Place all of the onigiri on the grill at the same time. Please be cautious when using a hot grill or pan.
7. Sear for a few minutes or until the surface of the kimchi yaki-onigiri gets crispy brown, then flip to grill both sides.
8. Grill the cheese yaki-onigiri until the surface is crispy brown, then flip and baste the cheese yaki-onigiri with the sauce from step 4. Grill the other side and baste it as well.

9. Place the yaki-onigiri on a serving platter. Wrap kimchi yaki-onigiri with a seaweed sheet if desired. Serve immediately.
10. Enjoy!

43. GUMBO BOWL

Ingredients (serves 4):

- 8 oz. smoked Andouille sausage, cut into 1/4-inch thick rounds
- 1/2 cup vegetable oil
- 2/3 cup flour
- 1 medium onion, chopped
- 2 celery stalks, chopped
- 1 medium green pepper, chopped
- 1 Tbsp. garlic, minced
- 1 cup okra, fresh or frozen, cut into 1/2-inch pieces
- 1 Tbsp. Creole seasoning
- 1 Tbsp. Worcestershire sauce
- 4 cups shrimp stock or chicken stock
- Salt and pepper, to taste
- 12 oz. shrimp, peeled and deveined

- 4 cups cooked long grain rice

- Hot sauce (optional)

Garnish:

- 4 green onions, sliced into small slivers

Instructions

1. In a skillet, brown the surface of the Andouille sausage for about 3 minutes, then drain fat and leave aside.
2. In a large sauce pan over low heat, heat the oil. Cook, stirring regularly, until the flour is a dark golden brown color, about 5 minutes.
3. Cook until the onion, celery, and green pepper are soft, about 6 minutes.
4. Cook for another 6 minutes after adding the garlic and okra.
5. Bring to a boil with the Creole spice, Worcestershire sauce, and shrimp or chicken stock.
6. Add the cooked sausage from step 1, cover, and cook for 30 minutes on low heat. Taste and adjust the flavor and consistency as needed with water, salt, and pepper.
7. Cook until the shrimp is just done, about 4 minutes.

8. 1 cup cooked rice in each serving bowl, ladle gumbo over rice, garnish with green onion Serve with a side of spicy sauce if desired.
9. Enjoy!

44. GYU-DON (BEEF BOWL)

Ingredients (serves 4):

- 1 lb. beef, thinly sliced (available at most Asian markets)
- 3 Tbsp. white wine or sake (rice wine)
- 2 Tbsp. sugar
- 1 Tbsp. mirin (Japanese sweet rice wine)
- 1/8 tsp. salt
- 4 Tbsp. soy sauce
- 1 tsp. grated ginger
- 1 large onion, sliced
- 1 cup ichiban dashi or 1 tsp. dashinomoto + 1 cup water
- 6 cups cooked short or medium grain white or brown rice

Garnish (optional):

- Pickled red ginger

Instructions

1. Marinate the beef in a basin with the wine or sake, sugar, mirin, salt, soy sauce, and grated ginger.
2. In a sauce pan, combine the onion and dashi. Cook on medium heat for 5 minutes.
3. Add the marinated beef to the sauce pan, cover, and simmer for another 5 minutes, or until the steak is fully cooked.
4. Cook the rice in each serving bowl and top with the cooked beef and onion.
5. Serve immediately with pickled red ginger, if desired.
6. Enjoy!

45. HALAL STYLE CHICKEN AND RICE

Ingredients (serves 4):

For Chicken:

- 2 Tbsp. fresh lemon juice
- 1 Tbsp. chopped fresh oregano
- 1/2 tsp. ground coriander seed
- 1-1/2 Tbsp. garlic, grated
- 1/4 cup olive oil
- 1/2 tsp. kosher salt
- 1/2 tsp. ground black pepper
- 2 lbs. boneless, skinless chicken thighs, trimmed of excess fat
- 1 Tbsp. vegetable oil

To Cook in the Rice Cooker:

- 2 cups (rice measuring cup) jasmine white rice
- Water to fill to water level 2 for "JASMINE" or 2-1/2 cups (rice measuring cup)
- 1/2 tsp. kosher salt
- 1/8 tsp. ground black pepper

To Prepare Separately:

- 1 tsp. granulated chicken bouillon
- 2 Tbsp. unsalted butter
- 1/2 tsp. turmeric
- 1/4 tsp. ground cumin

For Sauce:

- 1/2 cup mayonnaise
- 1/2 cup Greek yogurt
- 1 Tbsp. sugar
- 2 tsp. white vinegar
- 1 tsp. fresh lemon juice
- 1/4 cup chopped fresh parsley
- 1 tsp. ground black pepper
- Kosher salt to taste

Garnish and Condiments:

- 1/2 head iceberg lettuce, shredded
- 1 large tomato, diced
- Hot sauce (optional)

Instructions

1. Prepare the chicken by marinating it. Combine all of the ingredients given under "For Chicken" in a small bowl, except the chicken and vegetable oil. Half of the marinade should be placed in a 1-gallon plastic bag with the chicken. Seal the bag tightly and spread the marinade evenly over the chicken with your fingertips, making sure all regions are covered. Marinate in the refrigerator for at least 30 minutes or up to 4 hours. The remaining marinade should be kept refrigerated.

2. Prepare the rice. Use the measuring cup that came with your rice cooker to correctly measure the rice. Once the rice has been rinsed, drain it and set it in the inner frying pan.

3. Fill the container with water to the "JASMINE" water level, or as directed in the ingredients list. Use the rice spatula to stir in the salt and pepper in the inner frying pan with the rice.

4. Use the "JASMINE" (if available) or "WHITE RICE" setting to cook the rice.

5. Prepare the chicken while the rice is cooking. Take the marinated chicken out of the bag and blot it dry with paper towels. In a large skillet, heat the vegetable oil over medium-high heat. Cook for 4 minutes on one side, or until lightly browned. Cook for 6 minutes on the other side, then flip and cook for another 6 minutes on the other side. Allow to cool for 5 minutes before transferring to a cutting board.

6. Transfer cooked chicken to a medium bowl and chop into bite-size bits. Cover with plastic wrap and set aside the reserved marinade.

7. Make the sauce first. Combine all of the ingredients mentioned under "For Sauce," except the salt, in a small bowl. To combine the ingredients, whisk them together. Set aside after seasoning to taste with salt.

8. Prepare the rice seasoning when the rice has finished cooking. Melt butter in a large skillet over medium heat. Cook, stirring constantly, until the turmeric and cumin are aromatic but not browned, about 1 minute. Turn off the heat, transfer the cooked rice to the pan, and stir in the chicken bouillon. Serve the seasoned rice on individual serving plates.

9. Cook the chicken until it is done. Place the chicken in a skillet with the marinade from step 6. Cook, stirring regularly, over medium-high heat until thoroughly cooked. Remove from heat and serve over rice. On the side, place lettuce and tomato.

10. Drizzle the sauce over the chicken and serve with a side of hot sauce if desired. Enjoy!

46. HELLO KITTY HAYASHI RICE (HASHED BEEF WITH RICE)

Ingredients (serves 2-3):
To Cook in the Rice Cooker:

- 2 cups (rice measuring cup) short or medium grain white rice
- Water to fill to water level 2 for "WHITE RICE"

For Stew:

- 1/2 lb. chuck or rib eye beef
- 1/8 tsp. salt
- 1/8 tsp. black pepper
- 1/2 onion
- 1 Tbsp. olive oil
- 2 Tbsp. unsalted butter
- 1/8 tsp. salt
- 1 Tbsp. all-purpose flour
- 1 pkg. (8 oz. / pkg.) white mushrooms, sliced, 1/4" thick

For Sauce:

- 2 servings demi-glacé sauce concentrate (2-4 tsp. depending on the products)
- 2 Tbsp. tomato paste
- 4 tsp. Worcestershire sauce
- 2 tsp. soy sauce
- 4 tsp. ketchup
- 2 tsp. light or golden brown sugar
- 2/3 cup beef broth
- 1/3 cup red wine
- 1 bay leaf
- salt to taste
- For Coloring: (may substitute with blue food color)
- 3/4 cup shredded red cabbage
- 1/4 cup water
- 1/8 tsp. baking soda

For Decoration (for 2 servings):

- 1 egg white
- 1/2 tsp. corn starch
- 1 tsp. vegetable oil
- 1/2 red bell pepper, flattest side
- 1" square yellow bell pepper

- 3" x 3" nori sheet (approx.)
- 4 kernels yellow corn, cooked
- You will need dinner plates about 10" each.

Instructions

1. Cut the meat into thin slices. Use partially frozen meat to effortlessly thinly slice the meat. Wrap the meat in plastic wrap and place it in the freezer overnight if it's uncooked. Defrost in the refrigerator for 2-3 hours, or until semi-frozen. Wafer-thin slices of beef Season with 1/8 tsp salt and black pepper in a mixing bowl.
2. Prepare the rice. Use the measuring cup that came with your rice cooker to correctly measure the rice. Drain the rice and set it in the inner cooking pan after rinsing it until the water runs clean.
3. For "WHITE RICE," add water to water level 2. Use the "REGULAR" (if available) or "WHITE RICE" setting to cook the rice.
4. Prepare the blue dye for Hello Kitty's overalls while the rice is cooking. In a small saucepan, combine red cabbage and water. Cook, stirring periodically, for 5 minutes. Using a strainer, strain the cabbage and add baking soda to the liquid. Remove from the equation.
5. Prepare Hello Kitty's nose and ribbon. In a 1-inch-deep sauce pan, boil water (not listed in the ingredient list), then insert red and yellow bell peppers, skin side down, and simmer for 6 minutes. Chill peppers for 3 minutes in a dish of cold water (not listed in the ingredients list). Drain the water and peel the thin skin off the bell peppers. Remove from the equation.
6. Construct the overalls. Mix one tsp colored liquid from step 4 with corn starch in a small bowl. The egg white should be thoroughly whisked. Strain the egg white into the mixing bowl with the colored liquid using a sieve.
7. Spread vegetable oil with a paper towel in a nonstick frying pan over medium low heat. When the pan is heated, remove it from the heat and add the colored egg whites. Make a 6" circle by tilting the pan in a circular motion. Cook at a low temperature. Flip the crepe carefully and cook the second side in the same manner. Remove the pan from the heat and set it aside.
8. Make the sauce first. Vertically with the grain, slice onion into 1/4-inch wide strips. Except for the red wine, bay leaf, and salt, combine all sauce components.
9. In a large fry pan, heat the olive oil and butter over medium heat. Sauté the sliced onions with 1/8 tsp salt. Sprinkle all-purpose flour over the onion when it's soft and toss for a minute. Cook for 1 minute to remove the alcohol from the wine.
10. Stir in the bay leaf, the beef from step 1, the mushrooms, and the sauce mixture. Cover with a lid, lower the heat to a low level, and cook for 8 minutes. Remove from heat and set aside until ready to plate.
11. Create the Hello Kitty elements. To use as a template, draw Hello Kitty on a piece of paper (about 6" h × 5" w). Prepare the following for each decoration:
12. Cut nori sheet in half, layer sheets, then carefully cut out 6 whiskers and 2 eyes for whiskers and eyes.
13. Make a nose out of a yellow pepper by cutting out an oval.

14. To make the huge bow, cut two bow sections and one center knot from a red bell pepper.
15. To make the little bow, cut two bow sections and one center knot from a red bell pepper.
16. Rice should be shaped. Use parchment paper to cover the Hello Kitty drawing. Place warm rice on the face area of the parchment paper, cover with plastic wrap, correct shape, and move to the plating dish using plastic wrap as a guide.
17. Make the body out of rice cylinders. For her overalls, cut the blue egg white crepe from step 7 in half. Place two corn kernels for buttons on top of the rice and cover with the crepe.
18. Using plastic wrap, form rice cylinders for legs and attach to each head on the serving dish. For her hands, make little rice balls.
19. To finish Hello Kitty, put all of the pieces together.
20. Hello Kitty should be surrounded by the Hayashi stew (reheat if necessary).
21. Enjoy!

47. HELLO KITTY RICE PIZZA

Ingredients (makes four 4" x 5" pizza):
To Cook in the Rice Cooker:

- 2 cups (rice measuring cup) short or medium grain white rice
- Water to fill to water level 1 for "WHITE RICE"

For Pizza:

- 1/2 red bell pepper, flattest side
- 1" square yellow bell pepper slice
- 3.5" square nori sheet (approx.)
- 8 Tbsp. parmesan cheese, grated
- 1/2 tsp. salt
- 4 tsp. basil leaves, dried
- 2 egg
- 4 tsp. pizza sauce
- 4 sheets cheese wrap or 8 deli-style slices
- 1 Tbsp. olive oil

Garnish (optional):

Instructions

1. Use the measuring cup that came with your rice cooker to correctly measure the rice. Drain the rice and set it in the inner cooking pan after rinsing it until the water runs clean.
2. For "WHITE RICE," add water to water level 2. Use the "REGULAR" (if available) or "WHITE RICE" setting to cook the rice.

3. Prepare Hello Kitty's ribbon and nose while the rice is boiling. In a 1-inch-deep saucepan, boil water (not listed in the ingredient list), then insert red and yellow bell peppers, skin side down, and simmer for 6 minutes. Chill peppers for 3 minutes in a dish of cold water (not listed in the ingredients list). Drain the water and peel the thin skin off the bell peppers. Remove from the equation.
4. Get Hello Kitty's face ready. To use as a template, draw Hello Kitty's face (about 4" high). Prepare the following for each decoration:
5. Cut nori sheet in half, layer sheets, then carefully cut out 6 whiskers and 2 eyes for whiskers and eyes.
6. Make a nose out of a yellow pepper by cutting out an oval.
7. To make the bow, cut two bow sections and one center knot from a red bell pepper.
8. Set aside the remaining bell peppers, which have been minced.
9. Make the rice pizza according to the recipe. Transfer the rice to a large mixing bowl once it has finished cooking. Mix in the minced bell peppers from step 4, parmesan cheese, salt, and basil. Allow for a 5-minute cooling period.
10. In a separate dish, whisk the egg, then pour it over the combined rice from step 5 and stir well to blend.
11. Using oiled parchment paper, cover the Hello Kitty drawing. Place a quarter amount of mixed rice for the face onto the parchment paper and cover with plastic wrap, tightly pressing and adjusting shape to fit outline with hands, using the design as a guide. On each parchment paper, repeat procedures to make three more rice crusts. Remove from the equation.
12. Get the cheese ready. Trim the outline of the Hello Kitty template to make a little smaller version. Cut out a face form from parchment paper using this smaller pattern. Place a cheese slice on another piece of parchment paper and cut out four faces with the design. If required, use two slices of cheese each pizza. Remove from the equation.
13. In a large fry pan, heat the olive oil over medium low heat. Place the formed rice on the pan with the top side down. Place a lid on top and bake for 2-3 minutes, or until golden brown on the bottom.
14. Flip the rice pizza carefully to bake both sides, then spread one tsp of pizza sauce on top. Place the cheese that has been prepared on top. To melt the cheese, cover and cook for 1-2 minutes. Place the rice pizza on a serving plate and top with the bell peppers and nori from the previous step.
15. Serve with a broccoli garnish if desired.
16. Enjoy!

48. ICE RICE GELATO

Ingredients (makes about 1 pint):

- 1 cup cooked short or medium grain white rice
- 1 cup milk
- 4 Tbsp. sugar
- 1/2 tsp. vanilla extract
- 1 tsp. lemon zest
- 1 cup heavy cream
- Fruit of your choice (optional)

Instructions

1. Purée the rice, 1/2 cup milk, and sugar in a blender or food processor.
2. Combine the remaining milk, vanilla extract, and lemon zest in a mixing bowl.
3. To make gelato, add heavy cream to the mixture if you have an ice cream maker. Follow steps 3–7 if you don't have an ice cream machine.
4. Keep the heavy cream aside and freeze the mixture from step 2 for at least 3 hours in a large ice cube tray.
5. After 3 hours, whisk heavy cream to a gentle peak in a mixing dish.
6. Make a smoothie with frozen ice cubes in a food processor or blender.
7. Whip up the whipped cream and add it to the smoothie. Place in a jar and freeze for 3 hours or more, depending on how hard you want it.
8. Enjoy with fresh fruit!

49. ITALIAN SAUSAGE AND PEPPERS OVER TOMATO RICE

Ingredients (serves 2-3):

To Cook in the Rice Cooker:

- 1 cup (rice measuring cup) long grain white rice
- 5 oz. tomato juice
- 3 oz. water
- 1/4 tsp. salt

To Prepare Separately:

- 1 Tbsp. olive oil
- 1/2 lb. sweet Italian sausages, whole
- 1 medium yellow onion, sliced
- 1/2 red bell pepper, cleaned, seeded and sliced
- 1/2 yellow bell pepper, cleaned, seeded and sliced
- 1/2 green bell pepper, cleaned, seeded and sliced
- 1 tsp. dried oregano
- 1/4 tsp. salt
- 1/8 Tbsp. fresh ground pepper
- 1/4 tsp. red wine vinegar
- 1 canned anchovy filet, minced (optional)
- 2 Tbsp. Italian parsley, chopped (optional)

Ingredients (serves 4-6):

To Cook in the Rice Cooker:

- 2 cups (rice measuring cup) long grain white rice
- 10 oz. tomato juice
- 6 oz. water
- 1/2 tsp. salt

To Prepare Separately:

- 2 Tbsp. olive oil
- 1 lb. sweet Italian sausages, whole
- 2 medium yellow onions, sliced
- 1 red bell pepper, cleaned, seeded and sliced
- 1 yellow bell pepper, cleaned, seeded and sliced
- 1 green bell pepper, cleaned, seeded and sliced

- 2 tsp. dried oregano
- 1/2 tsp. salt
- 1/4 Tbsp. fresh ground pepper
- 1/2 tsp. red wine vinegar
- 2 canned anchovy filets, minced (optional)
- 4 Tbsp. Italian parsley, chopped (optional)

Instructions

1. Use the measuring cup that came with your rice cooker to correctly measure the rice. Once the rice has been rinsed, drain it and set it in the inner frying pan.
2. Using the rice spatula, combine the tomato juice, water, and salt with the rice. Use the "MIXED" setting to cook the rice.
3. In a large sauté pan, heat olive oil while the rice is cooking. Brown the sausages on all sides in a skillet. Reduce the heat to low and remove the sausages from the pan, slicing them into large bite-sized pieces and placing them on a warm platter.
4. Cook, stirring occasionally, until the onions are tender, about 5 minutes.
5. Add bell peppers and dried oregano to onions and simmer for another 5 minutes, or until peppers soften.
6. Add salt, pepper, red wine vinegar, anchovies, and half of the Italian parsley once the peppers have softened.
7. Stir the sausages into the pepper mixture to cook them through.
8. When the rice is done, use a rice spatula to fluff the remaining parsley into the rice and serve on warm plates. If there is any tomato paste left over from the juice on top of the rice, mix it in with the parsley. Place the sausage and pepper mixture on top of the rice. Serve right away.

50. JAMBALAYA

<For 5 or 10 cup Zojirushi Rice Cookers>
Ingredients (serves 4-6):

To Cook in the Rice Cooker:

- 3 cups (rice measuring cup) long grain white rice
- 1 tsp. salt
- 1/2 tsp. dried thyme leaves
- 1/4 tsp. dried chili flakes
- 8 oz. low sodium chicken broth
- 4 oz. diced canned tomatoes in puree
- Water as needed
- 1 medium onion, minced

To Prepare Separately:

1 Tbsp. olive oil

1 clove garlic, minced

8 oz. medium shrimp

6 oz. smoked sausage, sliced 1/4" thick

<For 3 cup Zojirushi Rice Cookers>
Ingredients (serves 2-3):

To Cook in the Rice Cooker:

- 1.5 cups (rice measuring cup) long grain white rice
- 1/2 tsp. salt
- 1/4 tsp. dried thyme leaves
- 1/8 tsp. dried chili flakes
- 4 oz. low sodium chicken broth
- 2 oz. diced canned tomatoes in puree
- Water as needed
- 1/2 medium onion, minced

To Prepare Separately:

- 1/2 Tbsp. olive oil
- 1/2 clove garlic, minced
- 4 oz. medium shrimp
- 3 oz. smoked sausage, sliced 1/4" thick

Instructions

1. Use the measuring cup that came with your rice cooker to correctly measure the rice. Drain and place in the inner cooking pan after a brief rinse.
2. Mix the salt and spices into the chicken stock in a separate bowl, then pour it into the inner frying pan.
3. Fill the water level 3 of "MIXED RICE" for 5 and 10 cup rice cookers, and up to water level 1.5 for 3 cup rice cookers with the diced tomatoes and puree, and if necessary, add water to fill the water level 3 of "MIXED RICE" for 5 and 10 cup rice cookers.
4. Cook on the "MIXED" setting with the minced onion on top.
5. When the rice cooker starts counting down, sauté the shrimp and sausage with olive oil and garlic in a frying pan and transfer to a bowl.
6. Open the lid when the rice is done cooking and transfer the rice to the bowl from step 5. Combine all ingredients in a large mixing bowl and serve right away.

51. JAPANESE BEEF CURRY

Ingredients (serves 4-6):

To Cook in the Rice Cooker:
For Curry:

- 2 Tbsp. vegetable oil
- 12 oz. stew beef
- 1 large onion, sliced
- 3 carrots, cut into bite-sized pieces
- 1 tsp. garlic, grated
- 1/2 tsp. ginger, grated
- 2 Tbsp. tomato paste
- 4 cups beef broth
- 2 Tbsp. Worcestershire sauce
- 2 tsp. soy sauce
- 2 bay leaves
- 1 tsp. honey
- 1-1/2 tsp. salt
- 1/8 tsp. black pepper
- 1 Russet potato, peeled, cut into bite-sized pieces
- 3 Tbsp. butter
- 3 Tbsp. all-purpose flour
- 3 Tbsp. curry powder

- 1/2 tsp. garam masala

Instructions

1.
   Use the measuring cup that came with your rice cooker to correctly measure the rice. Drain the rice and set it in the inner cooking pan after rinsing it until the water runs clean.
2. For "WHITE RICE," add water to the appropriate water level. Use the "HARDER" (if available) or "WHITE RICE" option to cook the rice.
3. Heat the oil in a large saucepan over medium heat and brown the steak. Place the chicken on a platter and put it aside.
4. Cook onion, carrots, garlic, and ginger in the same pot for 5 minutes over medium heat.
5. Combine the tomato paste and beef broth in a blender. Bring to a boil, scraping off any scum that rises to the surface, then add cooked beef, Worcestershire sauce, soy sauce, bay leaves, honey, salt, and pepper. Simmer for 15 minutes with the cover on.
6. Cook for another 30 minutes after adding the potatoes to the saucepan and covering it with a lid.
7. In a frying pan, combine the butter and flour and cook, stirring constantly, for 2 minutes over medium low heat. Cook for 1 minute after adding the curry powder.
8. Cook for 10 minutes after adding the mixture from step 7 to the beef broth mixture. Stir occasionally.
9. Remove the skillet from the heat and add garam masala, seasoning with salt and pepper (not listed in the ingredients list). Remove and discard bay leaves with care from the sauce.
10. When the rice is done cooking, fluff it gently with a rice spatula and serve on individual dishes.
11. Over rice, serve the curry.
12. Enjoy while it's still hot!

52. JAPANESE STYLE CURRY DORIA

Ingredients (serves 4):

- 2 Tbsp. butter
- 3 cups cooked rice
- 1/4 tsp. salt
- For White Sauce:
- 4 Tbsp. butter
- 4 Tbsp. all purpose flour
- 2 cups milk
- 1 tsp. chicken bouillon powder
- 1/8 tsp. black pepper

To Top Rice Before Baking:

- 1-1/2 to 2 cups curry or prepared Japanese curry
- 1 cup mozzarella cheese, shredded

For Garnish (optional):

- 2 tsp. curly parsley, minced

Instructions

1. A 9" x 13" casserole dish is required.
2. Set aside a small amount of oil (not listed in the ingredients list) to lightly coat the inside of the casserole dish.
3. 2 tbsps butter, melted in a large frying pan over medium heat Cook for 1 minute after adding the cooked rice and salt to the pan. Remove the rice from the heat and place it in an oiled casserole dish.
4. Preheat the oven to 400 ° Fahrenheit.
5. Make the white sauce according to the package directions. Melt 4 tbsps butter in a frying pan over low heat. Stir in the flour until it is completely smooth.
6. Combine the milk, chicken bouillon powder, and black pepper in a mixing bowl. Bring to a boil over medium heat, then simmer for 1 minute, stirring constantly. Remove the pan from the heat and pour the sauce over the rice in the casserole dish.
7. Spread the curry sauce on top of the white sauce and sprinkle with mozzarella cheese.
8. Bake for 15 minutes, or until cheese melts and curry is boiling, in a preheated oven.
9. When the baking is finished, sprinkle with optional minced parsley and serve right away. Enjoy!

53. JASMINE RICE WITH TOFU, BROCCOLI AND EDAMAME

Ingredients (serves 4)
To Cook in the Rice Cooker:

- 2 cups (rice measuring cup) jasmine rice
- Water to fill to water level 2 for "JASMINE" or 2-1/2 cups (rice measuring cup)
- 1 tsp. salt

To Prepare Separately:

- 4 Tbsp. soy sauce or tamari soy sauce
- 2 tsp. rice vinegar
- 1 (12 oz.) pkg. firm tofu, cut into 1/2 inch cubes
- 1 cup broccoli florets, cooked, cut in bite-sized pieces
- 1/2 cup edamame, shelled, cooked
- 1 cup cherry tomato, quartered

Instructions

1.
   Use the measuring cup that came with your rice cooker to correctly measure the rice. Place the inner cooking pan within the outer frying pan.
2. Fill the container with water to the "JASMINE" water level, or as directed in the ingredients. Use the rice spatula to mix the salt into the inner cooking pan with the rice. Use the "JASMINE" (if available) or "WHITE RICE" setting to cook the rice.
3. In a mixing bowl, add soy sauce or tamari, rice vinegar, and cubed tofu while the rice is cooking. Allow tofu to marinade in the soy sauce mixture for a few hours.
4. Warm the broccoli and edamame separately in microwave-safe containers until hot to the touch–about 1 minute on high.
5. When the rice is done cooking, fluff it with a rice spatula and spread it out on a big platter.
6. Add tomatoes and hot veggies to the rice once it has cooled to the touch. Transfer the marinated tofu to a separate bowl and toss the rice with the soy sauce mixture until evenly coated. Finally, gently toss in the marinated tofu with the rice.
7. Fill warm bowls with the mixture and serve immediately.
8. This dish can be refrigerated and eaten cold if desired.
9. Enjoy!

54. KEIHAN (JAPANESE CHICKEN SOUP WITH RICE)

Ingredients (serves 4):

For Shiitake Mushrooms:

- 4 medium dried shiitake mushrooms
- 1/2 cup water to soak shiitake (reserve)
- 1 Tbsp. sake (rice wine)
- 1 Tbsp. soy sauce
- 1 Tbsp. mirin (Japanese sweet rice wine)
- 1 tsp. sugar

For Chicken Soup:

- 2 medium chicken breasts
- 4 cups chicken stock
- 1 Tbsp. sake (rice wine)
- 1/2 tsp. salt
- 1 Tbsp. soy sauce

To Cook in the Rice Cooker:

- 2 cups (rice measuring cup) short or medium grain white rice
- Water to fill to water level 2 for "WHITE RICE"

For Shredded Egg Crêpes:

- 3 eggs
- 1/2 tsp. corn starch, mixed with 1/2 tsp. water
- 1/2 tsp. sugar
- 1 tsp. sake (rice wine)
- 1/8 tsp. salt

Topping:

- 1 tsp. dried orange peel
- 1/4 cup green onion, chopped
- 4 Tbsp. minced takuan (pickled daikon radish) or green papaya pickles (may substitute with your favorite pickles)
- A handful of shredded nori (seaweed)

Instructions

1. To rehydrate the shiitake mushroom, soak it in water for 30 minutes to an hour. The shares will be held in reserve.

2. In a medium sauce pan, place the chicken breasts. Bring the chicken stock, sake, salt, and soy sauce to a boil. Cook over low heat for 10 minutes, or until chicken is done, skimming off any scum that rises to the surface. Take the pan from the heat and set it aside to cool.
3. Use the items mentioned under "To Cook in the Rice Cooker" to make white rice. To learn how to cook white rice, go here.
4. Slice the shiitake mushrooms and simmer for 6 minutes, or until most of the liquid has drained, in the saved stock, sake, soy sauce, mirin, and sugar. Remove the pan from the heat and set it aside.
5. Crêpes with shredded egg Combine the eggs, corn starch solution, sugar, sake, and salt in a large mixing basin. Make four 7-inch egg crêpes in a medium nonstick frying pan over medium heat. To cool, stack the crêpes on a dish with parchment paper between each one. Remove the parchment paper and thinly slice the crêpe stack once it has cooled.
6. Remove the chicken from the broth when it is cool enough to handle, shred it, and set it aside. Do not throw away the soup.
7. When the rice is done cooking, fluff it gently with a rice spatula and serve it in individual serving bowls. Crêpes topped with shredded chicken, mushroom, and shredded egg
8. Reheat the chicken soup you saved and pour it over the toppings. To taste, garnish with orange peel, green onions, pickles, and nori.
9. Enjoy!

55. KIMCHI FRIED RICE

Ingredients (serves 4):

To Cook in the Rice Cooker:

- 2 cups (rice measuring cup) short or medium grain white rice
- Water to fill to water level 2 for "WHITE RICE"

To Prepare Separately:

- 3 Tbsp. vegetable oil
- 1 cup kimchi, chopped into bite-sized pieces
- 10 oz. canned tuna in oil, drained
- 4 Tbsp. kimchi pickling liquid
- salt to taste
- 1/8 tsp. black pepper

Garnish:

- 4 eggs
- 1 tsp. sesame seeds

- 8 sheets Korean seaweed (2.5" x 3"), cut in strips
- 2 stalk green onion, cut into thin slices

Instructions

1. Using the measuring cup that came with your rice cooker, accurately measure the rice. Drain the rice and set it in the inner cooking pan after rinsing it until the water runs clean.
2. For "WHITE RICE," add water to the appropriate water level. Use the "REGULAR" (if available) or "WHITE RICE" setting to cook the rice.
3. When the rice cooker's timer goes off, heat the vegetable oil in a big sauté pan and saute the chopped kimchi for 2 minutes.
4. Cook for another 2 minutes after adding the tuna and kimchi pickling liquid.
5. When the rice is done cooking, add it to the pan and stir it in evenly with the other ingredients. Season with salt and pepper to taste.
6. Make four eggs with the sunny side up. To serve, spoon fried rice onto warm plates and top with an egg. Sesame seeds, Korean seaweed, and green onion are sprinkled over top.
7. Enjoy while it's still hot!

56. KINOKO NO TSUKUDANI (MUSHROOM RICE TOPPING)

Ingredients (serves 4):

To Cook in the Rice Cooker:

- 2 cups (rice measuring cup) short or medium grain white rice
- Water to fill to water level 2 for "WHITE RICE"

For Tsukudani:

- 4 oz. shiitake mushroom
- 4 oz. white mushroom
- 4 oz. enoki mushroom
- 1 Tbsp. fresh ginger, finely julienned
- 2 tsp. sugar
- 3-1/2 Tbsp. soy sauce
- 1-1/2 Tbsp. mirin (Japanese sweet rice wine)
- 2 Tbsp. water

Instructions

1. Use the items mentioned under "To Cook in the Rice Cooker" to make white rice. To learn how to cook white rice, go here.
2. Prepare the tsukudani while the rice is cooking. Trim shiitake stems and cut into half or quarters vertically, depending on thickness. Cut enoki mushroom into two inch long parts and slice shiitake caps and white mushrooms into 1/4 inch thick slices.
3. Place all of the mushrooms, along with the other ingredients for tsukudani, in a frying pan and sauté over medium heat.
4. Cook, stirring occasionally, until most of the liquid has been absorbed, about 10-12 minutes.
5. Tsukudani should be served over freshly cooked rice, and the leftovers should be kept refrigerated.

57. KITSUNE-DONBURI (FRIED BEAN CURD AND EGG BOWL)

Ingredients (serves 2):

- 1.8 oz. fried bean curd (not seasoned)
- 2 green onions
- 1/2 cup ichiban dashi or 1/2 tsp. dashinomoto + 1/2 cup water
- 1 Tbsp. sake (rice wine)
- 1 Tbsp. mirin (Japanese sweet rice wine)
- 1 Tbsp. light brown sugar
- 1 Tbsp. soy sauce
- 3 eggs
- 2-1/2 cups cooked short or medium grain white or brown rice

Instructions

1. Fill frying pan halfway with water (not included in ingredients), bring to a boil, and cook fried bean curd for 2 minutes to drain excess oil. Drain the water and set it aside to cool.
2. Green onions should be cut diagonally into 2 inch length pieces.
3. Cut the fried bean curds into 1/2"x 2-1/2" strips once they have cooled enough to handle.
4. Place dashi, sake, mirin, brown sugar, soy sauce, and fried bean curd strips in a separate pan. Bring to a boil, then reduce to medium and continue to cook for 3 minutes.
5. Toss in the green onion to the pan.
6. In a mixing dish, lightly beat the eggs. 2/3 of the beaten egg should be equally distributed over the fried bean curd mixture. Cook for about a minute, or until the egg coagulates.
7. Pour the rest of the egg into the mixture. Turn off the heat when the egg begins to coagulate, around 30 seconds. Allow one minute to set before covering with a lid.
8. Warm the rice in serving dishes. Drizzle with sauce to taste and top with fried bean curd omelet.
9. Enjoy!

58. KURIGOHAN (JAPANESE CHESTNUT RICE)

Ingredients (serves 4-6):

To Prepare in Advance:

- 250g (about 10-12) raw chestnuts in their shell

To Cook in the Rice Cooker:

- 3 cups (rice measuring cup) short or medium grain white rice
- Water to fill to water level 3 for "WHITE RICE"
- 2 tsp. mirin (Japanese sweet rice wine)
- 1 tsp. salt

Ingredients (serves 2-3):

To Prepare in Advance:

- 125g (about 5-6) raw chestnuts in their shell
- To Cook in the Rice Cooker
- 1.5 cups (rice measuring cup) short or medium grain white rice
- Water to fill to water level 1.5 for "WHITE RICE"
- 1 tsp. mirin (Japanese sweet sake)
- 1/2 tsp. salt

Instructions

1. Soak the chestnuts for 30 minutes in boiling water. Starting from the bottom, cut around the chestnut with a knife, then peel away the hard shell and skin.
2. Use the measuring cup that came with your rice cooker to correctly measure the rice. Drain the rice and set it in the inner cooking pan after rinsing it until the water runs clean. Pour in the mirin and salt, then top it with water to the "WHITE RICE" water level.
3. Mix in the peeled chestnuts from step 1 well. Use the "MIXED" setting to cook the rice.
4. When the rice has done cooking, remove the lid and fluff the rice to release it before serving.

59.LAYERED TRIFLE TOWER

Ingredients (serves 10-14):

For Sponge Cake:

- 6-7 cups Whole Wheat Sponge Cake, cut into 3/4-inch cubes
- 1/4-1/3 cup marsala sherry or cranberry juice
- 5 Tbsp. seedless raspberry jam

For Custard:

- 7 Tbsp. sugar
- 5 Tbsp. cornstarch
- 6 egg yolks
- 3 cups whole milk
- 2 Tbsp. butter
- 1 tsp. vanilla extract

For Fruit Layer:

- 1.5 lb. sliced fresh strawberries
- 12 oz. fresh blueberries
- For Whipped Cream:
- 16 oz. whipped cream

For Decoration:

- Mint leaves
- You will need a 3 qt. trifle bowl.

NOTE:

The sponge cake can only be made in the following Rice Cooker models: NS-TGC10/18 or NS-TSC10/18.

Instructions

1. Make the sponge cake with whole wheat flour. To learn how to make the cake, click here.
2. Prepare the custard while you're making the sponge cake. In a saucepan, whisk together the sugar and cornstarch. Mix in the egg yolks thoroughly.
3. Gradually add the milk, then cook over medium heat for a few minutes, or until the first bubbles appear on the surface. To keep the mixture from adhering to the bottom of the pan, stir regularly.
4. Remove the pan from the heat and drain through a fine mesh strainer. Mix in the butter and vanilla extract well. Set aside, covered.

5. The cake should be layered. Transfer the sponge cake to a platter and set aside to cool. Half of the cubes should be used to cover the bottom of the trifle bowl. Sherry or cranberry juice might be used as a finishing touch. Microwave for 15 seconds on high (1200 w) to warm raspberry jam. Brush the cubes with the softened jam.
6. On top, arrange one-third of the sliced fresh strawberries and fresh blueberries.
7. Half of the custard should be layered on top of the fruit.
8. Pipe one-third of the whipped cream on top of the custard with a pastry bag or plastic bag.
9. To add another set of layers, repeat steps 4–7. Finish with the rest of the whipped cream and fruits. Refrigerate for at least 2 hours and up to 24 hours after covering.
10. Serve garnished with mint leaves. Enjoy!

60. LOCO MOCO

Ingredients (serves 4):
To Cook in the Rice Cooker:

- 2 cups (rice measuring cup) short or medium grain white rice
- Water to fill to water level 2 for "WHITE RICE"

To Prepare Separately:
- 1 lb. ground beef
- 1/2 cup onion, minced
- 1 egg
- 1/2 cup panko bread crumbs
- 1/2 tsp. salt
- 1/2 tsp. freshly ground pepper
- 1 Tbsp. vegetable oil
- 4 eggs for sunny side up or over easy

Brown Gravy:
- 1/2 cup butter
- 1/2 cup flour
- 1 quart beef broth
- 1/4 cup ketchup
- 1 Tbsp. soy sauce
- 1 Tbsp. Worcestershire sauce
- Salt and black pepper to taste

Garnish (Optional):

- Iceberg lettuce
- Tomato slices

Instructions

1. Use the measuring cup that came with your rice cooker to correctly measure the rice. Place the rice in the inner cooking pan after rinsing it until the water is clear.
2. For "WHITE RICE," add water to the appropriate water level." Use "REGULAR" (if available) or "WHITE RICE" to cook the rice "the scene
3. Assemble the gravy. In a saucepan over medium-low heat, melt the butter. Stir in the flour for 5 minutes, or until the mixture turns golden-brown in color.
4. Combine the beef broth, ketchup, soy sauce, and Worcestershire sauce in a large mixing bowl.
5. Continue to whisk while the sauce comes to a boil, then reduce to a low heat and cook for 30 minutes, or until desired thickness is attained, stirring regularly. To taste, season with salt and pepper. Remove from the oven and keep warm.
6. Combine beef, onion, one egg, panko, salt, and pepper in a large mixing bowl.
7. Make four flat oval patties by dividing the mixture in half. In a pan, heat the oil and cook the patties for 5 minutes over medium heat, then flip and cook on the other side until done.
8. Eggs can be fried sunny side up or over easy.
9. When the rice is done, divide it onto serving plates and top with cooked hamburger patties. Serve the gravy with a fried egg on top.
10. Serve with iceberg lettuce and tomato slices on the side.

61. MAKI SUSHI (SUSHI ROLL)

Ingredients:

- Cooked Sushi rice
- Nori (seaweed)

Instructions

1. On top of a bamboo mat, lay a nori sheet (makisu). On top of the nori sheet, spread the sushi rice. Place the items on the rice lengthwise.
2. Roll the sushi up the bamboo mat, pressing forward to form a cylinder.
3. Remove the bamboo mat from the sushi by pressing it hard.
4. Cut the sushi rolls into bite-size pieces (usually 8 pieces).

62. NEW ORLEANS STYLE RED BEANS AND RICE

Ingredients (serves 4):

To Cook in the Rice Cooker:

- 1 Tbsp. extra virgin olive oil
- 1/2 tsp. salt
- 2 tsp. Louisiana style hot sauce
- 1/2 tsp. dried thyme
- 1 Tbsp. celery, minced
- 1 Tbsp. onion, minced
- 1 Tbsp. green bell pepper, minced
- 1 clove garlic, minced
- 4 Tbsp. Andouille sausage, minced
- 4 Tbsp. canned red kidney beans
- 2 cups (rice measuring cup) long grain white rice
- 2 1/2 cups (rice measuring cup) chicken broth

Instructions

1. Prepare the materials for rice cooking. Blend olive oil, salt, spicy sauce, thyme, celery, onion, bell pepper, garlic, sausage, and kidney beans in a mixing dish and well combine.
2. Use the measuring cup that came with your rice cooker to correctly measure the rice. Once the rice has been rinsed, drain it and set it in the inner frying pan.

3. Toss the rice with the chicken broth. Make sure the sausage combination is equally distributed on top of the rice and that it is completely buried in the liquid. Mixing with rice is not a good idea.
4. Close the lid on the rice cooker and place the inner cooking pan inside. Use the "MIXED" setting to cook the rice.
5. When the rice is done cooking, fluff it with a rice spatula to loosen it up.
6. Serve immediately on a heated platter.
7. Optional: Serve with your favorite meat or seafood on top of the rice.
8. Enjoy!

63. NIÇOISE BROWN RICE SALAD

Ingredients (serves 4):
To Cook in the Rice Cooker:

- 1 cup (rice measuring cup) short or medium grain brown rice
- Water to fill to water level 1 for "BROWN RICE"
- 1/4 tsp. salt

For Dressing:

- 1 Tbsp. capers, rinsed
- 1 Tbsp. anchovy paste
- 1/2 tsp. garlic paste
- 3 Tbsp. Italian parsley leaves, chopped
- 2 Tbsp. lemon juice
- 1/4 cup olive oil

For Salad:

- 12 green beans, trimmed
- 3 green onions, thinly sliced
- 1 English cucumber, diced
- 2 x 5 oz. cans tuna in oil, drained, flaked
- 1/3 cup Kalamata olives, pitted
- 2 hard-boiled eggs, cut in 1/6
- 6 cherry tomatoes, cut in halves

Ingredients (serves 8):
To Cook in the Rice Cooker:

- 2 cup (rice measuring cup) short or medium grain brown rice

- Water to fill to water level 2 for "BROWN RICE"
- 1/2 tsp. salt

For Dressing:

- 2 Tbsp. capers, rinsed
- 2 Tbsp. anchovy paste
- 1 tsp. garlic paste
- 6 Tbsp. Italian parsley leaves, chopped
- 4 Tbsp. lemon juice
- 1/2 cup olive oil

For Salad:

- 24 green beans, trimmed
- 6 green onions, thinly sliced
- 2 English cucumber, diced
- 4 x 5 oz. cans tuna in oil, drained, flaked
- 2/3 cup Kalamata olives, pitted
- 4 hard-boiled eggs, cut in 1/6
- 12 cherry tomatoes, cut in halves

Instructions

1. Use the measuring cup that came with your rice cooker to correctly measure the rice. Quickly rinse the rose, drain, and set in the inner cooking pan.
2. Fill the corresponding water level for "BROWN RICE" with water. Then, using the rice spatula, add salt and mix well. Use the "BROWN" setting to cook the rice.
3. Combine all dressing ingredients in a large mixing basin.
4. Cook beans for 3 to 4 minutes in boiling salted water (not listed in the ingredients list) or until crisp-tender. Drain the beans and place them in cold water right away. Cut into quarter-length pieces.
5. When the rice is done, transfer it to a big plate and set it aside. When the rice is cool enough to handle, add it to the bowl with the dressing from step 3, along with the green onions and cucumber, and gently stir.
6. Serve the rice salad on plates. Arrange tuna, olives, eggs, and cherry tomatoes in a serving dish. Serve right away.
7. Enjoy!

64. NIGIRI SUSHI

Ingredients (serves 4, makes 48 pieces):

- 3 cups* cooked sushi rice
- 48 bite-sized pieces of topping (sashimi-quality fish, seafood or any sliced food of your choice) in 1.5" x 3.5" strips, with thickness up to 1/2"
- Wasabi paste (Japanese horseradish), optional
- Water to wet hands to prevent rice from sticking:
- 1 cup cold water
- 1 Tbsp. rice vinegar

Garnish and Condiments:

- Soy sauce
- Pickled ginger
- Wasabi paste
- Garlic, sliced and roasted
- Basil
- *3 cups raw rice, about 2-lbs. cooked rice

Instructions

1. Hands should be thoroughly washed, and a plating dish should be nearby.
2. In a small bowl, combine 1 cup cold water and 1 tbsp rice vinegar. In this hand water, wet both hands.
3. In your left hand, lay a piece of sliced topping flat on your palm.
4. Lightly grab a bite-sized ball of sushi rice using the tips of your right hand's fingers (0.6-0.7 oz., 15-20g). Avoid squeezing the rice.
5. Scoop a little amount of wasabi paste with your right index finger while holding the rice ball in your palm.
6. In your left palm, smear the wasabi on the middle of the sliced topping.
7. Place the rice ball on the topping on your right palm.
8. Make an indentation in the middle of the rice ball with your left thumb. (This keeps the rice stable and creates a little air pocket in the rice, giving it a fluffy feel.)
9. To end up with the topping side up, roll the sushi on your left hand towards your fingertips.
10. With your left thumb, shape the top edge of the sushi.
11. The edge of the sushi is the shorter side.
12. Gently fold your left hand to shape the sushi on the sides without moving your thumb, while holding the topping in place with your right index and middle fingers. The right fingers act as a lid for the mold on the left hand. To exert pressure, do not utilize.
13. Turn the sushi 180 ° clockwise.
14. Steps 10-12 should be repeated.

15. With your right hand, hold the sides of the sushi and place the finished sushi on the serving dish.
16. When viewed from the side, your sushi rice should resemble a boat.
17. Serve right away.

65. OATMEAL PEAR SURPRISE

Ingredients (serves 4):
For Oatmeal:

- 1 cup (rice measuring cup) steel cut oats
- Water to fill to water level 1 for "STEEL CUT OATMEAL" or 2-1/2 cups (rice measuring cup)

To Prepare Separately:

- 1 (15 oz.) can pear halves in juice, reserve juice
- 1 tsp. ground cinnamon
- 1 (6 oz.) pkg. raspberries
- 4 Tbsp. honey
- 1 cup yogurt

Please use the measuring cup that came with your rice cooker to measure the rice.

Instructions

1. Using the measuring cup that came with your rice cooker, correctly measure steel cut oats. Steel-cut oats should be placed in the inner frying pan. Fill the cup halfway with water for "STEEL CUT OATMEAL," or as directed in the ingredients.
2. Place the inner cooking pan in the rice cooker's main body and turn it on. Use the "STEEL CUT OATMEAL" (if available) or "PORRIDGE" setting to cook the steel cut oats.
3. Transfer one cup of steel cut oats to a bowl once they've finished cooking. Only 1 cup of steel cut oats will be used in this recipe. Combine the ground cinnamon and pear juice in a mixing bowl. Mix thoroughly and leave aside for at least 30 minutes to cool. Take care not to overmix the ingredients.
4. Cut the pear halves into dice. Toss the chopped pear, raspberries, and honey in a separate bowl lightly.
5. Step 3: Distribute the chilled oatmeal between 4 serving glasses.
6. Step 5: Spread a layer of yogurt on top of the oatmeal.
7. Place the fruit mixture from step 4 on top.
8. Enjoy!

66. OHAGI (JAPANESE SWEET RICE WITH ADZUKI PASTE)

Ingredients (makes 10):
To Cook in the Rice Cooker:

- 2 cups (rice measuring cup) sweet rice
- Water to fill to water level 2 for "SWEET RICE"

For Seasoning Rice:

- 1/4 tsp. salt
- For Adzuki Paste:
- 5 oz. adzuki beans
- 2/3 cup sugar
- 1/4 tsp. salt

For Matcha Ohagi:

- 1/2 tsp. matcha (green tea powder)
- 1/2 tsp. powdered sugar

NOTE:

This recipe cannot be made in Rice Cooker models NP-GBC05, NS-LAC05, NS-WXC10/18, NS-VGC05, NS-PC10/18, NS-RNC10/18 and NHS-06/10/18 as they do not have the Sweet rice setting.

Instructions

1. Rinse the rice, drain it, and strain it for at least 30 minutes. Allowing the rice to drain will help the rice texture in this dish.
2. To make the adzuki paste, combine all of the ingredients in a blender and blend until smooth. Adzuki beans should be carefully rinsed before being placed in a sauce pan with 2 cups of water (not included in the ingredients list). Bring to a boil over medium heat, then remove from heat.
3. In the sauce pan with the adzuki beans, add 2 cups of fresh water. Cook for an additional 1 hour and 30 minutes over medium low heat, or until the beans are soft enough to break with your fingertips. When surface scum appears, skim it off. During cooking, keep the beans immersed in water and add more if necessary.
4. In the inside cooking pan, place the rice. Fill the water level for "SWEET RICE" with water and cook the rice on the "SWEET RICE" setting.
5. Add half of the sugar to the pan when the beans are cooked, stir with a wooden spatula, and simmer for 5 minutes. Cook for another 10 minutes, or until the mixture has the consistency of mashed potatoes. Add the salt, remove from the heat, and set aside.

6. When the rice is done cooking, move it to a large mixing basin, season it with salt, and mash it with a potato masher. To keep the rice texture, mash halfway through.
7. Warm the mashed rice and spread it out on a baking sheet fitted with parchment paper. With a damp spatula, spread the rice out and divide it into ten pieces.
8. Make matcha ohagi rice balls. Place a piece of plastic wrap over a small bowl, add one piece of cooked rice, and use a wet spoon to make a dimple in the center. As a filling, place roughly 1 tbsp of adzuki paste in the center.
9. By lightly squeezing your hands together, hold the rice over the plastic wrap and form an oval-shaped rice ball. Make a total of 5
10. Make red bean ohagi rice balls. Make 5 oval-shaped rice balls without any filling using the remaining rice. Divide the remaining adzuki paste into five equal portions. Place a piece of plastic wrap over a small bowl and form a dimple in the center with one of the adzuki paste chunks.
11. Place the rice ball from step 10 in the center, place the adzuki paste on top of the plastic wrap, and lightly squeeze your hands together to form a flat oval shape, covering the rice with the adzuki paste. To make a total of 5, combine the following items. Serve on a serving platter (s).
12. In a separate dish, combine matcha and powdered sugar and, using a tea strainer, sprinkle over matcha ohagi rice balls from step 8.
13. Serve on a serving platter (s). Serve right away to experience the rice's delicate texture.

67. ONIGIRAZU RICE SANDWICH

Ingredients (makes 8 onigirazu):
To Cook in the Rice Cooker:

- 2 cups (rice measuring cup) short or medium grain white rice
- Water to fill to water level 2 for "WHITE RICE"

For Tuna and Cucumber Filling:

- 1 can (5 oz.) tuna in oil, drained, broken into small pieces
- 2 Tbsp. mayonnaise
- 1 tsp. wasabi paste
- 1/8 tsp. black pepper
- 1/2 cup cucumber, julienned
- 1/2 tsp. salt
- For Ham and Cheese Filling:
- 2 sliced cheddar cheese
- 2 sliced ham, thick cut
- 2 tsp. mayonnaise
- 1/2 cup arugula

For Wrap:

4 sheets nori (seaweed), 7.5" x 8" each

Instructions

1. Use the items mentioned under "To Cook in the Rice Cooker" to make white rice. To learn how to cook white rice, go here.
2. Mix cucumber with salt in a separate bowl and put aside for 10 minutes, then squeeze and drain excess water by hand. Refrigerate both bowls to keep them chilled.
3. To make the tuna and cucumber filling, combine all of the ingredients in a mixing bowl. Using a paper towel, squeeze any residual tuna oil. Combine in a mixing bowl with mayonnaise, wasabi, and black pepper.
4. When the rice is done cooking, move it to a separate bowl and fluff it lightly with a rice spatula. Allow 5 to 7 minutes for the rice to cool slightly.
5. Assemble the onigirazu with the ham and cheese. Cut a 7 to 8-inch-long piece of plastic wrap and place it on a cutting board. Place a nori sheet in the center of the plastic wrap.
6. Place one sliced cheese diagonally in the center of the nori.
7. 1/8 cup cooked rice, spread in the center of the cheese
8. Spread 1 tbsp mayonnaise over the rice and top with 1/4 cup arugula.
9. Place 1/8 cup cooked rice on top of the arugula.
10. Pull two opposite corners of the nori towards the center using the plastic wrap. To seal the nori to the rice, press down. Then peel back the plastic wrap with care.
11. Pull the remaining corners of the nori to the center with the plastic wrap and gently press down to seal and keep its shape. To prepare another ham and cheese onigirazu, repeat the instructions.
12. Assemble the onigirazu with the tuna and cucumber. Place a sheet of nori on top of a sheet of plastic wrap on a cutting board. 1/8 cup rice, half cup tuna, half cup cucumber, 1/8 cup rice, 1/8 cup tuna, half cup cucumber, 1/8 cup cucumber, 1/8 cup cucumber, 1/8 cup cucumber, 1/8 cup cucumber, 1/8 cup cucumber, 1/8 cup cucumber,
13. Fold and shape the onigirazu by repeating steps 8 and 9. To create another tuna and cucumber onigirazu, repeat the instructions.
14. Slice onigirazu in half with a knife while the plastic wrap is still attached.
15. Whether you're packing to go or eating right away, there's something for everyone.

68. FRIED RICE

READY IN: 1hr 5mins

SERVES: 4-6

YIELD: 10 cups

UNITS: US

INGREDIENTS

- 2 cups uncooked rice
- 1 cup cooked bacon or 1 cup cooked sausage
- 1 cup cooked chicken
- 1 cup carrot
- 2 eggs, scrambled and chopped up
- 1/4 cup soy sauce
- 2 tsps fresh ginger
- 2 tsps fresh garlic
- 4 -6 spring onions
- 1 3/4 cups chicken broth
- 2 tsps peanut oil
- 1/2 cup cilantro

DIRECTIONS

1. Using cold water, rinse the rice. As needed, change the water until it is almost white. When you're finished, place the rice in the bottom of the rice cooker.
2. Sausage, chicken, carrots, soy sauce, ginger, garlic, chicken broth, peanut oil, and the white part of the spring onions should all be combined. The green part of the spring onions, the cilantro, and the eggs can be saved for another time.
3. Fill the rice cooker halfway with water. Step 2: Pour in the mixture. DON'T COMBINE THE TWO. On the bottom, the rice will cook, while the mixture will cook on top.
4. Cook the rice according to the instructions on the rice cooker. I used the tougher cook setting on mine and set it to white rice (it leaves the rice a bit crunchier). With my rice cooker, it takes roughly 40 minutes.
5. Add the rest of the spring onions, cilantro, and the cooked eggs to the rice after it's done cooking. Close the cover after stirring the rice to combine the ingredients. Set the temperature to "warm" for 10 minutes.
6. Enjoy!

69. OYAKO-DONBURI (CHICKEN AND EGG BOWL)

Ingredients (serves 2):

- 0.3 lb. chicken thigh meat, boneless and skinless
- 1/4 onion, thinly sliced
- 2/3 cup ichiban dashi or 1/2 tsp. dashinomoto + 2/3 cup water
- 1 Tbsp. sake (rice wine)
- 2 Tbsp. mirin (Japanese sweet rice wine)
- 1 tsp. sugar
- 2 Tbsp. soy sauce
- 4 eggs
- 2-1/2 cups cooked short or medium grain white or brown rice

Garnish (optional):

1. Mitsuba (Japanese cryptotaenia) or cilantro

Instructions

1. Chicken thigh should be cut into bite-sized pieces.
2. Add the chicken, onion, dashi, sake, mirin, salt, and soy sauce to a frying pan. Bring the water to a boil. Reduce the heat to medium and cook for another 5 minutes.
3. In a basin, lightly beat the egg. 2/3 of the beaten egg should be equally distributed over the chicken and onion combination. Cook for about a minute, or until the egg coagulates.
4. Fill the pan with the remaining egg. Turn off the heat when the egg begins to coagulate, around 30 seconds. Allow one minute to set before covering with a lid.
5. Warm the rice in serving dishes. Drizzle with sauce to taste and top with a chicken omelet.
6. Mitsuba can be used as a garnish if desired.
7. Enjoy!

70. PAD THAI SHRIMP MIXED RICE

Ingredients (serves 4):
To Cook in the Rice Cooker:

- 2 cups (rice measuring cup) jasmine rice
- 2 oz. ketchup
- 2 oz. fish sauce
- 3 Tbsp. lime juice
- 2 Tbsp. brown sugar
- 1/2 tsp. red chili flakes
- 8 oz. water

To Prepare Separately:

- 2 Tbsp. peanut oil
- 2 Tbsp. shallot, minced
- 5 cloves garlic, minced
- 2 carrots, grated
- 3 eggs, slightly beaten
- 12 oz. raw shrimp, shelled and cut into thirds
- 4 green onions, cut into 1" slivers
- 1/4 cup cilantro, chopped
- 1/4 cup unsalted roasted peanuts, slightly crushed
- 1 lime, quartered

Instructions

1. Place the rice in the inner cooking pan after correctly measuring it with the measuring cup that came with your rice cooker.
2. Using the rice spatula, combine ketchup, fish sauce, lime juice, brown sugar, red chili flakes, and water in the inner cooking pan. Use the "MIXED" setting to cook the rice.
3. In a big sauté pan, heat the peanut oil until it is hot while the rice is cooking. Cook until the shallots and garlic are tender, about 2 minutes.
4. Cook until the grated carrots are tender, about 1 minute.
5. Add the beaten egg to one side of the pan and move the ingredients to the other. Cook until hard, cutting into pieces with a spatula.
6. Cook for 2 minutes, or until shrimp is just slightly done. Remove all of the ingredients from the pan and keep them heated until the rice is done.
7. When the rice is done cooking, use a rice spatula to gently fold in the cooked shrimp and egg mixture.

8. Fill individual serving bowls with rice. Green onions, cilantro, peanuts, and a lime slice should be garnished in each bowl.

71. PAELLA

<For 5 or 10 cup Zojirushi Rice Cookers>
Ingredients (serves 4-6):

To Prepare in Advance:

- 1 Tbsp. extra virgin olive oil
- 4 cloves garlic, minced
- 1 cup minced onion
- 1 tsp. salt
- 2 bay leaves, crushed
- 1/4 tsp. saffron
- 1 tsp. paprika
- 1 cup diced fresh tomato
- 4 oz. chicken broth
- 1 lb. mussels
- 1 lb. clams
- 1/2 lb. shrimp, peeled and deveined

To Cook in the Rice Cooker:

- 2 cups (rice measuring cup) short or medium grain white rice

To Prepare Separately:

- 1 cup frozen green peas
- 2 Tbsp. chopped parsley
- Lemon wedges

<For 3 cup Zojirushi Rice Cookers>
Ingredients (serves 2-3):

To Prepare in Advance:

- 1/2 Tbsp. extra virgin olive oil
- 2 cloves garlic, minced
- 1/2 cup minced onion
- 1/2 tsp. salt
- 1 bay leaf, crushed

- 1/8 tsp. saffron
- 1/2 tsp. paprika
- 1/2 cup diced fresh tomato
- 2 oz. chicken broth
- 1/2 lb. mussels
- 1/2 lb. clams
- 1/4 lb. shrimp, peeled and deveined

To Cook in the Rice Cooker:

- 1 cup (rice measuring cup) short or medium grain white rice
- To Prepare Separately:
- 1/2 cup frozen green peas
- 1 Tbsp. chopped parsley
- Lemon wedges

Instructions

1. In a sauté pan, heat the oil and sweat the garlic and onions until they are just browned, then add the salt, bay leaf, saffron, and paprika.
2. Bring the tomatoes and chicken broth to a boil. Combine the mussels and clams in a large mixing bowl.
3. Cover and steam for 2 minutes, then add the shrimp and steam for another 2 minutes.
4. When the seafood is done, drain the cooking liquid and set it aside.
5. In a large mixing bowl, combine the cooked seafood and frozen peas; cover and set aside at room temperature while the rice cooks.
6. Use the measuring cup that came with your rice cooker to correctly measure the rice. Drain the rice and set it in the inner cooking pan after rinsing it until the water runs clean. To reach the water level "2" for "MIXED RICE" in 5 and 10 cup rice cookers, and up to the water level "1" in 3 cup rice cookers, add the saved cooking liquid from step 4. Use chicken broth or water if more liquid is required. Use the "MIXED" setting during cooking.
7. Microwave the shrimp and green peas for 30 seconds after the rice is done cooking, then mix in the cooked rice. (Do not place the seafood in the inner cooking pan since the shell may scratch the nonstick surface.) Serve in heated bowls with lemon wedges and garnished with chopped parsley.

72. PROSCIUTTO RICE BALLS

Ingredients (makes 8 rice balls):
To Cook in the Rice Cooker:

- 2 cups (rice measuring cup) short or medium grain white rice
- Water to fill to water level 2 for "WHITE RICE"

For Rice Balls:

- 4 slices prosciutto
- 3 Tbsp. grated parmesan cheese
- 8 small basil leaves

Instructions

1. Use the items mentioned under "To Cook in the Rice Cooker" to make white rice. To learn how to cook white rice, go here.
2. When the rice is done, add the parmesan cheese and gently fold it in with the rice spatula. Remove from the equation.
3. Cut a 7 to 8-inch-long piece of plastic wrap and set it in a small basin. 1/8 of the rice from step 2 should be placed on top of the plastic wrap. By lightly squeezing your hands together, gather the plastic wrap over the rice and form an oblong rice ball. The rice ball should be hard enough not to fall apart, yet fluffy enough not to be smashed. Make seven more rice balls by repeating this process.
4. Unwrap each rice ball and lay a basil leaf on top.
5. Cut each prosciutto slice in half lengthwise, remove each rice ball from its plastic wrapper, and wrap prosciutto around the basil leaves and rice balls. Re-wrap the rice balls in plastic and press softly to shape them.
6. Remove the plastic wrap and place the plate on the counter.
7. Enjoy!

73. PUTTANESCA RICE SALAD

Ingredients (serves 4-6):

- To Cook in the Rice Cooker
- 1 cup (rice measuring cup) long grain white rice
- Water to fill to water level 1 for "LONG GRAIN WHITE," or 1-1/4 cups (rice measuring cup)
- 1/4 tsp. salt

To Add to Cooked, Cooled Rice:

- 2 Tbsp. sundried tomatoes, soaked in hot water for 10 minutes, liquid squeezed and roughly chopped
- 2 Tbsp. capers, roughly chopped
- 6 fillets anchovies, finely chopped
- 10 pitted black and green olives, sliced
- 1/2 cup fresh baby spinach and/or baby arugula leaves
- 1 Tbsp. olive oil

To Add Before Serving:

- 1 Tbsp. freshly squeezed lemon juice

Instructions

1.
   Use the measuring cup that came with your rice cooker to correctly measure the rice. Once the rice has been rinsed, drain it and set it in the inner frying pan.
2. Fill the container halfway with water for "LONG GRAIN WHITE," or as directed in the ingredients. In the inner cooking pan, add the salt and stir well from the bottom. If available, cook the rice on the "LONG GRAIN WHITE" or "MIXED" option.
3. When the rice is done cooking, fluff it with a rice spatula and spread it out on a big platter. Refrigerate for 30 minutes to cool.
4. When the rice has cooled, add the additional ingredients, except the lemon juice, and gently stir.
5. Refrigerate for a further 20-30 minutes to allow flavors to meld. Add the lemon juice right before serving and mix lightly to incorporate. Enjoy!

74. QUINOA AND CHICKEN SUPER SALAD

Ingredients (serves 4):
To Cook in the Rice Cooker:

- 1 cup (rice measuring cup) quinoa
- Water to fill to the water level 1 for "QUINOA"
- 1 tsp. chicken consommé powder

For Salad:

- 10 oz. roast chicken or canned chicken, cut into bite-sized pieces
- 1 bunch asparagus, trimmed ends
- 1/2 red bell pepper, diced small
- 1/4 red onion, diced small

For Dressing:

- 2 Tbsp. olive oil
- 1 Tbsp. lemon juice
- 1/3 tsp. salt
- 1/4 tsp. cumin powder
- 1/8 tsp. black pepper

Instructions

1. The Zojirushi Micom Rice Cooker & Warmer NL-BAC05 was used to create this recipe. Please refer to your Quick Start Guide for instructions on how to prepare quinoa in your model. This recipe will not work in the Pressure IH Rice Cooker (models NP-HTC10/18 and NP-NVC10/18).
2. Use the measuring cup that came with your rice cooker to correctly measure the quinoa and transfer it to the inner cooking pan. If the quinoa hasn't been washed, strain it through a fine mesh strainer and rinse it with water before adding it to the inner cooking pan. Cook using the "QUINOA" setting and adding water to the relevant water level.
3. When the quinoa has finished cooking, stir in the chicken consommé powder with a rice spatula and spread out on a big platter. Remove from the equation.
4. Mix together all of the dressing ingredients in a large mixing basin.
5. Cook asparagus for 2 to 3 minutes in boiling salted water (not listed in the ingredients list) or until crisp-tender. Drain the asparagus and place them in cold water right away. Cut each piece into a quarter-length section.
6. Lightly blend the chicken and quinoa, asparagus, red bell pepper, and red onion in the bowl with the dressing. Serve right away.
7. Enjoy!

75. QUINOA BURGER DELUXE

Ingredients (serves 4):

To Cook in the Rice Cooker:

- 1 cup (rice measuring cup) quinoa
- Water to fill to the water level 1 for "QUINOA"
- For Quinoa:
- 1/2 onion, minced
- 3 Tbsp. parmesan cheese, grated
- 1/4 tsp. salt
- 1/8 tsp. black pepper
- 3/4 cup Panko bread crumbs (Japanese bread crumbs)
- 1 tsp. garlic, grated
- 3 Tbsp. parsley, minced
- 4 eggs, beaten
- 2 Tbsp. olive oil

For Sauce:

- 1 Tbsp. ketchup
- 1 Tbsp. Worcestershire sauce
- 1 Tbsp. soy sauce
- 1 Tbsp. honey
- 1 Tbsp. water

Note:

The Zojirushi Micom Rice Cooker & Warmer NL-BAC05 was used to create this recipe. Please refer to your Quick Start Guide for instructions on how to prepare quinoa in your model. This recipe will not work in the Pressure IH Rice Cooker (models NP-HTC10/18 and NP-NVC10/18).

Instructions

1. Use the measuring cup that came with your rice cooker to correctly measure the quinoa and transfer it to the inner cooking pan. If the quinoa hasn't been washed, strain it through a fine mesh strainer and rinse it with water before adding it to the inner cooking pan. For "QUINOA," add water to the appropriate water level.
2. Use the "QUINOA" setting during cooking.
3. Transfer the cooked quinoa to a large mixing bowl and let aside to cool slightly.

4. When the quinoa has cooled, combine it with the onion, parmesan cheese, salt, pepper, bread crumbs, garlic, and parsley in a mixing bowl. When the mixture is cool enough to handle, add the beaten eggs and stir thoroughly.
5. In a frying pan, heat the olive oil. Divide the ingredients into four equal portions and form four big patties. Cook patties for 3 minutes on each side in a frying pan over medium low heat. Turn off the heat and transfer to a serving platter to cool. Keep the grease in a separate container.
6. Assemble the sauce. In the same frying pan, combine all of the Sauce ingredients. Stir to combine, then reduce to a low heat. Turn off the heat, remove the pan from the heat, and pour over the patties.
7. Serve with rice or make burgers with them.
8. Enjoy!

76. RICE AND BEANS WITH BACON AND COLLARD GREENS

Ingredients (serves 2-3):

To Cook in the Rice Cooker:

- 1 cup (rice measuring cup) long grain white rice
- 8 oz. low sodium chicken broth
- 1/4 tsp. dried thyme
- 1/16 tsp. ground black pepper
- 1/2 Tbsp. shallot, minced
- 1 bay leaf, whole
- 1/4 cup (rice measuring cup) mixed dried beans, soaked in water overnight
- 1 strip bacon, cooked, drained of oil and chopped

To Prepare Separately:

- 1/2 cup fresh tomatoes, diced
- 1/4 cup collard greens (may substitute with spinach), cooked, drained and roughly chopped
- Hot pepper sauce (optional)

Ingredients (serves 4-6):

To Cook in the Rice Cooker:

- 2 cups (rice measuring cup) long grain white rice
- 16 oz. low sodium chicken broth
- 1/2 tsp. dried thyme
- 1/8 tsp. ground black pepper
- 1 Tbsp. shallot, minced

- 1 bay leaf, whole
- 1/2 cup (rice measuring cup) mixed dried beans, soaked in water overnight
- 2 strips bacon, cooked, drained of oil and chopped

To Prepare Separately:

- 1 cup fresh tomatoes, diced
- 1/2 cup collard greens (may substitute with spinach), cooked, drained and roughly chopped
- Hot pepper sauce (optional)

Instructions

1.
   Use the measuring cup that came with your rice cooker to correctly measure the rice. Once the rice has been rinsed, drain it and set it in the inner frying pan.
2. Using the rice spatula, combine the chicken broth, thyme, pepper, and shallot in the inner frying pan.
3. On top of the rice, arrange the bay leaf, beans, and cooked bacon. Mixing with rice is not a good idea. Make sure that none of the ingredients are submerged in liquid. Use the "MIXED" setting to cook the rice.
4. When the rice is done cooking, remove the bay leaf and fluff the rice with a rice spatula.
5. Toss in the diced tomatoes and collard greens gently with a rice spatula. Serve immediately with a side of hot pepper sauce, if desired.
6. Enjoy!

77. RICE CROQUETTE

Ingredients (40 rice balls / serves 10):
To Cook in the Rice Cooker:

- 3 cups (rice measuring cup) short or medium grain white or brown rice
- Water to fill to water level 3 for "WHITE RICE" or "BROWN RICE"

To Prepare Separately:

- 3 oz. akamiso (brown colored miso)
- 1/4 cup mirin (Japanese sweet rice wine)
- 2 Tbsp. sake (rice wine)
- 1/2 tsp. shoyu (soy sauce)
- 3 Tbsp. sugar
- 1/2 lb. ground beef
- 1/2 cup finely chopped onions
- 2 Tbsp. vegetable oil
- 1 Tbsp. grated ginger
- 1/2 cup minced parsley or 1/4 cup thinly sliced chives
- 1 cup flour
- 1 Tbsp. garlic powder
- 1/4 tsp. sea salt
- 2 cups breadcrumbs
- 5 large eggs, lightly beaten, mixed with 5 Tbsp. water
- Vegetable oil for deep-frying
- Wedges of lemon

Instructions

1. Use the measuring cup that came with your rice cooker to correctly measure the rice. Drain and place white rice in the inner cooking pan after rinsing until water clears, or brown rice in the inner cooking pan after a fast rinse.
2. Depending on whether you're using "WHITE RICE" or "BROWN RICE," add water to the appropriate water level. White rice should be cooked on the "HARDER," "REGULAR" (if available), or "WHITE RICE" setting, whereas brown rice should be cooked on the "BROWN" setting.
3. In a bowl, combine the miso, mirin, sake, shoyu, and sugar while the rice is cooking.
4. Add oil to a hot skillet and sauté the onion until it is gently brown. Cook for 1 minute after adding the ginger. Cook the beef, breaking it up with a fork as it cooks, until it is crumbled and white. Cook, stirring constantly, until the miso mixture is no longer runny. If desired, remove any surplus oil. Set it aside and keep it warm.

5. Fold in the beef miso sauce and parsley/chives once the rice is done cooking. Make 40 rice balls (1 oz. each) while still hot, then freeze overnight.
6. Combine flour, garlic powder, and salt in a mixing basin. Separate the flour mixture, breadcrumbs, and lightly beaten eggs into three medium bowls. Pass the balls through the flour, then the egg, and then through the flour, then the egg, one at a time. The ball should then be passed through the breadcrumbs.
7. In a wok or deep saucepan heated to 340oF, pour 2-3 inches of oil, deep enough to cover the rice balls. Deep-fry the rice balls for 4 to 5 minutes, or until the outside is crispy and golden, never using more than half of the oil. With lemon wedges, serve the crisp and golden rice croquette.

78. RICE OMELET (JAPANESE OMU-RICE)

Ingredients (serves 2):

- 1 lb. cooked rice, warm, about 1-1/2 cups raw
- 4 oz. chicken thigh, boneless
- 5 mushrooms
- 2 Tbsp. butter
- 2 oz. onion, chopped
- 3 Tbsp. ketchup
- 1/4 cup chicken broth
- 1/2 tsp. salt
- 1/4 tsp. pepper
- 4 eggs
- 2 Tbsp. milk
- 2 Tbsp. vegetable oil

For Sauce:

- 1/4 cup ketchup
- 1 Tbsp. Worcestershire sauce

Instructions

1. Chicken should be diced into small pieces, and mushrooms should be sliced.
2. In a skillet over medium-high heat, melt the butter and cook the chicken, onion, and mushroom for 3 minutes.
3. Continue to simmer until the liquid has evaporated, adding 3 tbsps ketchup, chicken broth, salt, and pepper.
4. Toss in the cooked, warm rice and stir thoroughly. Set aside the chicken rice that has been cooked in the pan.

5. Combine eggs and milk in a mixing basin.
6. Wipe out the skillet and heat 1 tbsp of oil in it over medium heat, making sure the entire pan is coated. Half of the egg mixture should be poured into the pan.
7. Circularly move a spatula through the egg mixture until the egg is halfway cooked through.
8. Turn off the heat and place half of the chicken rice in the center of the egg mixture.
9. Fold one side of the egg over the rice by tilting the skillet to the side. Slide the omelet to the opposite side of the skillet by pushing and sliding it.
10. Flip the omelet onto a serving platter when it reaches the edge of the skillet, so the sides of the egg fold beneath the rice.
11. If necessary, adjust the shape using a paper towel. To create another omelet, repeat steps 6-11.
12. In a small bowl, combine the ketchup and Worcestershire sauce and pour over each omelet.
13. Serve immediately.

79. RICE SPRINKLES ONIGIRI

Ingredients (makes 8 onigiri):
To Cook in the Rice Cooker:

- 2 cups (rice measuring cup) short or medium grain white rice
- Water to fill to water level 2 for "WHITE RICE"

For Vegetable Furikake:

- 1 Tbsp. sesame oil
- 1 small carrot, diced
- 1/3 cup daikon, diced
- 2 cups kale leaves, chopped into small pieces
- 1 Tbsp. shoyu (soy sauce)
- 1 Tbsp. mirin (Japanese sweet rice wine)
- 1/2 tsp. sugar
- 1/4 tsp. salt
- 1 tsp. toasted white sesame seeds

Instructions

1.
   Use the items mentioned under "To Cook in the Rice Cooker" to make white rice. To learn how to cook white rice, go here.
2. Furikake can be made while the rice is cooking. In a frying pan, heat sesame oil over medium heat. Sauté the carrots, daikon, and kale in the pan for 3 minutes.
3. Add the shoyu, mirin, sugar, and salt to the pan and cook for another 3 minutes, or until the liquid has nearly completely evaporated, before adding the sesame seeds.
4. When the rice is done cooking, move it to a separate bowl, sprinkle with the furikake from step 3, and fold gently with the rice spatula.
5. Cut a 7 to 8-inch-long piece of plastic wrap and set it in a small basin. On top of the plastic wrap, sprinkle 1/8 cup of mixed rice. By lightly squeezing your hands together, gather the plastic wrap over the rice and form a triangle rice ball. The rice ball should be hard enough not to fall apart, yet fluffy enough not to be smashed. Make seven more onigiri by repeating the previous method.
6. Remove the plastic wrappers from the onigiri and place them on a dish.
7. Enjoy!

80. RICE WITH SAUSAGE, ONION, KETCHUP AND SUNNY-SIDE-UP EGG

Ingredients (serves 4 to 6)
To Cook in the Rice Cooker:

- 3 cups (rice measuring cup) short or medium grain white or brown rice
- Water to fill to water level 3 for "WHITE RICE" or "BROWN RICE"

To Prepare Separately:

- 2 Tbsp. vegetable oil
- 1 cup chopped onion
- 1/2 cup chicken stock
- 1 tsp. sea salt
- 1 tsp. Worcestershire sauce
- 10 oz. sweet-style sausage, cut into 1/2-inch square cubes
- 1 cup frozen mixed vegetable
- 1/4 cup ketchup
- 4 to 6 medium eggs
- Freshly ground black pepper

Instructions

1. Using the measuring cup that came with your rice cooker, accurately measure the rice. Place white rice in the inner cooking pan after rinsing until water clears, or brown rice in the inner cooking pan after a fast rinse.
2. Depending on whether you're using "WHITE RICE" or "BROWN RICE," add water to the appropriate water level. White rice should be cooked on the "HARDER," "REGULAR" (if available), or "WHITE RICE" setting, whereas brown rice should be cooked on the "BROWN" setting.
3. When the rice is done cooking, strain it and rinse it under cold tap water to chill it down and eliminate any excess starch. Before stir-frying the rice, drain it and let it aside for 20 minutes. If you're using rice that's already been cooked and stored in the fridge, skip this step.
4. Heat the vegetable oil in a large skillet or wok and sauté the onions for 5 to 10 minutes over medium-low heat. While the onions are cooking, season with 1/2 tsp salt. Cook the sausage over high heat until all of the pieces look to be fully cooked. Cook the mixture over moderately high heat until the stock is half absorbed, then add the chicken stock, Worcestershire sauce, and ketchup.
5. Combine the rice, frozen vegetables, and the remaining sea salt in a mixing bowl. Cook until the mixture is well heated. Lastly, season with freshly ground black pepper.

6. In a nonstick or ordinary skillet, cook four to six sunny-side-up eggs.
7. Divide the rice into 4 to 6 bowls and top each with a sunny-side-up egg.

81. PORTABELLA MUSHROOM RICE WITH BEEF AND BROCCOLI

Ingredients (serves 2-3):

To Cook in the Rice Cooker:

- 1.5 cups (rice measuring cup) Jasmine rice
- 12 oz. beef broth
- 1/2 Tbsp. soy sauce
- 1/2 garlic clove, thinly sliced
- 1/4 tsp. ground black pepper
- 1/2 cup baby portabella mushroom, 1/8" thick slices

To Prepare Separately:

1/3 lb. chuck, round or sirloin beef, thinly sliced

1/2 Tbsp. soy sauce

1/2 Tbsp. olive oil

1/8 tsp. ground black pepper

1.5 cups broccoli florets, pre-cooked, chopped in bite-size pieces

Ingredients (serves 4-6):

To Cook in the Rice Cooker:

2. 3 cups (rice measuring cup) Jasmine rice
3. 24 oz. beef broth
4. 1 Tbsp. soy sauce
5. 1 garlic clove, thinly sliced
6. 1/2 tsp. ground black pepper
7. 1-1/4 cups baby portabella mushroom, 1/8" thick slices

To Prepare Separately:

1. 3/4 lb. chuck, round or sirloin beef, thinly sliced
2. 1 Tbsp. soy sauce
3. 1 Tbsp. olive oil
4. 1/4 tsp. ground black pepper

5. 3 cups broccoli florets, pre-cooked, chopped in bite-size pieces

Instructions

1.
   Place the rice in the inner cooking pan after correctly measuring it with the measuring cup that came with your rice cooker.
2. Using the rice spatula, combine beef broth, soy sauce, garlic, and black pepper in the inner cooking pan.
3. Place mushroom slices on top of the rice and soak them in the broth. Mushrooms and rice should not be combined. Use the "MIXED" setting to cook the rice.
4. In a mixing bowl, combine the sliced beef, soy sauce, olive oil, and black pepper while the rice is cooking. Allow to marinate for a while. Cover broccoli florets with plastic wrap in a microwave-safe bowl.
5. When the rice has done cooking, fluff it lightly using a rice spatula. Sear the marinated meat in a heavy frying pan over medium heat. Stir frequently to avoid burning – about 1 minute.
6. To reheat the broccoli florets, microwave them on "high" for about 40 seconds.
7. With the rice spatula, carefully fold the browned beef and hot broccoli florets into cooked rice. Serve right away.
8. Enjoy!

82. SALMON CHAZUKE

Ingredients (serves 2):

1. 2 filets salmon (approx. 3 oz. each)
2. Salt to taste
3. 2 cups cooked rice (short or medium grain white rice)
4. 1/2 sheet nori seaweed
5. 2 shiso leaves (perilla) or basil
6. 1 tsp. soy sauce
7. 1 tsp. wasabi paste
8. 1 Tbsp. green tea leaves
9. 2-1/2 cups hot water (175°F)

Instructions

1. Season the salmon filets with salt and pepper. For 5 minutes, preheat the Gourmet Roaster. Roast fish for 8 minutes, or until gently browned on top. Remove the skin and bones from the salmon and break it up into flakes with two forks.
2. To remove extra starch, strain cooked rice through a sieve and rinse with hot water. Drain the rice thoroughly.
3. Nori seaweed and shiso leaves should be shredded.
4. Place rice, fish flakes, and soy sauce in two serving bowls. Nori seaweed, shiso leaves, and wasabi paste are sprinkled over top.
5. To assist the topping hold its shape, make a cup of green tea and pour it around the inside edge of the bowls. Serve right away.

83. SALMON TERIYAKI WITH MIXED VEGETABLES OVER RICE

Ingredients (serves 4-6):

To Cook in the Rice Cooker:

1. 3 cups (rice measuring cup) short or medium grain white or brown rice
2. Water to fill to water level 3 for "WHITE RICE" or "BROWN RICE"

To Prepare Separately:

Sauce:

1. 1 cup mirin (Japanese sweet rice wine)
2. 1/2 cup sake (rice wine)
3. 1/2 cup shoyu (soy sauce)
4. 1/4 cup sugar
5. 4 garlic cloves
6. 1 tsp. Italian hot dried chile flakes
7. 1 1/4 lbs. salmon with skin, cut into 4 to 6 pieces
8. 2 1/8 tsp. sea salt
9. 1 Tbsp. vegetable oil
10. 2 cups frozen mixed vegetables
11. 1 Tbsp. white sesame seeds

Instructions

1. Place the rice in the inner cooking pan after correctly measuring it. Rinse white rice until the water runs clear, or rinse brown rice once.
2. Depending on whether you're using "WHITE RICE" or "BROWN RICE," add water to the appropriate water level. White rice should be cooked on the "HARDER," "REGULAR" (if available), or "WHITE RICE" setting, whereas brown rice should be cooked on the "BROWN" setting.
3. Over medium heat, bring the mirin and sake to a simmer in a small saucepan. Bring the sugar and shoyu to a slow heat to dissolve the sugar. Reduce the heat to low, add the garlic, and continue to cook for another 7 minutes. Remove from the heat, stir in the chili flakes, and set aside to cool to room temperature.
4. 1 tsp salt on each side of the salmon pieces and set aside for 20 minutes. Rinse the salmon under cold running water, drain, and pat dry with a paper towel. Over medium heat, heat a nonstick or conventional skillet. Apply a small layer of oil to the skillet's bottom. Season the salmon with 1/8 tsp salt and set it skin-side down in the skillet. Cook the salmon until the skin is golden brown over medium-low heat. Turn the salmon over and cook for another 7 minutes over low heat, or until it is almost cooked through. Spread 6 to 8 tbsps of the prepared sauce equally over each fish in the skillet, allowing the sauce to sizzle. Make sure the sauce doesn't burn. Turn the heat off.

5. Divide the cooked rice into 4 to 6 bowls and set aside. 1 tbsp of the prepared sauce should be spooned over the rice. Place a piece of salmon on top of each rice portion. Divide the remaining sauce in the skillet and pour it over the fish. Make sure the skillet is clean.

6. Return the skillet to the burner and heat it on high. Add the vegetable oil and the frozen mixed vegetables when the oil begins to sizzle. Cook the vegetables for 1 to 2 minutes over high heat, stirring constantly. Remove the skillet from the heat and stir in 1–2 tbsps of the prepared sauce. Return the skillet to the heat and stir the vegetables and sauce together.

7. In the 4 to 6 bowls, arrange the cooked veggies next to the fish. Serve with a sprinkle of white sesame seeds on top of each bowl.

84. SALSA VERDE STYLE BROWN RICE

Ingredients (serves 4-6)

To Cook in the Rice Cooker:

1. 2 cups (rice measuring cup) short grain brown rice
2. Water to fill to water level 2 for "BROWN RICE"

To Prepare Separately:

1. 12 oz. fresh or frozen spinach
2. 1/4 cup water from cooking or defrosting spinach, or as needed
3. 1 shallot, peeled
4. 1 clove garlic, peeled
5. 2 Tbsp. caper in brine, drained
6. 1 Tbsp. fresh parsley, chopped
7. 1 Tbsp. fresh tarragon, chopped
8. 1/4 cup Parmesan cheese, grated
9. 4 canned anchovy filets

For Garnish:

1-2 oz. Grating cheese such as Ricotta salata cheese

Instructions

1.
   Use the measuring cup that came with your rice cooker to correctly measure the rice. Once the rice has been rinsed, drain it and set it in the inner frying pan.
2. Fill the pot halfway with water for "BROWN RICE," and cook the rice on the "BROWN" setting.

3. Prepare the salsa verde mixture while the rice is cooking. Cook fresh spinach in salted water that is rapidly boiling (not included in ingredient list). If you're using frozen spinach, thaw it in the microwave first. 1/4 cup spinach water is set aside for mixing.
4. Blend spinach, spinach water, and all other ingredients (excluding garnish) until smooth in a blender.
5. To warm the sauce, pour the pureed sauce into a sauce pot and heat gradually. Keep heated until the rice is finished cooking.
6. When the rice is done cooking, add the sauce and mix gently with the rice spatula.
7. Serve in individual serving bowls with shredded cheese on top. Serve immediately.
8. Enjoy!

85. SHIITAKE-GOHAN (SHIITAKE MUSHROOM RICE)

Ingredients (serves 4-6):
To Prepare in Advance:

1. 5 medium dried shiitake mushrooms
2. 1 cup water to soak shiitake (reserve)
3. 2 Tbsp. sake (rice wine)
4. 2 Tbsp. shoyu (soy sauce)
5. 2 Tbsp. mirin (Japanese sweet sake)

To Cook in the Rice Cooker:

1. 3 cups (rice measuring cup) short or medium grain white rice
2. Water to fill to water level 3 for "WHITE RICE"

To Prepare Separately:

- Stone parsley to taste
- Sliced ginger to taste

Ingredients (serves 2-3):
To Prepare in Advance:

- 2-1/2 medium dried shiitake mushrooms
- 1/2 cup water to soak shiitake (reserve)
- 1 Tbsp. sake (rice wine)
- 1 Tbsp. shoyu (soy sauce)
- 1 Tbsp. mirin (Japanese sweet sake)

To Cook in the Rice Cooker:

- cups (rice measuring cup) short or medium grain white rice

- Water to fill to water level 1.5 for "WHITE RICE"

To Prepare Separately:

- Stone parsley to taste
- Sliced ginger to taste

Instructions

1. To rehydrate the shiitake mushroom, soak it in water for 30 minutes to an hour. The shares will be held in reserve. Cook the shiitake mushrooms in the saved stock, sake, shoyu, and mirin for a few minutes.
2. Use the measuring cup that came with your rice cooker to correctly measure the rice. Drain the rice and set it in the inner cooking pan after rinsing it until the water runs clean. Fill the pot halfway with water and add the stock from step 1 to the "WHITE RICE" water level.
3. Mix in the cooked shiitake from step 1 well. Use the "MIXED" setting to cook the rice.
4. When the rice has done cooking, remove the lid and fluff the rice to release it before serving.
5. Garnish with stone parsley and thinly sliced ginger.

86. SHRIMP AND RICE CEVICHE

Ingredients (serves 4-6):

To Cook in the Rice Cooker:

- 1 cup (rice measuring cup) jasmine rice
- Water to fill to water level 1 for "JASMINE" or 1-1/4 cups (rice measuring cup)
- 1/2 tsp. salt

To Prepare Separately:

- 1 lb. fresh or frozen medium shrimp, peeled, deveined and cut in half length-wise (about 30 shrimps)
- 1/4 cup orange juice
- 1/2 cup fresh lime juice
- 2 Tbsp. red onion, finely chopped
- 1 medium carrot, thinly sliced and cut in halves
- 2-4 red radishes, thinly sliced
- 1 medium tomato, cut into bite sized pieces
- 1 stalk celery, cut into bite sized pieces
- 2 green onions, thinly sliced
- 1 small fresh jalapeño pepper, finely chopped
- 1/4 cup tomato juice
- 1/4 tsp. Worcestershire sauce
- 1 Tbsp. cilantro, chopped
- 1/2 tsp. salt
- 1/4 tsp. ground pepper

For Garnish:

- 1/2 ripe but firm avocado, pitted, peeled and diced

Instructions

1. Start by preparing the shrimp. Mix the orange and lime juice together in a small bowl. Soak the shrimp in the juice mixture for at least 1 hour to "cook."
2. Combine all remaining ingredients (excluding garnish) in a separate bowl. Allow for at least 30 minutes of marinating time in the refrigerator.
3. Use the measuring cup that came with your rice cooker to correctly measure the rice. Once the rice has been rinsed, drain it and set it in the inner frying pan.

4. Fill the container with water to the "JASMINE" water level, or as directed in the ingredients. Use the rice spatula to mix the salt into the inner cooking pan with the rice. Use the "JASMINE" (if available) or "WHITE RICE" setting to cook the rice.
5. When the rice is done cooking, fluff it lightly with a rice spatula and spread it out on a big platter to cool for 30 minutes.
6. Mix the shrimp and veggie mixture together thoroughly.
7. *This mixture can be made up to a day ahead of time.
8. 2/3 of the rice should be divided into large glass bowls once it has cooled. Evenly distribute the ceviche mixture over the rice. Place the leftover rice on top of the ceviche and top with avocado on each plate.

87. SHRIMP YAKIMESHI, STIR-FRIED RICE

Ingredients (serves 4-6):
To Cook in the Rice Cooker:

- 3 cups (rice measuring cup) short or medium grain white or brown rice
- Water to fill to water level 3 for "WHITE RICE" or "BROWN RICE"

To Prepare Separately:

- 3 Tbsp. vegetable oil
- 4 large eggs, lightly beaten
- 2 large garlic cloves, minced
- 3 scallions, both green and white parts, cut thin diagonally
- 10 oz. small shrimp, cleaned, shelled, frozen or fresh, cut into half diagonally
- 1 tsp. sea salt
- 2/3 cup frozen edamame soybeans or green peas, cooked in boiling water for 1 minute, cooled under cold tap water and drained
- 2 to 3 tsp. shoyu (soy sauce)
- 1/2 tsp. white pepper powder or freshly ground black peppercorn

Instructions

1. Use the measuring cup that came with your rice cooker to correctly measure the rice. Drain and place white rice in the inner cooking pan after rinsing until water clears, or brown rice in the inner cooking pan after a fast rinse.
2. Depending on whether you're using "WHITE RICE" or "BROWN RICE," add water to the appropriate water level. White rice should be cooked on the "HARDER," "REGULAR" (if available), or "WHITE RICE" setting, whereas brown rice should be cooked on the "BROWN" setting.

3. When the rice is done cooking, strain it and rinse it under cold tap water to chill it down and eliminate any excess starch. Before stir-frying the rice, drain it and let it aside for 20 minutes. If you're using rice that's already been cooked and stored in the fridge, skip this step.
4. In a wok or a big skillet, heat 2 tbsps vegetable oil and fry the eggs over moderately high heat. When the bottoms of the eggs have firmed up, give them a few hefty stirs with a spatula and transfer to a bowl. The egg is still delicate at this point, with a combination of firm cooked and runny parts.
5. Cook the garlic and scallion in the remaining 1 Tbsp. vegetable oil in the wok or skillet until fragrant, about 20 seconds over high heat. Add the shrimp and salt and heat, turning constantly with a spatula, until the outsides of the shrimp are white.
6. Cook, stirring constantly with a spatula, until the rice is thoroughly warm. Cook until the green peas or soybeans are cooked through. Add the eggs that were set aside. Shoyu with white or black peppercorns are used to season.
7. While still hot, divide and serve in 4 to 6 bowls.

88. SMOKED SALMON SUSHI STYLE

Ingredients (makes 12 pieces):
For Sushi Rice:

- 2 cups sushi rice
- 3 Tbsp. rice vinegar
- 1-1/2 Tbsp. sugar
- 1/2 tsp. salt

To Prepare Separately:

- 8 oz. sliced lox or cold-smoked salmon
- 1 stalk green onion, thinly sliced

Garnish:

- Fresh dill
- You will need a medium sized rigid loaf pan (aluminum, glass or ceramic; 8-1/2" x 4-1/2" size).

- 2 cups raw rice, about 1 lb. 7 oz. cooked rice

Instructions

1.

Sushi rice can be made with the items provided. To learn how to make sushi rice, click here.
2. Wax paper should be used to line the loaf pan.

3. Place one layer of ingredients at a time. Half of the smoked salmon slices should be on the bottom of the pan. Half of the sushi rice should be added and leveled. Cover rice with plastic wrap and firmly press down with fingers and a rubber spatula.

4. Remove the plastic wrap and set it aside for step 5. Cover rice with green onions and the remaining half of the smoked salmon.

5. Cover the smoked salmon with the remaining rice. Cover with plastic wrap and firmly press down with fingers and a rubber spatula.

6. Allow 15 minutes for the mixture to set at room temperature. Invert the loaf pan onto a cutting board, leaving the bottom side up, to remove the sushi.

7. Over lined paper, cut into bite-sized squares. Remove the paper and serve with dill on top.

8. Enjoy!

89. MUSUBI

Ingredients (serves 4):
To Cook in the Rice Cooker:

- 2 cups (rice measuring cup) short or medium grain white rice
- Water to fill to water level 2 for "WHITE RICE"

To Prepare Separately:

- 1 can SPAM lite or original
- For Egg Style Musubi:
- 1 egg
- 1/4 tsp. sugar
- 1/8 tsp. salt
- 1 tsp. vegetable oil
- 4 sheets nori seaweed, 4"x 8" sheets

For Teriyaki Style Musubi:

- 1/2 Tbsp. shoyu (soy sauce)
- 1/4 tsp. sugar
- 1/2 Tbsp. mirin (Japanese sweet rice wine)
- 4 strips nori seaweed, 2" x 8" strips

Instructions

1.

Use the items mentioned under "To Cook in the Rice Cooker" to make white rice. To learn how to cook white rice, go here.

2. When the rice is done cooking, move it to a separate bowl and fluff it lightly with a rice spatula. Remove from the equation.
3. In a small mixing bowl, crack the egg and add 1/4 tsp sugar and 1/8 tsp salt.
4. Heat a small frying pan over medium-high heat for 1 minute. Cook for 30 seconds or until half done after spreading vegetable oil and pouring the egg mixture from step 3. Cook for another 10 seconds after flipping the egg.
5. Cut cooked egg in quarters on a cutting board, then trim to 3.5" x 2" size, similar to a SPAM® piece. Remove from the equation.
6. Remove the SPAM from the can and cut it into 8 pieces horizontally. In a large frying pan, cook SPAM® on both sides over medium high heat until crispy brown, about 2-3 minutes per side. Turn off the heat and place 4 pieces on a plate to cool.
7. "Teriyaki Style Musubi" should be made. Sauté the remaining 4 pieces of SPAM in the pan with the shoyu, sugar, and mirin from the "Teriyaki Style Musubi" components over low heat. Cook for 1-2 minutes after flipping SPAM and coating it with sauce. Turn off the heat and transfer to a separate dish to cool.
8. Put together the "Egg Style Musubi." Place a 4"x 8" nori sheet on a cutting board and lay rice about 1/2" thick, the size of one piece of SPAM (3.5" x 2").
9. Place one fried egg slice from step 5 on top of the rice.
10. On the egg, place a piece of grilled plain SPAM from step 6.
11. Spread another half-inch layer of rice on top of the SPAM.
12. Nori should be rolled and wrapped, and the shape should be fixed with your hands. To create 3 more musubi, repeat steps 8-12. Allow for 5 minutes of resting time before cutting into halves and plating.
13. Assemble the "Musubi in Teriyaki Style." Place a 7 to 8-inch-long piece of plastic wrap on a cutting board. Place a handful of rice on top of the grilled teriyaki-flavored SPAM from step 7 on the plastic wrap.
14. By lightly squeezing your hands together, gather the plastic wrap around the contents and form an oval rice ball. The rice ball should be hard enough not to fall apart, yet fluffy enough not to be smashed. To make three more rice balls, repeat steps 13 and 14.
15. Remove the plastic wrap and wrap a 2" x 8" nori strip around the middle of each musubi.
16. Enjoy!

90. SPICY BASMATI RICE WITH LENTILS AND SPINACH

Ingredients (serves 4-6):

To Cook in the Rice Cooker:

- 2 cups (rice measuring cup) basmati rice
- 1/2 cup (rice measuring cup) red lentils
- 16 oz. water
- 1/2 tsp. salt
- 2 tsp. spicy Madras curry powder
- 3 oz. onion, minced
- 3 cloves garlic, sliced

To Prepare Separately:

- 2 oz. cherry tomatoes, cut in half lengthwise
- 2 oz. roasted slivered almonds, unsalted
- 1 pinch salt
- 1 pinch ground black pepper
- 10 oz. frozen spinach
- 4 green onions, thinly sliced
- To taste, spicy Madras curry powder (optional)

Instructions

1.
   Use the measuring cup that came with your rice cooker to correctly measure the rice. Drain and place in the inner cooking pan after a brief rinse. Using the measuring cup that came with your rice cooker, measure the red lentils separately and rinse once. Remove from the equation.
2. Using the spatula, combine water, salt, and spicy Madras curry powder in the inner frying pan with the rice. Place the minced onions, sliced garlic, and red lentils from step 1 on top of the rice, making sure they are well submerged. Mixing with rice is not a good idea.
3. Use the "MIXED" setting to cook the rice.
4. Combine cherry tomatoes, almonds, salt, and pepper in a bowl while the rice cooks. Allow it to marinate at room temperature for a few hours.
5. When the rice is done, thaw frozen spinach in a microwave for 1 minute at 1,100 watts, finely chop, squeeze off excess water, and fold it into the rice with a rice spatula.
6. Fill warm bowls halfway with rice, then top with tomato/almond mixture and chopped green onions.
7. As desired, add a pinch of hot Madras curry powder. Serve right away.
8. Enjoy!

91. SPICY CURRY FLAVORED VEGETABLE YAKIMESHI, STIR-FRIED RICE

Ingredients (serves 4-6):
To Cook in the Rice Cooker:

- 3 cups (rice measuring cup) short or medium grain white or brown rice
- Water to fill to water level 3 for "WHITE RICE" or "BROWN RICE"

To Prepare Separately:

- 1/4 cup vegetable oil
- 1 cup minced onion
- 3 cloves garlic, finely minced
- 1/4 cup carrots, finely minced
- 2 cups frozen mixed vegetables
- 2 oz. Swiss chard, cut into thin strips crosswise with white stem
- 1-1/2 tsp. sea salt
- 2 to 3 Tbsp. curry powder (select a type of powder for the degree of spiciness preferred)

Instructions

1. Use the measuring cup that came with your rice cooker to correctly measure the rice. Place white rice in the inner cooking pan after rinsing until water clears, or brown rice in the inner cooking pan after a fast rinse.
2. Depending on whether you're using "WHITE RICE" or "BROWN," add water to the appropriate water level. For white rice, use the "HARDER," "REGULAR," or "WHITE RICE" settings, while for brown rice, use the "BROWN" setting.
3. When the rice is done cooking, strain it and rinse it under cold tap water to chill it down and eliminate any excess starch. Before stir-frying the rice, drain it and let it aside for 20 minutes. If you're using rice that's already been cooked and stored in the fridge, skip this step.
4. Preheat a wok or a big skillet over high heat. When the pan is hot, add the vegetable oil and sauté the onions and carrots for about 10 minutes over medium-low heat. Cook for about 20 seconds, or until the garlic is aromatic.
5. Stir in the curry powder several times. Increase the heat to high and stir in the frozen veggies and Swiss chard, along with the salt, until the vegetables are well cooked and covered in oil.
6. Cook until the rice is heated through and looks nicely browned, then add the rinsed or cooled rice. If required, season the rice with salt.
7. While still hot, divide and serve in 4 to 6 bowls.

92. SPRING FLOWER SUSHI ROLL

Ingredients (makes 4 rolls):
For Sushi Rice:

- Cooked Sushi rice
- 6 Tbsp. canned beets (about one 5 oz. can), minced, reserve liquid
- 2 Tbsp. liquid from the canned beets

For Filling:

- 5 thick asparagus
- 11 sheets nori (seaweed), about 7.5" x 8" size
- 12 canned whole baby corn (about one 15 oz. can)
- For Dipping and Condiments (optional):
- Soy Sauce
- Wasabi
- Gari (pickled ginger)
- You will need a bamboo sushi mat (makisu) or parchment paper.

Instructions

1. Warm sushi rice, minced beets, and liquid from canned beets are combined in a big mixing dish. Place plastic wrap over the bowl and set it aside.
2. Remove and discard the hard ends of the asparagus. Blanch for 3 minutes in salted water (not listed in the ingredients) and then cool under cold running water. Set aside 4 thin slices of asparagus cut lengthwise.
3. Seven nori sheets should be cut into three equal strips.
4. Fill the shells with the filling. On a bamboo mat, place a nori strip. Place 4 tbsps of sushi rice on a nori sheet with a wet measuring spoon. Cover the rice with plastic wrap and spread it out evenly with your fingertips, leaving about 1/4 inch along the longer edge.
5. Roll the sushi up the bamboo mat, pressing forward to form a cylinder. Make 14 more identical thin rolls by repeating the process.
6. Put together the flower roll. Place a nori sheet in its whole on top of a bamboo mat. Place one of the thin rolls from step 5 at the front edge of the nori sheet, then a strip of asparagus above it. Place four more thin rolls and four more asparagus strips alternately. Between the first and second thin rolls, place three baby corns lengthwise.
7. Roll the sushi up the bamboo mat, pressing forward to form a huge cylinder. Check the sides of the sushi roll as you roll it to make sure the baby corns are in the middle. Remove the bamboo mat from the roll by pressing it firmly.
8. Make three more rolls by repeating steps 6 and 7. Flower sushi rolls should be cut into bite-sized pieces (usually 8 pieces).

9. Serve with soy sauce, wasabi, and gari if desired. Enjoy!

93. STEEL CUT OATMEAL

Ingredients (serves 2-3):

- 1 cup (rice measuring cup) steel cut oats
- Water to fill to water level 1 for "STEEL CUT OATMEAL" or 2-1/2 cups (rice measuring cup)
- 1 cup (rice measuring cup) half & half
- 3-4 Tbsp. brown sugar

Note: Please use the rice measuring cup that came with your rice cooker.

Instructions

1. Using the measuring cup that came with your rice cooker, correctly measure steel cut oats. Steel-cut oats should be placed in the inner frying pan. Fill the cup halfway with water for "STEEL CUT OATMEAL," or as directed in the ingredients.
2. Place the inner cooking pan in the rice cooker's main body and turn it on. Use the "STEEL CUT OATMEAL" (if available) or "PORRIDGE" setting to cook the steel cut oats.
3. Open the cover, stir, and add the remaining ingredients when the rice cooker is set to Keep Warm.
4. Warm the dish before serving.
5. The texture can be softened by using the Timer function and soaking the oats overnight. When cooking with milk or other dairy products, do not use the Timer feature since they may deteriorate.
6. If your rice cooker doesn't have a porridge setting, keep an eye on it while it's cooking because it can overflow.
7. Enjoy!

94. SUMMER CURRY WITH BROWN RICE

Ingredients (serves 4-6):
To Cook in the Rice Cooker:

- 2 cups (rice measuring cup) short or medium grain brown rice
- Water to fill to water level 2 for "BROWN RICE"

To Prepare Separately:

- 2 Tbsp. butter
- 1 medium onion
- 2 cloves garlic, chopped
- 2 tsp. chopped ginger
- 1/2 lb. ground pork
- Salt
- Pepper
- 1 zucchini
- 1 green (or 1/2 green and 1/2 red) bell pepper
- 1 medium potato
- 4 Tbsp. cornstarch
- 2 Tbsp. curry powder
- 2 cans (14 oz. each) vegetable broth
- 1 bay leaf
- 1 Tbsp. ketchup
- 1 Tbsp. Worcestershire sauce
- 3 Tbsp. milk
- 1/4 to 1 apple, grated
- 1/4 cup frozen green peas
- Cilantro if preferred

Instructions

1. Use the measuring cup that came with your rice cooker to correctly measure the rice. Once the rice has been rinsed, drain it and set it in the inner frying pan.
2. Fill the corresponding water level for "BROWN RICE" with water. Use the "BROWN" setting to cook the rice. If your rice cooker doesn't have a brown rice setting, use the rice measuring cup to add 3 cups of water.
3. Slice onion thinly and cut zucchini, bell pepper, and potato into bite-size pieces. In a skillet, melt butter and sauté garlic, ginger, and onion. When the onions have softened, add the ground pork and season with salt and pepper to suit. When the meat is done, add the zucchini, bell pepper, and potato, and simmer for a few minutes more before transferring to a large pot.

4. Combine cornstarch and curry powder in a pot and stir to combine. Stir vigorously for one minute, being careful not to burn. Simmer for 20 minutes over low heat with the vegetable stock, bay leaf, ketchup, and Worcestershire sauce.
5. Once the veggies are fully cooked, add the milk, grated apple, and green peas and continue to boil for another 5 minutes. Depending on your preferences, adjust the number of apples. The sweeter it is, the more apples there are.
6. When the rice is done cooking, fluff it with a rice spatula and place a scoop on a big, deep plate. Pour in the curry and, if desired, garnish with chopped cilantro. Serve immediately.

---

95. SUSHI RICE

Ingredients (serves 4-6):
To Cook in the Rice Cooker:

- 3 cups (rice measuring cup) short or medium grain white rice
- Water to fill to water level 3 for "SUSHI RICE"
- To Prepare Separately:
- 4 Tbsp. rice vinegar
- 3 Tbsp. sugar
- 1 tsp. salt

Instructions

1. Use the measuring cup that came with your rice cooker to correctly measure the rice. Place rice in inner cooking pan after rinsing until water is clear.
2. For "SUSHI RICE," add water to the appropriate water level. Use the "SUSHI" option to cook the rice.
3. In a small bowl, whisk together the rice vinegar, sugar, and salt until the sugar dissolves. Remove from the equation.
4. When the rice is done cooking, transfer it to a big, shallow dish. (Avoid using metal because it may react with the vinegar.) Use a spatula to spread the vinegar mixture evenly over the rice. While the rice is still hot, combine the vinegar seasoning.
5. Fan the rice quickly with a hand or electric fan while you fold in the vinegar mixture. Continue to fan and mix the rice until it has reached room temperature and is glossy.

96. SWEET RICE COOKED WITH ADZUKI BEANS

Ingredients (serves 4-5):

- 3 cups (rice measuring cup) sweet rice
- oz. adzuki beans
- Water
- Salt with parched sesame, to taste

Instructions

1. Rinse rice and drain for 30 minutes or more in a strainer.
2. In a colander, rinse the adzuki beans, then place them in a saucepan with 2 cups of water and bring to a boil for 2 minutes. Add 3 cups of water and continue to boil for another 20 minutes, or until the beans are soft enough to break with your fingertip. The beans should be drained, but the stock should be kept.
3. Fill the Inner Cooking Pan with the rice from step 1, the soup stock from step 2, and enough water to reach water level 3 for "SWEET RICE." Stir well from the bottom of the pan, then top with the adzuki beans from step 2 and smooth up the surface.
4. Select the "SWEET" setting using the MENU button, then hit start.
5. Open the lid and loosen the rice once it has finished cooking. Serve in a bowl with a sprinkle of salt and a sprinkling of parched sesame seeds on top.

97. TAKIKOMI-GOHAN (MIXED RICE)

Ingredients (serves 2-3):
To Cook in the Rice Cooker:

- 1 Tbsp. light soy sauce
- 1 Tbsp. mirin (Japanese sweet rice wine)
- 1/3 tsp. salt
- 1/3 tsp. dashinomoto
- 1 oz. chicken (or dried young sardines), cut into 1/2-inch cubes
- 1/3 slice Age (fried tofu), cut into strips, place in strainer and pour hot water over it and gently squeeze to drain excess oil
- 0.7 oz. carrots
- 0.7 oz. Konnyaku
- 0.7 oz. Gobo
- 2 cups (rice measuring cup) short or medium grain white rice
- Water to fill to water level 2 for "WHITE RICE" or "MIXED RICE"
- 2 dried shiitake mushrooms, soaked in water for 30 minutes to an hour to reconstitute (reserve the soaking water as stock)

To Prepare Separately:

- Boiled string beans or stone parsley to taste

Instructions

1. Combine the soy sauce, mirin, salt, and dashinomoto in a mixing bowl. Soak the chicken in the mixture and let it age. This soup liquid should not be thrown away.
2. Slice the carrots and Konnyaku into small strips while they soak. Konnyaku should be soaked in boiling water and then drained. Gobo should be shredded, soaked in water to remove the bitter taste, and then drained. Cut the reconstituted shiitake into tiny strips after removing the firm tips.
3. In a large mixing bowl, combine the soup stock from step 1 with the water used to soak the dried shiitake mushrooms.
4. Use the measuring cup that came with your rice cooker to correctly measure the rice. Drain the rice and set it in the inner cooking pan after rinsing it until the water runs clean. Step 3: Pour in the soup stock. Mix well after adding water to the appropriate water level for "WHITE RICE" or "MIXED RICE."
5. On top of the rice, equally distribute the ingredients from stages 1 and 2. Use the "WHITE RICE" or "MIXED RICE" setting to cook the rice.
6. When the rice has done cooking, remove the lid and fluff the rice with a fork to loosen it up.
7. Serve in a bowl with string beans and stone parsley on top.

98. TACO RICE BOWL

Ingredients (serves 4):

- 1 Tbsp. vegetable oil
- 1 tsp. garlic, minced
- 1 medium onion, chopped
- 12 oz. ground beef
- 2 Tbsp. soy sauce
- 1 tsp. chili powder
- 1 tsp. ground cumin
- 1/2 tsp. salt
- 1/4 tsp. black pepper
- 4 cups cooked white or brown rice
- 8 oz. shredded cheddar cheese
- 2 cups shredded iceberg lettuce
- 1 cup chopped tomatoes

- 1/2 cup salsa

Instructions

1. In a medium sauté pan, heat the vegetable oil over medium heat. Add the garlic and onion and cook for about 3 minutes. Increase the heat to high, add the ground beef to the pan, break it up with a spatula, and cook for 5 minutes.
2. Combine the soy sauce, chili powder, cumin, salt, and pepper in a mixing bowl. Cook for 3 minutes, or until the liquid has almost completely evaporated.
3. 1 cup cooked rice should be added to each serving bowl. Serve with cooked meat on top.
4. Top the meat with cheese and lettuce, tomatoes, and salsa.
5. Enjoy!

99. TAMAGO-DONBURI (EGG BOWL)

Ingredients (serves 1):

- 1/8 onion, thinly sliced
- 1/3 cup ichiban dashi or 1/3 tsp. dashinomoto + 1/3 cup water
- 1 Tbsp. sake (rice wine)
- 1 Tbsp. mirin (Japanese sweet rice wine)
- 1/8 tsp. salt
- 1/3 Tbsp. soy sauce
- 2 eggs
- 1-1/4 cups cooked short or medium grain white or brown rice

Topping:

- Green onion, thinly sliced
- Nori (seaweed) (optional)

Instructions

1. Add onion, dashi, sake, mirin, salt, and soy sauce to a small pan (use one that is the same diameter or slightly smaller than your serving bowl) and simmer for 5 minutes over medium heat.
2. In a small mixing dish, lightly beat the eggs. In the same pan as the onion mixture, crack the eggs.
3. Wait approximately a minute for the eggs to begin to coagulate. With a spatula, slowly press the edge of the egg mixture to the center of the pan, cover with a lid, and lower heat to low; cook for another 30 seconds.

4. Place cooked rice in serving bowl and top with omelette and sauce.
5. Green onion and nori are optional garnishes.
6. Enjoy!

100. TEMAKI SUSHI

Ingredients (serves 3):

- 3 cups cooked sushi rice
- 8 sheets nori (Seaweed), cut in halves
- Soy sauce
- Wasabi
- Gari (pickled ginger)
- Suggested Ingredients:
- Tuna
- Shrimp, boiled
- Smoked salmon
- Ham
- Cheese
- Salmon roe
- Japanese cucumber (or English cucumber)
- Cornichon
- Green onion
- Perilla (Ooba)
- Daikon sprouts
- Red leaf Lettuce

Instructions

1. Get the ingredients ready. This stage will generally take the longest, but after it's done, the chef won't have to do any more cooking.
2. Cook and prepare the sushi rice, taking care to leave time for it to cool completely because it tastes better cold than heated.
3. Slice your preferred component, whether it's fish, veggies, or meat, into elongated strips that will fit better in your hand-roll.
4. If your visitors request it, make sure to have soy sauce, wasabi, and ginger on hand.
5. Finally, take some time to arrange all of your components on a large plate in an elegant manner. It's the small touches that make a big difference in a successful visual presentation.
6. On one hand, place a sheet of nori and a ball of rice at the edge.
7. Arrange the ingredients on top of the rice in a diagonal pattern.
8. Fold the nori wrap in half at the corner.

9. Wrap into a cone form after that. You should be rolling perfect pieces in no time if you practice enough.
10. This is so much fun—and everyone gets to enjoy their masterpieces!

Tips:

Don't overdo it with hand-rolled sushi! Using your ingredients sparingly is the key to better-looking sushi.

Enjoy!

101. TEMARI-SUSHI

Ingredients (makes 20 pieces):
For Sushi Rice:

- 2 cups cooked sushi rice
- 3 Tbsp. rice vinegar
- 1-1/2 Tbsp. sugar
- 1/2 tsp. salt

Other Ingredients:

- 10 edamame beans, frozen and shelled
- 5 medium shrimp, deveined and precooked
- 1 Tbsp. rice vinegar
- 2 Tbsp. water
- 1/8 tsp. salt
- 5 slices smoked salmon (about 5 oz.)
- 1 green onion
- Garnish and Condiments:
- Soy sauce
- Wasabi paste
- Gari (pickled ginger)
- *2 cups raw rice, about 1 lb. 7 oz. cooked rice

Instructions

1. Sushi rice can be made with the items provided. To learn how to make sushi rice, click here.
2. Preheat the rest of the ingredients. Place edamame in cold water after blanching. Remove the shrimp tails and cut them in half lengthwise.

3. In a bowl, combine rice vinegar, water, and salt. In a large mixing dish, combine the drained edamame and cut shrimp and soak for 15 minutes to up to 6 hours in the refrigerator.
4. Green onion should be minced and smoked salmon pieces should be cut in half. Remove from the equation.
5. For the shrimp temari and smoked salmon temari, divide the sushi rice in half.
6. Place a huge square of plastic wrap on a level surface and cut it into a square.
7. One slice of salmon should be placed in the center of the plastic wrap.

8. On top of the salmon, place a small scoop of sushi rice. Gather the plastic wrap around the rice ball, twist it, and roll it into a ball form.
9. Make a small depression on top and set rice side down on the serving plate. Then remove the plastic wrap.
10. Make ten salmon temari-sushi pieces by repeating steps 6–9.
11. Follow the same techniques as the salmon temari to make 10 pieces of shrimp temari-sushi.
12. For salmon temari, top with chopped green onion; for shrimp temari, top with edamame.
13. Both should be served with soy sauce, wasabi, and gari. Enjoy!

102. TEN-DON (TEMPURA BOWL)

Ingredients (serves 4):
To Cook in the Rice Cooker:

- 2 cups (rice measuring cup) short or medium grain white rice
- Water to fill to water level 2 for "WHITE RICE"
- To Prepare Separately:
- 4 servings Tempura , battered with 2 Tbsp. extra flour
- Sauce:
- 6 Tbsp. soy sauce
- 4 Tbsp. mirin (Japanese sweet rice wine)
- 2 Tbsp. sugar

Instructions

1. Use the measuring cup that came with your rice cooker to correctly measure the rice. Drain the rice and set it in the inner cooking pan after rinsing it until the water runs clean.
2. For "WHITE RICE," add water to the appropriate water level. Use the "REGULAR" (if available) or "WHITE RICE" setting to cook the rice.

3. Tempura can be made with a thicker batter by adding an additional 2 tbsps flour to the batter and keeping it heated.
4. Put the soy sauce, mirin, and sugar in a small saucepan and bring to a low simmer over medium heat.
5. When the rice is done, divide it among the serving bowls and top with tempura. Drizzle the prepared sauce over the top and serve right away.

103. TENMUSU

Ingredients (makes 9 rice balls):
To Cook in the Rice Cooker:

- 2 cups (rice measuring cup) short or medium grain white rice
- Water to fill to water level 2 for "WHITE RICE"

To Prepare Separately:

- 9 medium shrimp Tempura with 2 Tbsp. extra flour

Sauce:

- 3 Tbsp. soy sauce
- 2 Tbsp. mirin (Japanese sweet rice wine)
- 1 Tbsp. sugar
- Seasoning and Wrap:
- 1 tsp. salt
- 2 sheets nori seaweed

Instructions

1. Use the measuring cup that came with your rice cooker to correctly measure the rice. Drain the rice and set it in the inner cooking pan after rinsing it until the water runs clean.
2. For "WHITE RICE," add water to the appropriate water level. Use the "REGULAR" (if available) or "WHITE RICE" setting to cook the rice.
3. By adding an extra 2 tbsps of flour to the batter, you can make a thicker tempura batter.
4. Put the soy sauce, mirin, and sugar in a small saucepan and bring to a low simmer over medium heat.
5. When the rice is done cooking, move it to a medium mixing basin, season with salt, and stir thoroughly with a rice spatula. Place 1/2 cup cooked rice on a piece of plastic wrap in a small bowl.

6. Place a tempura shrimp in the center of the rice and dip it in the sauce. By lightly squeezing your hands together, hold the rice over the plastic wrap and form a rectangle rice ball. Arrange the shrimp so that their tails protrude from the rice ball's top. The rice ball should be hard enough not to fall apart, yet fluffy enough not to be smashed.
7. Wrap each sheet of nori seaweed around the rice balls in 6 strips. This recipe makes 9 rice balls.

104. TERIYAKI RICE BURGER

Ingredients (serves 5):

To Cook in the Rice Cooker:

- 2 cups (rice measuring cup) short or medium grain white rice
- Water to fill to water level 2 for "WHITE RICE"
- 1/2 tsp. salt

Chicken Patties:

- 4 oz. tofu, drained
- 1/2 lb. ground chicken
- 1/2 Tbsp. sake (Japanese rice wine)
- 2 cloves garlic, minced
- 2 stalks green onion, minced
- 2 Tbsp. beaten egg
- 1/4 tsp. salt
- 1/4 tsp. ground black pepper
- Potato starch, as needed for dusting (may substitute with cornstarch)
- 2 Tbsp. olive oil

Rice Buns:

- 3 Tbsp. red paprika, diced into 1/4"
- 3 Tbsp. yellow paprika, diced into 1/4"
- 2 Tbsp. jalapeno, minced
- 1 Tbsp. white sesame seeds
- 1/4 tsp. salt
- 1 Tbsp. olive oil
- Teriyaki Sauce:
- 3 Tbsp. soy sauce
- 2 Tbsp. sake (Japanese rice wine)
- 1 Tbsp. Mirin (Japanese sweet cooking rice wine)

- 1 Tbsp. sugar
- 1 1/2 Tbsp. honey

Topping (optional):

- 1/4 cup spring mix leaves
- 5 thinly sliced red onion
- 5 slices tomato
- 5 slices cheese

Instructions

1. Microwave tofu for 2 minutes at 500 watts on a microwave-safe dish. Remove the tofu from the microwave, cover with a different dish or weight, and set aside for 20 minutes. Remove the tofu from the water and set it aside.
2. Use the measuring cup that came with your rice cooker to correctly measure the rice. Place rice in inner cooking pan after rinsing until water is clear. Add water to the "WHITE RICE" water level, then add salt and stir well. Use the "WHITE RICE" or "QUICK" option to cook the rice.
3. While the rice is cooking, mash the drained tofu in a large mixing dish with a fork. With clean hands, combine the ground chicken, sake, garlic, green onion, egg, salt, and pepper.
4. Make five 1/2" thick round patties out of the mixture. Dent the center of each patty slightly. Set aside after lightly dusting with potato starch.
5. To make the teriyaki sauce, combine all of the ingredients in a mixing bowl. In a small sauce pan, combine all of the ingredients. Simmer for 7-8 minutes over very low heat, scraping the particles off the surface as needed, until sauce thickens. Make sure the sauce doesn't burn or overcook. Remove the pan from the heat and set it aside.
6. When the rice is done cooking, use the rice spatula that came with your rice cooker to fluff in the red paprika, yellow paprika, jalapeo, white sesame seeds, and salt.
7. Place one rice mixture in a gallon size 10" x 14" plastic bag and the other rice mixture in a gallon size 10" x 14" plastic bag. Spread the rice into a square, slightly crushing it.
8. Roll the rice mixture into a 1/2" thickness with a rolling pin over the bag. Cut the rice buns out of the plastic bag with a 3" round cookie cutter or an empty container. To make a total of 10 buns, repeat steps 6 and 7. (If required, gather and re-roll leftover rice mixture.)
9. In a frying pan, heat 1/2 tbsp olive oil over medium-low heat. Cook 5 rice buns for 3-4 minutes on each side, or until toasty and crispy on both sides. Place on a cooling rack to cool. Repeat with another 1/2 tbsp olive oil and the remaining rice buns.
10. Preheat the oven to 350°F and prepare the chicken patties. In a frying pan, heat 2 tbsps olive oil over medium-low heat and add the prepared patties. Brown both sides for about 3-5 minutes each side or until cooked through, covered with lid.
11. Please be wary of the hot pan and the splattering oil. When flipping patties, wipe the lid clean of moisture and grease.
12. Assemble the burger by running each cooked patty through the prepared teriyaki sauce. If desired, add spring mix greens, chopped red onion, tomato, and cheese. Serve right away.

13. Enjoy!

105. THAI GREEN CHICKEN CURRY

Ingredients (serves 4-6):

To Cook in the Rice Cooker:

- 2 cups (rice measuring cup) Jasmine rice
- Water to fill to water level 2 for "JASMINE" or 2 1/2 cups (rice measuring cup) water

For Paste:

- 1/4 tsp. cumin seeds, toasted
- 1/2 tsp. coriander seeds, toasted
- 1/4 tsp. white peppercorns, toasted
- 1 stalk lemongrass, white part only, thinly chopped
- 1 Tbsp. galangal (may substitute with ginger), chopped
- 1 small shallot, chopped
- 1 Tbsp. garlic, chopped
- 10 prik kee noo (Thai green chili pepper) (may substitute with small green chilies of your choice), chopped, adjust amount for preferred hotness
- 1/2 kaffir lime peel (may substitute with lime peel)
- 1 kaffir lime leaf, torn (optional)
- 1/2 tsp. kapi (Thai shrimp paste) (optional)
- 2 Tbsp. fresh coriander roots, chopped
- 10 Thai basil leaves (may substitute with basil leaves), chopped
- 1/2 tsp. sea salt

For Curry:

- 1 lb. boneless and skinless chicken breast, cut into bite-sized pieces
- 1-1/2 Tbsp. fish sauce
- 1 (14 oz.) can coconut milk
- 1 cup chicken stock
- 3-4 Thai eggplants (may substitute with small Asian eggplants), cut into bite-sized pieces
- 1 (8 oz.) can of sliced bamboo shoots, drained
- 2 tsp. palm sugar (may substitute with light brown sugar)
- 3 fresh kaffir lime leaves, torn (optional)
- 4 sprigs Thai basil leaves (may substitute with basil leaves), reserve stem for garnish
- 1/2 prik chee fah daeng (red mild chili) (may substitute with red bell pepper), sliced

Instructions

1. Using the measuring cup that came with your rice cooker, accurately measure the rice. Once the rice has been rinsed, drain it and set it in the inner frying pan.
2. Fill the container with water to the "JASMINE" water level or as directed in the ingredients. Use the "JASMINE" (if available) or "WHITE RICE" setting to cook the rice.
3. Blend all ingredients for "For Paste" in a hand blender or a tabletop blender. If required, add more water.
4. In a bowl, combine the chicken breasts with 1/2 tbsp of fish sauce, cover, and set aside.
5. Half of the coconut milk should be placed in a large sauce pan and cooked over medium heat until the water has evaporated and the volume has been reduced to half or the oil has surfaced, around 6 to 8 minutes.
6. Stir in the paste from step 3 and cook for 3 minutes, or until aromatic.
7. Add the chicken, the remaining coconut milk, the chicken stock, the eggplants, the bamboo shoots, the remaining fish sauce, the sugar, and the lime leaves to the pan. Bring to a boil, then reduce to a low heat for 10 minutes.
8. When the chicken pieces are cooked and the eggplants are soft, toss in the prik chee far daeng, season with fish sauce (not listed in the ingredients list) to taste, and turn off the heat. Leave the stems of the basil leaves for garnish and stir the leaves into the curry.
9. When the rice is done cooking, fluff it gently with a rice spatula and serve on individual dishes.
10. Serve with rice and basil stems as a garnish.
11. Enjoy while it's still hot!

106. THAI OATMEAL SALAD WITH EGGPLANT

Ingredients (serves 4-6):
For Oatmeal:

- 1 cup (rice measuring cup) steel cut oats
- Water to fill to water level 1 for "STEEL CUT OATMEAL" or 2-1/2 cups (rice measuring cup)

For Salad:

- 1 eggplant
- 2 Tbsp. vegetable oil
- 1/2 red onion
- 1 bunch cilantro
- 8 oz. small tomatoes (cherry tomatoes or grape tomatoes)

For Dressing:

- 2 fresh bird's eye chili (Thai red chili pepper), (may substitute with small red chilies of your choice), chopped, adjust amount for preferred hotness
- 2 tsp. garlic, grated
- 2 Tbsp. lime juice
- 2 Tbsp. fish sauce
- 2 tsp. palm sugar (may substitute with light brown sugar)
- For Toppings (Optional):
- 1/3 cup chopped peanuts, roasted and unsalted
- Please use the rice measuring cup that came with your rice cooker.

Instructions

1. Using the measuring cup that came with your rice cooker, correctly measure steel cut oats. Steel-cut oats should be placed in the inner frying pan. Fill the cup halfway with water for "STEEL CUT OATMEAL," or as directed in the ingredients.
2. Place the inner cooking pan in the rice cooker's main body and turn it on. Use the "STEEL CUT OATMEAL" (if available) or "PORRIDGE" setting to cook the steel cut oats.
3. When the steel cut oats are done, fluff them lightly with a rice spatula and spread them out on a big plate. Steel cut oats can be prepared ahead of time and kept refrigerated for up to a day.
4. Cut the eggplant into one-inch cubes after peeling it. In a frying pan over medium heat, heat the vegetable oil and sauté the eggplants for 10-12 minutes, or until tender. Turn off the heat and transfer to a large mixing bowl to cool.
5. Red onion should be thinly sliced, and cilantro should be cut into one-inch long pieces. Toss the sautéed eggplants with the onion slices, cilantro, and tomatoes.
6. Prepare the salad dressing. In a small bowl, combine all dressing ingredients and set aside.

7. Step 5: Add the cooled steel cut oatmeal to the eggplant mixture. Toss in the dressing thoroughly.
8. Serve on a serving dish with chopped peanuts on top.
9. Enjoy!

107. TOFU JASMINE FRAGRANT RICE

Ingredients (serves 4-6)

To Cook in the Rice Cooker:

- 3 cups (rice measuring cup) jasmine rice
- Water to fill to water level 3 for JASMINE or 3-3/4 cups (rice measuring cup)
- 1 tsp. salt

To Prepare Separately:

- 1 lb. firm tofu, drained, cut into bite sized cubes
- 1/4 cup gluten free soy sauce
- 3/4 cup cilantro, chopped
- 3/4 cup peanuts, roasted, unsalted

For Garnish (optional):

- Lime wedges

Instructions

1.

   Use the measuring cup that came with your rice cooker to correctly measure the rice. Drain the rice and set it in the inner cooking pan after a short rinse.
2. Fill the container with water to the "JASMINE" water level, or as directed in the ingredients. Use the rice spatula to mix the salt into the inner cooking pan with the rice. Use the "JASMINE" (if available) or "WHITE RICE" setting to cook the rice.
3. In a bowl, add tofu cubes and soy sauce while rice cooks. Allow tofu to marinade in soy sauce for a few hours. Cilantro should be chopped, peanuts should be measured, and lime wedges should be cut.
4. When the rice has done cooking, fluff it lightly using a rice spatula. Toss in the tofu, soy sauce, cilantro, and peanuts gently.
5. Serve in heated bowls with a lime wedge on top. Serve right away.
6. Enjoy!

108. TOPPED SALMON QUINOA BOWL

Ingredients (serves 4):

To Cook in the Rice Cooker:

- 1 cup (rice measuring cup) tri-color quinoa
- Water to fill to the water level 1 for "QUINOA"

Pickled celery:

- 2 stalk celery hearts
- 2 Tbsp. water
- 4 Tbsp. apple cider vinegar
- 1/2 tsp. sugar
- 1/4 tsp. salt
- 1/0 tsp. black pepper

Salmon:

- 4 salmon fillets (about 0.3 lb. each)
- 1 tsp. salt
- 1 Tbsp. vegetable oil

Other toppings:

- 1/2 cup shallot, finely chopped
- 8 oz. baby portabella mushroom
- 1 Tbsp. vegetable oil
- 1 tsp. chili powder
- salt and pepper for taste
- 1 cup baby kale, chopped

Dressing:

- 1/3 cup mayonnaise
- 1 fresh lime juice
- 1 Tbsp. olive oil
- Zest of one lime

Garnish:

10 sprigs cilantro

Instructions

1. Use the measuring cup that came with your rice cooker to correctly measure the quinoa and transfer it to the inner cooking pan. If the quinoa hasn't been washed, strain it through a fine mesh strainer and rinse it with water before adding it to the inner cooking pan. For "QUINOA," add water to the appropriate water level. Use the "QUINOA" setting during cooking. When the quinoa is done, fluff it, cover it, and keep it warm.
2. Prepare the celery pickles. Place celery in a heat-resistant bowl and slice into thin diagonal slices. Place water, apple cider vinegar, sugar, salt, and pepper in a small sauce pan. Over medium heat, stir occasionally until the sugar has completely melted and the mixture has come to a boil. Immediately pour the heated liquid over the celery segments. Allow to cool to room temperature before serving.
3. Prepare the filet of salmon. Season the fillet evenly with salt and lay aside for 15 minutes.
4. Prepare the rest of the toppings. Cut the mushrooms into slices. Warm 1 tbsp of oil in a large frying pan over medium-high heat. Cook for 1 minute after adding the shallot and seasoning with chili powder, salt, and pepper. Add the mushroom slices and cook for 4 minutes, seasoning with salt and pepper as needed. Remove from heat and place on a platter. Remove the frying pan from the heat and wipe it clean.
5. Step 3: Rinse the salmon and blot it dry with a paper towel. Warm 1 tbsp of oil in the same pan over medium-high heat. Cook for 3 minutes, or until the skin is crisp, with the salmon skin side down. Cook for another 3 to 5 minutes, or until the fish is done. Place on a chopping board to cool.
6. Cooked salmon should be cut into 2-inch chunks. If desired, remove the bone and skin.
7. When the quinoa is done cooking, divide it into individual bowls. Add mushrooms, greens, pickled celery, and salmon on the top.
8. In a small mixing bowl, combine all of the dressing ingredients. 1 tbsp dressing drizzled over each quinoa bowl Chop the cilantro and sprinkle it over top. Any remaining dressing should be served on the side.
9. Serve when still hot.
10. Enjoy!

109. TRICOLOR SOBORO BOWL

Ingredients (each serves 3):

For Beef Soboro:

- 8 oz. ground beef (may substitute with ground chicken)
- 1/4 tsp. fresh ginger, grated
- 1 Tbsp. sugar
- 1 Tbsp. sake (Japanese rice wine)
- 1-1/2 Tbsp. soy sauce

For Egg Soboro:

- 3 eggs
- 1 Tbsp. mirin (Japanese sweet rice wine)
- 1/2 tsp. salt
- 1 tsp. sugar
- 1/2 Tbsp. vegetable oil

Snow Peas:

- 2 oz. snow peas
- Salt for blanching

Rice:

- 4 cups cooked short or medium grain white or brown rice

Instructions

1. In a frying skillet, brown the ground beef over medium heat. Break up the meat into smaller bits using a whisk. Use a silicone whisk if your pan isn't scratch-resistant.
2. When the meat has turned a pale hue, add the ginger, sugar, sake, and soy sauce and continue to mix and boil until the liquid has almost completely evaporated, about 4 minutes. Remove the pan from the heat and set it aside.
3. In a mixing dish, whisk together the eggs. Mix in the mirin, salt, and sugar thoroughly.
4. Heat a frying pan on low heat, then add the vegetable oil and egg mixture, whisking constantly until the mixture becomes fluffy scrambled eggs.
5. Blanch trimmed snow peas for 3 minutes in boiling water with salt. Drain and cut into strips on the diagonal.
6. Top cooked rice with beef soboro, egg soboro, and snow peas in each serving bowl.
7. Enjoy!

110. TRIPLE FLAVOR CHICKEN ONIGIRI

Ingredients (makes 6 onigiri):
To Cook in the Rice Cooker:

- 2 cups (rice measuring cup) short or medium grain brown rice
- Water to fill to water level 2 for "BROWN RICE"

For Filling:

- 6 oz. boneless and skinless chicken thigh
- 1/4 tsp. salt
- 1 Tbsp. teriyaki sauce
- 1 Tbsp. barbecue sauce
- 1 Tbsp. Buffalo wing sauce
- 1 tsp. vegetable oil

For Seasoning Rice:

- 1/2 tsp. salt
- For Finishing Touches:
- 1 whole sheet nori seaweed, cut into two 8" x 3.5" strips
- 1/2 tsp. dried parsley
- 1/2 tsp. white sesame

Instructions

1. Use the items mentioned under "To Cook in the Rice Cooker" to make brown rice. To learn how to make "brown rice," click here.
2. Prepare the chicken while the rice is cooking. Chicken thigh should be cut into 3/4-inch squares or smaller pieces.
3. 1/4 tsp salt, then divide the mixture into three equal halves. Mix up the teriyaki, barbeque, and Buffalo wing sauce in each half individually. 5–15 minutes of marinating
4. In a nonstick frying pan, heat the vegetable oil, then separate the seasoned chicken and cook for 4-6 minutes on medium low heat. Remove from the equation. To make the toppings, separate two pieces of each flavour chicken (optional).
5. When the rice is done cooking, move it to a separate bowl, season with 1/2 tsp salt, and fluff gently with a rice spatula. Place a plastic wrap on the dish and set it aside.
6. Cut a 7 to 8-inch-long piece of plastic wrap and set it in a small basin. Make 6 equal amounts of cooked rice. 1/6 of the rice should be placed on top of the plastic wrap. In the center of the rice, place 1/2 of the teriyaki chicken from step 4. Squeeze your hands together tightly and wrap the plastic wrap around the rice to form a triangular rice ball. The rice ball should be hard enough not to fall apart, yet fluffy enough not to be smashed.

7. To prepare another teriyaki chicken onigiri, repeat step 6. Make two more onigiri with BBQ chicken using the same manner. Buffalo chicken is used to make a unique form of onigiri. Cut a 7 to 8-inch-long piece of plastic wrap and set it in a small basin. Place half of the Buffalo chicken from step 4 in the center of the bowl, then top with 1/6 of the cooked rice and shape into a triangle.

8. Each onigiri should be wrapped in plastic wrap. Wrap a nori seaweed piece around each rice ball for teriyaki chicken. Sprinkle dried parsley on grilled chicken. Sprinkle white sesame on Buffalo chicken. Optional toppings from step 4 can be used to top teriyaki and Buffalo chicken onigiri.

9. Enjoy!

111. TROPICAL LONG GRAIN SALAD

Ingredients (serves 4):
To Cook in the Rice Cooker:

- 1 cup (rice measuring cup) long grain white rice
- Water to fill to water level 1 for "LONG GRAIN WHITE," or 1-1/4 cups (rice measuring cup)
- 1/4 tsp. salt

To Add to Cooked Rice:

- 1 Tbsp. olive oil

For Dressing:

- 2 Tbsp. orange marmalade
- 2 Tbsp. lime juice
- 1 Tbsp. white wine vinegar
- 1/8 tsp. salt or adjust taste to preference
- 1/8 tsp. pepper
- 1/3 cup olive oil
- To Add to Cooked, Cooled Rice:
- 1 lb. extra large cooked shrimp, peeled and deveined
- 1 mango, peeled, diced
- 1/3 cup chopped fresh mint
- 1/3 cup chopped cilantro
- 4 scallions, minced
- 1/4 cup unsweetened shredded coconut, lightly toasted

Ingredients (serves 8):

To Cook in the Rice Cooker:

- 2 cup (rice measuring cup) long grain white rice
- Water to fill to water level 2 for "LONG GRAIN WHITE", or 2-1/2 cups (rice measuring cup)
- 1/2 tsp. salt

To Add to Cooked Rice:

- 2 Tbsp. olive oil

For Dressing:

- 4 Tbsp. orange marmalade
- 4 Tbsp. lime juice
- 2 Tbsp. white wine vinegar
- 1/4 tsp. salt or adjust taste to preference
- 1/4 tsp. pepper
- 2/3 cup olive oil
- To Add to Cooked, Cooled Rice:
- 2 lb. extra large cooked shrimp, peeled and deveined
- 2 mango, peeled, diced
- 2/3 cup chopped fresh mint
- 2/3 cup chopped cilantro
- 8 scallions, minced
- 1/2 cup unsweetened shredded coconut, lightly toasted

Instructions

1.
   Use the measuring cup that came with your rice cooker to correctly measure the rice. Once the rice has been rinsed, drain it and set it in the inner frying pan.
2. Fill the container halfway with water for "LONG GRAIN WHITE," or as directed in the ingredients. Mix in the salt thoroughly. If available, cook the rice on the "LONG GRAIN WHITE" or "MIXED" option.
3. When the rice is done cooking, drizzle with olive oil, fluff with a rice spatula, and lay out on a big plate. Refrigerate for 30 minutes to cool.
4. Combine orange marmalade, lime juice, white wine vinegar, salt, pepper, and olive oil in a mixing bowl and stir well.
5. Place rice in the center of a large platter. Arrange the shrimp, mango, mint, cilantro, scallions, and coconut in a serving dish. Before serving, drizzle the dressing over the salad and mix to combine.
6. Enjoy!

112. TUNA & AVOCADO TOWER

Ingredients (serves 4):

- 2 cups cooked sushi rice
- 2 avocados, pitted, peeled, and cut into 1/2-inch cubes
- 1/4 cup freshly squeezed lemon juice
- 8 oz. fresh sashimi quality tuna, cut into 1/2-inch cubes
- Salad or sprouts as garnish (optional)
- You will need four 3-1/2" diameter ramekins.

Instructions

1. Sushi rice should be prepared according to the directions in the Sushi Rice recipe.
2. Toss avocado cubes with lemon juice.
3. Cover the bottoms of the ramekins with plastic wrap.
4. 1/4 of the avocados from step 2 should be spread evenly on the bottom of the ramekin.
5. Spread around 2 ounces of diced tuna over the avocado.
6. Add 1/2 cup sushi rice on top.
7. To press the rice, use the bottom of another ramekin. Repeat steps 3–7 with the remaining ramekins.
8. Place the ramekin on a platter upside down, with the rice layer on the bottom.
9. Serve with salad or sprouts on the side.

113. TUNA SEAFOOD PILAF

Ingredients (serves 4):

- 10 oz. canned tuna
- 3 Tbsp. butter
- 1/2 onion, small dice
- 8 oz. salad style shrimp, small to medium-sized
- 8 mushrooms, sliced
- 1/4 cup bell pepper, small dice
- 3 cups cooked rice
- 1/2 tsp. salt
- 1/4 tsp. black pepper
- 2 Tbsp. curly parsley, minced

Instructions

1. Using a fork, divide the tuna into large parts.
2. Melt butter in a large frying pan over medium heat and sauté onion for 2 minutes.
3. Sauté for 1 minute with the shrimp, tuna, mushrooms, and bell pepper in the pan.

4. Cook for another minute after adding the cooked rice, salt, and black pepper. Toss in the minced parsley lightly to mix. Turn off the heat.
5. Serve right away. Enjoy!

114. VEGETABLE BROWN RICE ZOSUI (JAPANESE RICE SOUP)

Ingredients (serves 3-4):
To Cook in the Rice Cooker:

- 1 cup (rice measuring cup) short or medium grain brown rice
- Water to fill to water level 1 for "BROWN RICE"

To Prepare Separately:

- 3 cups chicken broth
- 3 leaves cabbage, chopped
- 8 oz. bamboo shoots, sliced and boiled (drain if using canned bamboo shoots)
- 3 leaves rainbow Swiss chard, chopped
- 3 green onions, cut into bite-size pieces
- 3 Tbsp. soy sauce
- 1 Tbsp. mirin (Japanese sweet rice wine)
- 2 eggs

Instructions

1. Using the measuring cup that came with your rice cooker, accurately measure the rice. Once the rice has been rinsed, drain it and set it in the inner frying pan. Fill the corresponding water level for "BROWN RICE" with water. Use the "BROWN" setting to cook the rice.
2. Prepare the soup when the rice cooker starts counting down to completion. Place chicken broth, cabbage, bamboo shoots, and stem portion of Swiss chard in a large clay cooking pot or a Dutch oven and heat to medium high. When the broth has reached a boil, add the cooked brown rice and cover with a lid.
3. Cook for 3 minutes, then add the Swiss chard leaves, green onions, soy sauce, and mirin to the pot, cover, and cook until the soup boils again.
4. Eggs should be beaten with a fork in a small basin. Pour over the top of the soup, turn off the heat, and cover.
5. Allow 2 minutes for the eggs to fry before serving in bowls.

115. WAKAME-GOHAN (SEAWEED MIXED RICE)

Ingredients (serves 2):

To Cook in the Rice Cooker:

- 1 cup (rice measuring cup) short or medium grain white rice
- Water to fill to water level 1 for "WHITE RICE"

To Prepare Separately:

- 2 Tbsp. wakame seaweed, dried and cut
- 1/2 tsp. salt
- 2 tsp. mirin (Japanese sweet rice wine)
- 1 Tbsp. chives, minced
- 1 tsp. sesame oil
- 2 tsp. sesame seeds

Instructions

1. Use the measuring cup that came with your rice cooker to correctly measure the rice. Drain the rice and set it in the inner cooking pan after rinsing it until the water runs clean. For "WHITE RICE," add water to the appropriate water level. Use the "WHITE RICE" setting to cook the rice.
2. To form little flakes, crush the wakame seaweed between your palms.
3. When the rice is done cooking, add the wakame and the rest of the ingredients to the rice and fold gently with a rice spatula.
4. Allow 5 minutes to set after closing the lid.
5. Serve immediately.

116. WHOLE WHEAT SPONGE CAKE

Ingredients (for NS-VGC05):

- 1/4 cup whole wheat flour
- 1/4 cup all purpose flour (sifted)
- 2 eggs (separate white from yolk)
- 2-1/2 Tbsp. sugar
- Vanilla extract to taste
- 1/2 Tbsp. milk and 1 Tbsp. melted butter
- Butter (to coat the inner cooking pan)
- Fresh cream and fruits for decoration

Ingredients (for NS-TGC10/NS-TSC10):

- 1/3 cup whole wheat flour
- 1/3 cup all purpose flour (sifted)
- 5 eggs (separate white from yolk)
- 1/3 cup sugar
- Vanilla extract to taste
- 1 Tbsp. milk and 1-1/2 Tbsp. melted butter
- Butter (to coat the inner cooking pan)
- Fresh cream and fruits for decoration
- Ingredients (for NS-TGC18/NS-TSC18):
- 1/2 cup whole wheat flour
- 1/2 cup all purpose flour (sifted)
- 7 eggs (separate white from yolk)
- 1/2 cup sugar
- Vanilla extract to taste
- 1-1/2 Tbsp. milk and 2 Tbsp. melted butter
- Butter (to coat the inner cooking pan)
- Fresh cream and fruits for decoration

Instructions

1. Lightly and evenly grease the interior of the inner frying pan with butter.
2. In a mixing basin, beat egg whites until stiff but not separated, gradually adding sugar. Beat in the egg yolks and vanilla essence until thick.
3. With a rubber spatula, blend in both flours until smooth and fully incorporated. Gently fold in the milk and butter, being careful not to overmix.

4. Pour the batter into the greased inner cooking pan and tap it lightly on the counter to remove any trapped air. Place the pan in the rice cooker and set the setting to "CAKE." The bake time for NS-VGC05 and NS-TGC/TSC10 is 45 minutes, and 65 minutes for NS-TGC/TSC18.
5. When the cake is done baking, remove it from the pan and set it aside to cool.
6. Whipped cream is used to frost the cake, and fruit is added as a garnish.

117. WILD RICE AND CHICKEN LIVER CROSTINI

Ingredients (serves 8-10):

To Cook in the Rice Cooker:

- 1 cup (rice measuring cup) wild rice
- 1/4 tsp. salt
- 1/4 tsp. coarse ground black pepper
- 12 oz. water
- 4 fresh sage leaves, whole, do not chop
- To Prepare Separately:
- 2 Tbsp. extra virgin olive oil
- 16 oz. onions, chopped
- 24 oz. chicken liver, sliced
- 2 cloves garlic, minced
- 2 Tbsp. fresh sage, chopped
- 2 tsp. salt
- 1/4 tsp. black pepper
- 6 Tbsp. dry sherry
- 1 tsp. red wine vinegar

Instructions

1. To make crostini, slice French or Italian bread into 1/3" slices, drizzle with olive oil, and toast on both sides until golden brown.
2. Place the rice in the inner cooking pan after correctly measuring it with the measuring cup that came with your rice cooker.
3. Use the rice spatula to combine salt, pepper, and water in the inner cooking pan with the rice. On top of the rice, scatter entire sage leaves. Use the "BROWN" setting to cook the rice.
4. Prepare the chicken liver mixture while the rice is cooking. Heat the olive oil in a big sauté pan until it is extremely hot. Cook until the onions are a deep, caramel brown color.
5. Reduce to a low heat setting and add the sliced chicken liver, cooking until medium done. To break the liver into smaller bits, stir it together.
6. Stir in the minced garlic, sage, salt, pepper, sherry, and vinegar to roughly incorporate the liver and onion mixture.

7. When the rice is done cooking, remove the sage leaves and fold the liver mixture into the rice with a rice spatula. The mixture can be prepared ahead of time and kept refrigerated for up to a day.
8. Serve with crostini as a side dish.

118. WILD RICE SALAD

Ingredients (serves 4):
To Cook in the Rice Cooker:

- 1 cup (rice measuring cup) wild rice
- 1-1/2 cups (rice measuring cup) water

To Prepare Separately:

- 12 oz. chicken broth
- 1/2 tsp. salt
- 1 cup blended grains (couscous, orzo, baby garbanzo beans and red quinoa)
- 1/4 onion, minced
- 1 Tbsp. olive oil

For Dressing:

- 1 Tbsp. red wine vinegar
- 1/4 cup lemon juice
- 1 tsp. sugar
- 1/4 tsp. salt
- 1/4 tsp. pepper
- 3 Tbsp. olive oil
- 3 Tbsp. flat leaf parsley, chopped

Instructions

1. Use the measuring cup that came with your rice cooker to correctly measure the rice. Once the rice has been rinsed, drain it and set it in the inner frying pan. Using the same measuring cup, pour the water into the inner frying pan. Use the "BROWN RICE" setting to cook the rice.
2. In a skillet over medium high heat, bring chicken stock to a boil while the rice is cooking. Stir in 1/2 tsp salt and the mixed grains, then return the mixture to a boil. Reduce the heat to low, cover, and cook for 10 minutes.
3. In a large mixing bowl, combine the red wine vinegar, lemon juice, sugar, salt, pepper, olive oil, and parsley.
4. Toss cooked grains with minced onion and 1 tbsp olive oil, mix well, and set away.
5. Once the wild rice is done, combine it with the cooked grains and toss with the dressing (from step).

6. Serve refrigerated or at room temperature.

119. YAKI-ONIGIRI CHAZUKE (GRILLED RICE BALL SOUP)

Ingredients (serves 4):
To Cook in the Rice Cooker:

- 2 cups (rice measuring cup) short or medium grain white rice
- Water to fill to water level 2 for "WHITE RICE"

For Soup:

- 4 oz. Daikon radish
- 1 carrot
- 2 oz. string bean
- 4 cups ichiban dashi or 2 tsp. instant dashi + 4 cups water
- 1/2 tsp. salt
- 1 tsp. soy sauce

For Rice Balls:

- 1 Tbsp. ground or whole white sesame seeds
- Topping (optional):
- 2 stalks green onion, cut into diagonal thin slices
- A handful of shredded nori (seaweed)
- 1 tsp. wasabi paste

Instructions

1. Use the items mentioned under "To Cook in the Rice Cooker" to make white rice. To learn how to cook white rice, go here.
2. Cut the daikon radish and carrot into matchstick-sized pieces, and quarter the string beans. In a sauce pan, combine the daikon, carrot, string beans, and dashi; bring to a boil, then reduce to a low heat and cook for 3 minutes, then set aside.
3. When the rice has done cooking, transfer it to a separate bowl and mix in the sesame seeds carefully using a rice spatula.
4. Cut and insert a 7 to 8-inch-long piece of plastic wrap in a shallow basin. Cover the plastic wrap with a quarter cup of cooked rice. Squeeze your hands together lightly and hold the rice over the plastic wrap to form a triangle rice ball. The rice ball should be hard enough not to fall apart, yet fluffy enough not to be smashed. Make three more rice balls by repeating this process.

5. Use an electric grill or a frying pan to cook the rice balls. Preheat the Indoor Electric Grill (EB-CC15/EB-DLC10) for 6 minutes on "HI" or until the operation light turns off. Heat 1 tsp vegetable oil (not listed in the ingredient list) in a frying pan over medium heat.
6. Place the rice balls on the grill after removing the plastic wrap. Please be cautious when using a hot grill or pan. 3 minutes on each side, or until golden brown. Fill individual serving dishes with the mixture.
7. Pour the soup over each rice ball after it has been reheated.
8. Optional toppings can be added before serving.

120. YAKINIKU-DONBURI

Ingredients (serves 2):

- 2 Tbsp. sake (rice wine)
- 3 Tbsp. soy sauce
- 1-1/2 Tbsp. sugar
- 2 tsp. gochujang (Korean red chili pepper paste)
- 1 Tbsp. onion, grated
- 1/2 tsp. garlic, grated
- 1/4 tsp. ginger, grated
- 1/8 tsp. ground black pepper
- 0.6 lb. beef, your choice of cut
- 1 Tbsp. potato starch
- 1 tsp. dark sesame oil
- 1 tsp. vegetable oil
- 2-1/2 cups cooked short or medium grain white or brown rice

Garnish:

- Green leaf lettuce
- White sesame seeds

Instructions

1. Combine sake, soy sauce, sugar, gochujang, onion, garlic, ginger, and black pepper in a small pan. Over medium heat, bring to a boil. Take the pan from the heat and set it aside to cool.
2. 1/8-1/4 inch pieces of beef, cut against the grain
3. Adjust the thickness of each slice depending on the cut of meat chosen. Tougher pieces, such as loin filet, should be sliced thinly, while softer slices, such as flanks, should be sliced thickly.

4. Combine sliced meat, potato starch, and half of the sauce from step 1 in a plastic bag. Distribute the starch and sauce evenly over the bag with your fingers and marinate for 15 minutes to an hour.
5. Fill serving bowls halfway with warm rice and top with hand torn green leaf lettuce, then leave aside.
6. In a frying pan, heat sesame oil and vegetable oil over medium heat.
7. Cook for 40 seconds before flipping the meat and cooking for another 10 seconds, or until browned on both sides.
8. Drizzle the remaining sauce from step 1 over the cooked meat and sprinkle sesame seeds on top.
9. Enjoy!

121. JAPANESE DRY CURRY

Ingredients (serves 4):
To Cook in the Rice Cooker:

- 2 cups (rice measuring cup) short or medium grain white rice
- Water to fill to water level 2 for 'WHITE RICE"

To Prepare Separately:

- 1 large onion
- 1 carrot
- 1 Tbsp. olive oil
- 1 tsp. minced garlic
- 1 tsp. minced ginger
- 5 oz. ground pork
- 5 oz. ground beef
- 1 tsp. garam masala
- 1 Tbsp. curry powder
- 2 Tbsp. tomato ketchup
- 2 Tbsp. Worcestershire sauce
- 2 Tbsp. soy sauce
- 3 Tbsp. chicken stock
- 3 Tbsp. raisins
- 6 Tbsp. diced bell pepper, any color
- Garnish (optional):
- 4 hard boiled eggs, sliced

Instructions

1. Use the items mentioned under "To Cook in the Rice Cooker" to make white rice. To learn how to cook white rice, go here.
2. Onion and carrots should be minced. Sauté garlic, ginger, onion, and carrot for 5 minutes in a frying pan with oil over high heat.
3. Continue to simmer for 3 minutes more, or until the pork and beef are cooked through.
4. Toss the remaining ingredients into the pan, excluding the optional garnish. Cook for 5 minutes, or until most of the liquid has evaporated, over medium heat.
5. When the rice is done cooking, fluff it gently with a rice spatula and serve on individual dishes.
6. Serve the dry curry over rice and top with hard boiled egg pieces if desired.

SOME AROMA RICE COOKER RECIPES YOU CAN TRY

1. WILD RICE PILAF WITH ITALIAN SAUSAGE

SERVINGS: 4

PREP TIME: 10 MINUTES

COOK TIME: 50 MINUTES

INGREDIENTS

- 2 cups wild rice
- 1 tsp olive oil
- 1 tsp butter
- 4 Italian sausage links, sliced
- 1 cup sweet onion, diced
- 1 cup bell pepper, diced
- 1/2 cup celery, diced
- 1/3 cup tomato sauce
- 4 cups chicken stock
- 1 tsp smoked paprika
- 1 tbsp black pepper

DIRECTIONS

1. In the inner pot, use the Sauté-then-Simmer® function to heat the olive oil and butter.
2. Stir in the sausage once the butter has completely melted. 5 minutes, or until the sausage has browned, gently stir.
3. Add the onion, bell pepper, and celery to the pan and cook until the vegetables are somewhat softened.
4. Remove the lid and stir in the wild rice, tomato sauce, chicken stock, smoky paprika, and pepper.

5. When the rice is done, the cooker will automatically switch to Keep Warm mode. Serve while it's still hot!

---

2. SEAWEED SANDWICHES

SERVINGS: 4

PREP TIME: 15 MINUTES

COOK TIME: 45 MINUTES

INGREDIENTS

- 2 cups short-grain rice
- 12 oz. spam
- 4 eggs
- 8 lettuce leaves
- 4 sheets dried seaweed/nori
- 1 tbsp sesame oil
- 3 tbsp mayonnaise
- salt

DIRECTIONS

1. Press White Rice using 2 cups uncooked rice in your rice cooker. Allow 15 minutes for the rice to cook.
2. Cut the spam into little pieces that are easy to eat.
3. Place 4 eggs and sliced spam on the steam tray after the rice has been cooking for 15 minutes. Open the lid of the cooker with caution and place the steam tray inside. Allow the cooking cycle to continue with the lid closed.
4. Remove the eggs and spam from the steam tray when the cycle is finished and set aside to cool.
5. Season the rice with salt and sesame oil. Mix thoroughly.
6. Place the steamed eggs in a large mixing basin after peeling them. Combine the eggs and mayonnaise in a mixing bowl.
7. Arrange seaweed sheets on serving dishes, rough side up.
8. Top each seaweed sheet with 1/2 cup cooked rice, 2 slices of spam, 1 cup egg salad, and a tiny leaf of lettuce.
9. Roll the seaweed into a burrito/wrap by folding it from the bottom left to the upper left.
10. If preferred, drizzle each wrap with soy sauce, sriracha, or spicy mayonnaise.

3. SPLIT PEA SOUP

SERVINGS: 6

PREP TIME: 25 MINUTES

COOK TIME: 35 MINUTES

INGREDIENTS

- 1 tbsp olive oil
- 1 tbsp butter
- 1/2 bunch spring onion, sliced
- 1 potato, diced
- 1 liter vegetable stock
- 2 lbs. fresh peas
- 1/2 small bunch mint
- biscuits, baguettes or bread to serve

DIRECTIONS

1. In the inner pot, use the Sauté-then-Simmer® function to heat the olive oil and butter.
2. Add the spring onions and potatoes once the butter has completely melted and the oil is hot. While sautéing, gently stir for 5 minutes.
3. Pour in the vegetable stock, and the cooker will automatically convert to a low heat setting. Simmer the broth until the potatoes are fork tender.
4. Cook for an additional 5 minutes after adding the peas and mint leaves, then switch off the stove.
5. Allow the mixture to cool before blending or smoothing the texture of the soup with a hand mixer.
6. Ladle the soup into 6 heat-safe bowls, top with additional mint and sliced spring onions if desired, and serve with biscuits for dipping on the side.

4. LAMB WITH PEARL COUSCOUS

SERVINGS: 4

PREP TIME: 15 MINUTES

COOK TIME: 30 MINUTES

INGREDIENTS

- 2 racks of lamb (3 lbs.), frenched
- 2 tbsp salt
- 1 tsp pepper
- 1/2 tsp garlic powder
- 1/4 tsp dried rosemary
- 1/4 tsp dried thyme
- 1/4 tsp dried sage
- 1/3 cup beer
- 8 oz pearled couscous
- 2 1/4 cup chicken stock
- 1 small sweet onion, chopped
- 8 oz mushroom, sliced
- 6 oz baby spinach
- 1 tsp salt
- 1 tbsp olive oil

DIRECTIONS

1. Sprinkle salt, pepper, garlic powder, dried rosemary, dried thyme, and dried sage over each lamb rack. Place the lamb racks in a large mixing bowl or a big plastic bag and marinate in the refrigerator for at least 1 hour.
2. Remove the racks from the refrigerator after 1 hour and allow the lamb to come to room temperature.
3. Using the White Rice option, boil the pearl couscous, chicken stock, and olive oil in the inner pot. Remove the couscous from the inner pot once it has finished cooking and set it aside.
4. Preheat the olive oil in the Sauté-then-Simmer mode, then sauté the sweet onion and mushrooms until softened.
5. Add the cooked couscous and baby spinach, and season with 1 tsp of salt.
6. Preheat your grillet or a big saucepan over medium heat to 450°F.
7. Place one of the lamb racks in the pan, meat side down, and cover with a lid. Allow 6 minutes for the lamb to cook before carefully opening the cover and flipping the rack so that the other side is facing down. Cook for another 6 minutes after removing the lid. Remove the rack and do the same thing with the other lamb rack.

8. Place both lamb racks in the saucepan and reduce the heat to 300°F or low heat if cooking on the stovetop.
9. Pour in the beer, cover, and let aside to cook for about 10 minutes.
10. Remove the lamb from the pan when it is thoroughly cooked and let both racks cool and tenderize for 15 minutes before cutting.
11. To serve, pour the couscous onto a big platter and evenly distribute it. Then, on top of the couscous, put both lamb racks against each other. If there's any sauce or drippings left in the pan, pour them on top.

5. TAIWANESE STICKY RICE

SERVINGS: 2-4

PREP TIME: 15 MINUTES

COOK TIME: 40 HOURS

INGREDIENTS

- 3 cups rice
- 7 shiitake mushrooms, diced
- 2 tbsp dried shrimp
- 5 Chinese sausages, diced
- 3 cups water
- 2 tsp sugar
- 2 tbsp soy sauce

DIRECTIONS

1. Preheat the rice cooker's inner pot using the Sauté-then-Simmer option.
2. Once the inner pot is hot, add the Chinese sausage and cook for 10 minutes, or until both sides are browned.
3. Add the dried shrimp and shiitake mushrooms to the pan and continue to cook for another 5 minutes.
4. Stir in the rice, soy sauce, and sugar until everything is well combined. Cancel the Sauté-then-Simmer operation once everything is integrated.
5. Fill the inner pot with 3 cups of water, then select the White Rice function. Allow the rice to finish cooking before switching the rice cooker to Keep Warm mode.
6. Finally, serve and enjoy!

6. SAVORY BREAD PUDDING

SERVINGS: 6-8

PREP TIME: 30 MINUTES

COOK TIME: 1 HOUR

INGREDIENTS

- 1/2 loaf egg-based bread (such as challah or brioche), cut into cubes
- 4 eggs
- 1 cup onion, chopped
- 1 cup half and half
- 2 cups deli ham, chopped
- 1/2 cup butter, melted
- 1 cup cheddar cheese, grated
- 1/4 cup fresh parsley, chopped
- salt and pepper

DIRECTIONS

1. Whisk together eggs, half-and-half, salt, and pepper in a large mixing basin.
2. Add the bread cubes to the mixture. Stir gently to blend, then set aside for 20 minutes to allow the bread to steep.
3. Melt the butter in the rice cooker's inner pot and set the Sauté-then-Simmer setting. Allow the butter to melt before adding the chopped onion and sautéing until transparent and tender.
4. Add the ham and cook for another 10 minutes, or until the ham is slightly charred.
5. Pour the bread cubes that have been soaked into the inner pot. Stir in the cheddar cheese until all of the ingredients are properly combined.
6. Once the ingredients are combined, close the lid and allow the mixture to simmer until your unit changes to Keep Warm mode.
7. Serve the pudding hot, with spicy sauce or other condiments on the side if preferred.

7. FRENCH ONION SOUP

SERVINGS: 4-6

PREP TIME: 7 MINUTES

COOK TIME: 50 MINUTES

INGREDIENTS

- 5 medium sweet onion, thinly sliced
- 2 tbsp butter
- 4 garlic cloves, minced
- 1 10.5-oz can beef gravy
- 1/3 cup dry white wine
- 5 cups beef stock
- 1 tsp Worcestershire sauce
- 1 bay leaf
- 1 tsp dried thyme
- salt and pepper, to taste
- 2 cups grated Gruyere cheese
- cubed baguette

DIRECTIONS

1. Whisk together eggs, half-and-half, salt, and pepper in a large mixing basin.
2. Add the bread cubes to the mixture. Stir gently to blend, then set aside for 20 minutes to allow the bread to steep.
3. Melt the butter in the rice cooker's inner pot and set the Sauté-then-Simmer setting. Allow the butter to melt before adding the chopped onion and sautéing until transparent and tender.
4. Add the ham and cook for another 10 minutes, or until the ham is slightly charred.
5. Pour the bread cubes that have been soaked into the inner pot. Stir in the cheddar cheese until all of the ingredients are properly combined.
6. Once the ingredients are combined, close the lid and allow the mixture to simmer until your unit changes to Keep Warm mode.
7. Serve the pudding hot, with spicy sauce or other condiments on the side if preferred.

8. MAPLE GLAZED PORK BELLY

SERVINGS: 2-4

PREP TIME: 7 MINUTES

COOK TIME: 4 HOURS 10 MINUTES

INGREDIENTS

- 2 lbs pork belly
- salt and pepper, to taste
- pinch of cayenne pepper
- 1/4 cup balsamic vinegar
- 1/4 cup chicken stock
- 1/4 maple syrup
- 3 garlic cloves, minced
- 1 tbsp olive oil
- 1 tbsp Italian seasoning

DIRECTIONS

1. Season the pork belly with salt, pepper, and cayenne pepper after patting it dry with a paper towel. Refrigerate the seasoned pork belly for at least one night.
2. Combine the balsamic vinegar, chicken stock, maple syrup, garlic, olive oil, and Italian seasoning in a large mixing bowl.
3. Heat the oil using the Sauté-then-SimmerTM feature. After the oil has heated up, add the pig belly and cook until it is brown and crispy on both sides.
4. Place the balsamic vinegar mixture in the rice cooker and set it to Slow Cook. Cook for 4 hours on HIGH.
5. When the pork belly is done, slice it to the appropriate thickness and serve right away.

9. GINGERBREAD CAKE

SERVINGS: 2-4

PREP TIME: 7 MINUTES

COOK TIME: 30 MINUTES

INGREDIENTS

- 1 large egg
- 1 cup molasses
- 2 ½ cups cake flour
- 1 ½ tsp baking soda
- ½ cup sugar
- ½ cup butter
- 1 tsp ground cinnamon
- 1 tsp ground ginger
- ½ tsp ground cloves
- ½ tsp salt
- 1 cup hot water

DIRECTIONS

1. Cream the butter with a hand mixer on high speed until smooth and creamy. Mix in the sugar once the butter has reached a soft consistency.
2. Beat the egg and molasses together on medium-high speed until thoroughly combined.
3. Sift together all of the dry ingredients in a separate mixing dish. then combine the dry and wet components.
4. Pour in the hot water and mix well.
5. Pour the batter into the inner pot, then use your cooker's Cake or White Rice mode.
6. When the cycle is through, insert a toothpick into the center of the cake. Remove the inner pot from the rice cooker and set aside to cool if the toothpick comes out clean.
7. Allow to cool completely before serving on its own or with a frosting of your choice!

10. VEGAN MAC & CHEESE

SERVINGS: 2-4

PREP TIME: 7 MINUTES

COOK TIME: 30 MINUTES

INGREDIENTS

- 2 ⅔ cups macaroni
- 1 cup diced yellow potatoes
- ¼ cup peeled/diced butternut squash
- ⅓ cup chopped onion
- ¾ cup water
- ½ cup raw cashews
- ¼ cup coconut milk
- 1 tbsp lemon juice
- 1 tsp salt or more to taste
- ¼ tsp garlic powder
- 1 pinch paprika

DIRECTIONS

1. Use the Soup or White Rice feature to bring the water to a boil in the inner pot. Once the water has reached a steady boil, add the macaroni and simmer for about 15 minutes, or until al dente. Remove the macaroni from the pot and set it aside.
2. Continue to boil chopped vegetables in the Soup or White Rice function until they are cooked and soft.
3. Blend the cooked veggies with a quarter cup of water and the additional ingredients in a blender until smooth.
4. Toss the cooked macaroni with the puréed sauce. Season with salt to taste and serve right away.

11. LEMON ROSEMARY CHICKEN

SERVINGS: 2-4

PREP TIME: 7 MINUTES

COOK TIME: 45 MINUTES

INGREDIENTS

- 1 whole chicken (about 5 lbs.), spatchcocked
- 6 tbsp olive oil
- 4 tbsp fresh rosemary, minced
- 3 tbsp fresh parsley, minced
- 4 tbsp garlic cloves, minced
- 2 tbsp orange juice
- 2 tbsp lime juice
- 4 tbsp lemon zest
- ⅓ cup brown sugar
- 4 tsp salt
- 4 lemon slices

DIRECTIONS

1. Combine all ingredients in a large mixing dish, except the spatchcocked chicken.
2. Using a basting brush or your hands, coat both sides of the chicken with the mixture. Make sure the chicken is completely covered in the sauce.
3. Place the chicken in the inner pot, skin side up, and pour the remaining sauce over it.
4. Cook the chicken for 20 minutes on the Steam setting. Insert a meat thermometer into the thickest portion of the chicken to check for doneness during the cooking period.
5. After the Steam function has finished cooking for 20 minutes, switch to the White Rice function. Check the chicken for doneness with a meat thermometer. Cook on the White Rice function until the temperature of the thickest portion of the chicken reaches 165°F.

Remove the chicken from the inner pot and serve on a big plate after it has finished cooking.

12. CREAMY CHEESY CORN

SERVINGS: 3-5

PREP TIME: 2 MINUTES

COOK TIME: 10 MINUTES

INGREDIENTS

- 1 tbsp butter
- 2 (15.25oz) cans corn, drained
- 1/2 cup onion, chopped
- 1/2 cup heavy cream
- 1/2 cup cheddar cheese
- salt and pepper
- pinch of cayenne pepper

DIRECTIONS

1. In the inner pot, melt the butter using the Sauté setting. Once the butter has melted, add the chopped onion and cook for 3 minutes, or until transparent.
2. Add the corn, heavy cream, salt, pepper, and cayenne pepper and stir to combine.
3. Cook the mixture for another 5-7 minutes on Sauté mode, stirring occasionally.
4. Stir in the cheddar cheese until it is melted and well mixed.
5. If preferred, season with more salt and pepper.

13. KETO BUTTERNUT SQUASH RISOTTO

SERVINGS: 2

PREP TIME: 5 MINUTES

COOK TIME: 25 MINUTES

INGREDIENTS

- 2 cups butternut squash, cubed
- 1 tbsp olive oil
- 3 garlic cloves, minced
- 12 oz riced cauliflower, frozen or fresh
- 1/2 cup chicken broth
- 1/4 cup coconut milk
- salt and pepper, to taste

DIRECTIONS

1. Using the Sauté-then-Simmer® mode, heat the olive oil in the inner pot. Once the oven is preheated, add the cubed butternut squash and cook, tossing frequently with a long-handled wooden fork, for about 3-5 minutes, or until somewhat softened.
2. Combine the minced garlic, riced cauliflower, chicken broth, and coconut milk in a large mixing bowl. The cooker will switch to simmer mode on its own. Cook until the risotto is cooked, stirring periodically to prevent the bottom from burning.
3. Season to taste with salt and pepper, then serve and enjoy!

14. MUSHROOM LENTIL LOAF

SERVINGS: 12

PREP TIME: 10 MINUTES

COOK TIME: 1 HOUR

INGREDIENTS

- 1 cup dry lentils
- 3 cups vegetable broth
- 1 cup shredded carrots
- 1 ½ cups chopped sweet onion
- 3 cups diced brown mushrooms
- 2 tbsp minced garlic
- ¾ cups diced green bell pepper
- 1 cup breadcrumbs
- 1 cup flour
- 1 cup sunflower seeds, finely chopped
- 4 tbsp tomato paste
- 3 tbsp vegan Worcestershire
- 2 tbsp dried oregano
- 2 tbsp dried thyme
- 1 tbsp dried parsley
- 1 tbsp ground flax seed + 3 tbsp water
- Balsamic Glaze
- ⅓ cup ketchup
- 4 tbsp balsamic vinegar
- 1 tbsp maple syrup

DIRECTIONS

1. Rinse the lentils and combine with the vegetable broth in the inner pot of your rice cooker. Allow to cook on the White Rice setting until the cooker switches to Keep Warm automatically. Set aside to cool in a separate bowl.
2. Preheat the oven to 375 ° Fahrenheit and prepare a DoveWareTM dish with parchment paper. Set aside to thicken the ground flax seed and water mixture.
3. Finely chop the onion, garlic, mushroom, and pepper in a food processor.
4. Heat 2 tbsp oil in your rice cooker's Sauté-then-Simmer® mode, then sauté the onions. After the onions have browned, add the mushrooms, garlic, carrots, and green pepper, and continue to cook for another 10 minutes. Remove the pan from the heat and set it aside.
5. Mash half of the lentils in a food processor, then return them to the dish with the remaining ingredients and herbs.

6. Toss the flax seed mixture with the Worcestershire sauce and tomato paste in a mixing dish.
7. Combine all of the ingredients in a large mixing bowl and stir until the liquid is uniformly spread.
8. Using a spatula, spread out the mixture in the DoveWare.
9. In a small mixing bowl, combine all of the ingredients for the balsamic glaze. Cook for 40-45 minutes in the oven with the topping on top of the bread. Allow 10-15 minutes for cooling before serving.

15. VEGETARIAN CHILI MAC

SERVINGS: 6-8

PREP TIME: 10 MINUTES

COOK TIME: 35 MINUTES

INGREDIENTS

- 1 tbsp olive oil
- 1 sweet yellow onion, diced
- 2 cloves garlic, minced
- 2 tbsp chili powder
- 15 oz marinara sauce
- 15 oz black beans, drained and rinsed
- 1 cup frozen corn
- 2 cups vegetable broth
- 2 cups macaroni
- 1 cup cheddar cheese, shredded

DIRECTIONS

1. Preheat the cooker to Sauté-then-Simmer STS® and sauté the garlic and onion in the oil until tender and translucent.
2. In the inner saucepan, combine the chili powder, marinara sauce, black beans, corn, and vegetable broth. To incorporate everything, give it a good stir.
3. Stir in the macaroni until everything is well blended. To loosen the noodles, stir the chili every few minutes until it reaches a boil.
4. Once the chili has reached a boil, cover and cook for 15 minutes, or until the pasta is cooked and the liquid is thick and saucy.
5. When the pasta is finished, set the cooker to KEEP WARM. Stir in the shredded cheddar cheese until it is completely melted. Serve immediately.

16. CAULIFLOWER MAC AND CHEESE

SERVINGS: 8-10

PREP TIME: 5 MINUTES

COOK TIME: 45 MINUTES

INGREDIENTS

- 16 oz penne
- 1 head cauliflower, cut into florets
- 1 tbsp olive oil
- 2 tbsp butter
- 1 cup white onion, chopped finely
- 1 tsp cayenne
- 3 cups milk
- 1 cup vegetable stock
- 10-12 ounces smoked gouda, shredded
- 1 tbsp Dijon mustard
- salt and pepper, to taste

DIRECTIONS

1. Fill the multicooker with water up to the top measuring line. To bring it to a boil, close the cover and set the Steam function for 30 minutes.
2. Once the water has to a boil, remove the lid and add the pasta. Cook for 5 minutes after returning to a boil.
3. After 5 minutes of boiling the pasta, add the cauliflower florets and cook for another 3 minutes, or until the pasta is al dente and just soft.
4. Switch off the stove. Remove the inner pot with oven mitts, drain, and set the pasta and cauliflower aside. Place the pot back in the oven.
5. Add the oil and butter to the cooker's Sauté-then-Simmer STS® mode. Cook until the butter has melted.
6. Stir in the onion and cook for 5 minutes, or until it softens.
7. Combine the cayenne, milk, and stock in a mixing bowl. Cook until the water is boiling, then add the cheese and whisk until it is totally melted.
8. Season with salt and pepper and stir in the mustard. Turn the stove off.
9. Stir in the cauliflower and noodles until everything is well mixed. Serve right away.

Food Network provided the inspiration for this recipe.

17. WALNUT LONGAN CAKE

SERVING SIZE: 2

PREP TIME: 15 MINUTES

COOK TIME: 50 MINUTES

INGREDIENTS

- 1 ½ cups of rice flour
- ½ cup cake flour
- 1 ½ tsp. baking powder
- ½ tsp. baking soda
- 1 cup brown sugar
- 1 tbsp. molasses
- ½ cup hot water
- 1 ½ cup cold water
- ½ cup longan
- ½ cup walnut

DIRECTIONS

1. Sift the rice flour, cake flour, baking powder, and baking soda twice.
2. Melt brown sugar and molasses in a large mixing basin with hot water, then chill with cold water.
3. Mix all of the flour mixes into the sugar water until smooth.
4. Transfer the mixture to the inner saucepan and top with walnuts and longans.
5. Place your inner pot in the rice cooker and use the Cake function to cook it.
6. When the cooking cycle is over, chill the cake before removing it from the inner pot.
7. Slice it and set it aside to cool.

18. WILD RICE WITH TURMERIC BROTH

SERVING SIZE: 2

PREP TIME: 15 MINUTES

COOK TIME: 20 MINUTES

INGREDIENTS

- 2 medium carrots, scrubbed + cut into 1 inch pieces
- 1 tsp. oil salt and pepper for taste
- 1 tsp. coconut oil
- ½ shallot, finely diced
- 1 clove of garlic, minced
- 1 thumb-sized piece of ginger, peeled + minced
- 1 ½ tsp ground turmeric
- 2 cup filtered water
- ½ lemon, juice
- ½ cup cook wild rice
- sprouts, for garnish

DIRECTIONS

1. In your Aroma rice cooker, cook your wild rice with the brown rice faction.
2. Toss the carrots with oil, salt, and pepper in your inner pot. Cook the carrots in STS till they are brown and tender. Remove it from the equation.
3. Melt the coconut oil in the same inner pot. Add the shallots and cook them in STS until they are translucent and tender. Stir in the garlic and ginger until the mixture is aromatic. Stir in the turmeric until it is evenly distributed around the pot. Continue to whisk until the mixture resembles a paste (add more coconut oil if necessary).
4. Slowly pour in the water while stirring and sautéing the carrots. When the water is boiling, cover the pot and cook for 10 minutes.
5. When the cycle is over, open the top and stir in the lemon juice. Salt and pepper the soup to taste.
6. Put wild rice in a mixing basin. Pour the soup into the bowl and top with sprouts if desired.

19. IMMUNITY-BOOSTING BUDDHA BOWL

SERVING SIZE: 2

PREP TIME: 15 MINUTES

COOK TIME: 25 MINUTES

INGREDIENTS

- 1 cup cooked wild rice
- 8 ounces firm tofu, cut into triangles
- 2 medium sweet potatoes peeled and diced
- 1 tsp soy sauce
- 1 tsp sugar
- 2 tbsp water
- 2 tsp olive oil divided use
- Salt and pepper for taste
- 2 cups shredded green kale
- ½ avocado, peeled and cubed
- ½ red bell pepper, sliced
- sesame seeds for garnish

DIRECTIONS

1. Using the STS feature on your rice cooker, sauté green kale, bell pepper, and firm tofu one by one in oil. Salt & pepper to taste.
2. In the rice cooker, toss the sweet potatoes with the oil, sauté until lightly browned, then add the soy sauce, sugar, and water. Cook for another 10 minutes with the lid closed.
3. To assemble, place the cooked item on top of the avocado and sprinkle sesame seeds on top.

20. DIRTY WINGS TWO WAYS

SERVING SIZE: 2

PREP TIME: 5 MINUTES

COOK TIME: 30 MINUTES

INGREDIENTS
HONEY SOY STYLE:

- 15 party wings
- ½ cup honey
- 1 tbsp garlic powder
- 1 cup soy sauce
- 2 tbsp cooking wine
- 1 tbsp black pepper
- 2 tbsp olive oil
- salt to taste

BUFFALO STYLE

- 15 party wings
- ¼ cup unsalted butter
- 1 clove garlic, minced
- ¼ cup hot sauce
- ½ tsp salt
- 2 tbsp water

DIRECTIONS

1. In the inner pot, combine all of the ingredients (per taste) and cover.
2. Turn on the stove.
3. After the cooking cycle is completed, keep the dish warm for another 10 minutes before serving.

21. ONE-POT CAJUN CHICKEN PASTA

SERVING SIZE: 2

PREP TIME: 5 MINUTES

COOK TIME: 30 MINUTES

INGREDIENTS

- 3 strips of bacon, chopped
- 1 boneless, skinless chicken breasts, cubed
- 1 ½ tbsp Cajun seasoning, divided, or to taste
- ¼ cup chopped onion
- ½ cup brown mushroom, sliced
- ¼ bell peppers, stemmed, seeded, and thinly sliced
- ½ cup whipping cream, plus more as needed
- ½ cup chicken broth
- 1 tbsp Olive oil
- 1 cup penne
- ¼ cup grated parmesan cheese

DIRECTIONS

1. Combine the chicken broth, whipping cream, and olive oil in the inner pot.
2. Combine all other ingredients except the parmesan cheese in a large mixing bowl and stir thoroughly.
3. Close the lid and turn the switch off.
4. After the cooking cycle has completed. Stir in the parmesan cheese, allowing it to completely melt.

22. ARUGULA & MUSHROOM MACARONI AND CHEESE

SERVINGS: 12

PREP TIME: 10 MINUTES

COOK TIME: 1 HOUR

INGREDIENTS

- 16 oz shell macaroni
- ¼ cup plus 3 tbsp olive oil
- 12 oz white mushrooms, sliced
- about 8 cups baby arugula (roughly 32 ounce bag, more or less depending on your liking)
- 5 cloves garlic, minced
- salt & pepper, to taste
- 2½ cups half-and-half
- pinch of cayenne pepper
- 16 oz cream cheese, room temperature
- 7 oz extra sharp cheddar, shredded
- 4 oz Gruyere, shredded
- 1 cup Panko breadcrumbs

DIRECTIONS

1. Preheat the oven to 425 ° Fahrenheit.
2. Bring a large saucepan of water to a boil while the oven heats; add the macaroni and cook until al dente, about 6 minutes. If you prefer, you may use Sauté-then-Simmer STS® in your multicooker to complete this stage.
3. Strain the pasta, reserving 134 cups of the cooking liquid; set both aside. If you cooked your pasta in the multicooker, rinse and thoroughly dry the inner pot before replacing it in the cooker.
4. Select the Sauté-then-Simmer STS® feature on your cooker. Add 3 tbsps of oil, close the top, and cook for a few minutes.
5. Add the mushrooms and simmer for about 5 minutes with the lid open, until lightly browned and softening.
6. Toss in the arugula, garlic, and season to taste with salt and pepper.
7. Cook, stirring constantly with a long-handled wooden or heat-safe spoon, for 3 minutes, or until the arugula is wilted but still brilliant green.
8. Transfer the mushroom mixture to a separate bowl and put it aside.
9. Carefully remove the inner pot, rinse it carefully, and completely dry it before replacing it in the cooker.
10. Set your stove to the Sauté-then-Simmer STS® mode once more. With the lid open, bring the half-and-half and cayenne to a simmer.

11. Cook for for 15 minutes, stirring frequently, until it has reduced by about 1 cup.

12. Put the cooker on KEEP WARM and stir in the cream cheese until it melts.

13. Stir in the shredded cheddar and Gruyere cheeses until smooth and melted.

14. Stir in the macaroni and the reserved pasta water until everything is well combined.

15. Fold the mushroom and arugula mixture in gently. Mix until everything is well blended.

16. Remove the macaroni and cheese from the cooker and place it in the casserole dish.

17. Combine the bread crumbs and remaining olive oil in a separate bowl; sprinkle equally over the macaroni and cheese.

18. Bake for 10 minutes, or until a little browning has occurred. Allow at least 5 minutes for cooling before serving.

23. GARDENER'S PIE

SERVINGS: 12

PREP TIME: 10 MINUTES

COOK TIME: 1 HOUR 15 MINUTES

INGREDIENTS
FOR THE POTATOES:

- 4 large russet potatoes
- ¼ cup half-and-half
- 4 tbsp butter
- salt & pepper, to taste
- 1 egg yolk

FOR THE FILLING:

- 2 tbsp olive oil
- 1 white onion, chopped
- 2 carrots, peeled and diced small
- 3 cloves garlic, minced
- 8 oz white mushrooms, diced small
- salt and pepper, to taste
- 2 tbsp tomato paste
- 1 cup vegetable broth
- 1 tbsp Italian seasoning
- ¾ cup frozen corn kernels
- ¾ cup frozen peas

FOR THE GRAVY:

- 4 tbsp butter
- 10 oz white mushrooms, sliced
- ¼ cup flour
- salt & pepper, to taste
- 4 cups vegetable stock
- 1 tbsp Italian seasoning

DIRECTIONS

TO MAKE THE POTATOES:

1. Peel the potatoes and cut them into half-inch cubes.
2. Place the potatoes in a large pot and add enough cold water to cover them by 1 inch. Bring to a boil over high heat, covered.
3. Once the potatoes are boiling, cover them and reduce the heat to medium to keep it simmering. Cook for 10-15 minutes, or until a fork can easily pierce it. Drain and return to the boiling pot when they're done.
4. Mash the potatoes, then add the half-and-half, butter, salt, and pepper and mash until smooth; whisk in the yolk and set aside.

TO MAKE THE FILLING:

1. Preheat oven to 350°F.
1. Preheat the oven to 400°F while the potatoes are cooking.
2. Add the oil for the filling and set your stove to Sauté-then-Simmer STS®. Allow to heat for 5 minutes with the lid closed.
3. Once the oil is hot, add the onion and carrots and fry, turning frequently with a long-handled wooden or heat-safe spoon, for about 5 minutes, or until they begin to soften.
4. Add the garlic and simmer for about 1 minute, or until fragrant.
5. Add the mushrooms and season to taste with salt and pepper. Cook, stirring occasionally, for about 6 minutes, or until well cooked.
6. Stir in the flour until the veggies are completely coated; simmer for 2 minutes to remove the flour flavor.
7. Combine the tomato paste, vegetable broth, and Italian spice in a large mixing bowl. To blend, thoroughly stir everything together.
8. Replace the top and bring the mixture back to a boil. Once the sauce has to a boil, remove the lid and continue to cook for 10-12 minutes, stirring occasionally, until the sauce has thickened. Keep the lid ajar at all times.
9. Once the sauce has thickened, mix in the corn and peas well before turning off the heat.
10. Spoon the mixture into the casserole dish and cover with mashed potatoes, starting around the edges to seal the dish and prevent it from bubbling. Using a rubber spatula, smooth the surface.
11. Arrange the casserole dish on a baking sheet (in case it bubbles over).
12. Preheat oven to 350°F and bake for 25 minutes. After 25 minutes, increase the heat to broil and cook for an additional 5 minutes to brown the potatoes on top.

13. Allow for at least 15 minutes of cooling before serving.

REQUIREMENTS FOR THE GRAVY:

1. Rinse and dry the inner pot while the pie is cooking, then return it to the cooker.
2. Preheat the cooker on Sauté-then-Simmer STS® for a few minutes with the lid closed.
3. Remove the cover and pour in the butter. Cook until it has completely melted and is bubbling.
4. Season with salt and pepper and stir in the mushrooms with a long-handled wooden or heat-safe spoon.
5. Simmer for 10-15 minutes, stirring regularly, until the liquid has evaporated.
6. Add the flour and mix well. Cook for about 5 minutes, stirring occasionally.
7. Add the vegetable stock, 1 cup at a time, stirring and incorporating completely between each addition; season with Italian seasoning.
8. Continue to cook, stirring periodically, until the desired thickness is obtained, about 25 minutes.
9. When you're ready to serve, set the cooker to KEEP WARM.

Scoop the gardener's pie onto plates after it has slightly cooled, and cover with the mushroom gravy.

24. SPAGHETTI SQUASH CARBONARA

SERVINGS: 6

PREP TIME: 10 MINUTES

COOK TIME: 2 HOURS

INGREDIENTS

- 1 large spaghetti squash
- 6 slices bacon, cut into small pieces
- 6 cloves garlic, minced
- ½ cup chicken or vegetable broth
- 4 egg yolks
- 2 whole eggs
- 2 cups parmesan cheese, grated
- salt & pepper, to taste
- 1 cup frozen peas

DIRECTIONS

1. Preheat the oven to 375 ° Fahrenheit.

2. Use a fork to poke the squash all over, making sure the prongs go all the way through to the inside.
3. Bake the squash for 1 hour and 30 minutes straight in the oven. Only bake for 1 hour if you prefer your spaghetti squash to be a little crunchier.
4. When it's done, remove it from the oven with oven mitts and set it directly on a chopping board.
5. Allow to cool for an hour before cutting in half lengthwise. Scoop out the seeds and use a fork to shred the spaghetti. Place in a large mixing basin and put aside.
6. Preheat the cooker on Sauté-Then-Simmer STS® with the lid covered for a few minutes.
7. Add the bacon chunks and cook, turning regularly with a long-handled wooden/heat-safe spoon, until crispy.
8. Add the garlic once the bacon is browned and crispy. Cook for 1 minute, stirring constantly, until aromatic.
9. Pour in the broth and simmer until all of the liquid has evaporated.
10. In a medium mixing bowl, whisk together the egg yolks, whole eggs, and parmesan cheese while the broth is simmering. Remove from the equation.
11. Add the frozen peas after the liquid has been absorbed. Cook for a minute or two until completely thawed, then switch to Keep Warm.
12. Finally, pour in the egg mixture. Just enough to integrate the eggs, peas, and bacon, stir lightly. Make sure the eggs aren't scrambled.
13. Toss in the spaghetti squash and toss well to incorporate everything. To ensure that all of the squash is coated in the sauce, we recommend using tongs.
14. Garnish with more parmesan and freshly cracked black pepper right away.

25. CHICKEN ALFREDO STUFFED SHELLS

SERVINGS: 14 SHELLS, SERVES ABOUT 7

PREP TIME: 10 MINUTES

COOK TIME: 1 HOUR

INGREDIENTS

- 14 jumbo shells (about ½ of a 12 ounce box)
- 1 tbsp olive oil
- 1 chicken boneless skinless chicken breast, cut into small pieces
- 15 oz ricotta cheese
- 1 egg
- 1 tbsp Italian seasoning
- 1 tsp oregano
- ¾ cup parmesan cheese, grated
- salt & pepper, to taste
- 15oz jar alfredo sauce (roasted garlic if you can find it)
- ½ cup mozzarella cheese, shredded

DIRECTIONS

1. Half-fill the inner pot of the rice cooker with water (roughly to line 6). Close the lid and set the timer for 12 minutes on Steam (or 3 minutes longer than the cooking time on the package instructions).
2. When the cooker timer begins to count down, the water has reached a gentle boil. Open the cover and add the shells, stirring well to ensure they are completely submerged. Close the lid and cook, stirring regularly, until the timer sounds and the timer reaches 0 minutes.
3. Turn off the stove. CAREFULLY take the inner pot out of the rice cooker using oven mitts. Drain and set aside the pasta to cool. Replace the inner pot in the cooker without rinsing or wiping it down.
4. Add the olive oil to the inner pot and set the cooker to Sauté-Then-Simmer STS®. Allow the oil to heat for 5 minutes with the lid closed.
5. Add the chicken and simmer for 7 minutes, stirring constantly with a long-handled wooden or heat-safe spoon. Season with salt and pepper, then remove the pot from the cooker and set it aside. Scoop the chicken into a big mixing basin.
6. Toss the chicken with the ricotta, egg, Italian spice, and 12 cup parmesan cheese. Set aside after thoroughly mixing the ingredients.
7. In the inner pot of the rice cooker, spread roughly half of the alfredo sauce.
8. Fill each shell with about 2 tsps of the ricotta mixture and lay on top of the alfredo sauce in the inner pot. Continue until the ricotta mixture has been used up and the rice cooker is full. Fit as many as possible without stacking them on top of one another; they can be pushed together.

9. Top the filled shells with the remaining alfredo sauce. The remaining parmesan cheese and mozzarella should be sprinkled over top.
10. Close the lid and select the White Rice setting on the cooker. Cook the shells for the duration of the cooking cycle.
11. When you're finished, turn off the stove. Serve with the shells scooped out. Fresh parsley, red pepper flakes, and freshly cracked black pepper are sprinkled on top.

---

26. BROCCOLI CHEDDAR SOUP

SERVINGS: 8

PREP TIME: 15 MINUTES

COOK TIME: 45 MINUTES

INGREDIENTS

- 5 tbsp butter
- ½ yellow onion, chopped
- 2 carrots, peeled and chopped into small pieces
- 1 stalk celery, thinly sliced
- ¼ cup flour
- 2 cups milk
- 2 cups vegetable stock
- 1½ cups coarsely chopped broccoli florets
- 2½ cups sharp cheddar, shredded
- salt and pepper, to taste

DIRECTIONS

1. Select Sauté-Then-Simmer STS® on your multicooker. Close the lid and heat for a few minutes.
2. Place 1 tbsp of butter in the inner pot and melt it. Add the onion, carrots, and celery once the butter has melted.
3. Cook, stirring regularly with a long-handled wooden or heat-safe spoon, for about 7 minutes, or until soft.
4. Stir in the remaining butter and flour. To melt the butter and coat all of the vegetables with flour, stir continually.
5. Cook the flour for another 4 minutes, stirring constantly. It should be turning somewhat brown at this point.
6. Slowly pour in the milk, followed by the vegetable stock, while stirring constantly. To blend, stir everything together thoroughly.

7. Allow 30 minutes for the soup to come to a simmer. Keep in mind that the automated turn-off may cause your stove to go from Sauté-Then-Simmer STS® to Keep Warm mode. If this occurs, simply switch the cooker to STS® mode.
8. Toss in the broccoli florets that have been chopped. Cook for another 10 minutes, or until the broccoli is tender.
9. Put the cooker on Keep Warm mode. Stir in the cheese until it is completely melted and integrated.
10. Season to taste with salt and pepper, then serve.

27. BRUSCHETTA DIP

SERVINGS: ABOUT 10

PREP TIME: 5 MINUTES

COOK TIME: 20 MINUTES

INGREDIENTS

- 2 tbsp olive oil
- 3 cloves garlic, minced
- ½ red onion, chopped
- salt and pepper, to taste
- 1 tbsp basil
- 1 tbsp oregano
- 1 tsp garlic powder
- 28 oz can diced tomatoes
- 3 tbsp balsamic vinegar
- ½ cup parmesan cheese, grated (or nutritional yeast for vegan option)
- 1 loaf French or garlic bread, lightly toasted in the oven

DIRECTIONS

1. Select Sauté-Then-Simmer STS® on your multicooker. Fill the inner pot halfway with oil, close the lid, and cook for a few minutes.
2. Remove the top from the pot and add the garlic. Cook for 1 minute, or until aromatic.
3. Season with salt and pepper to taste, as well as basil, oregano, and garlic powder. Cook, stirring occasionally with a long-handled wooden or heat-safe spoon, until the onion is tender, about 5 minutes.
4. Combine the tomatoes and balsamic vinegar in a mixing bowl. Close the lid after giving it a good stir.
5. Simmer for 10-12 minutes, or until the bruschetta dip is bubbling and warmed through.
6. Serve in a big mixing basin with bread slices for dipping or spreading.

28. TERIYAKI ZUCCHINI NOODLES

SERVING SIZE: 2

PREP TIME: 5 MINUTES

COOK TIME: 20 MINUTES

INGREDIENTS

- 3 cloves garlic, minced
- 1 tbsp soy sauce
- 2 tbsps teriyaki sauce
- 2 tbsps olive oil
- 1 pound fresh or frozen zucchini noodles
- ½ sweet yellow onion, chopped small
- salt & pepper, to taste
- fresh cilantro, chopped to garnish
- sesame seeds, to garnish

DIRECTIONS

1. Preheat your Aroma multicooker on Sauté-then-Simmer STS® for around 5 minutes with the lid on.
2. Combine the garlic, soy sauce, teriyaki sauce, and oil in a bowl while the cooker is heating. With a fork, whisk it thoroughly.
3. Remove the lid from the pot and add the zucchini noodles. Cook for about 2 minutes, stirring often with a long-handled wooden or heat-safe spoon until just cooked but still crunchy. NOTE: If using frozen zucchini noodles, cook for 5 minutes or until all of them are separated and cooked. In the saucepan containing the zucchini noodles, there will almost certainly be residual water. Turn the cooker off, take the inner pot from the cooker using an oven mitt, and carefully drain the excess water. Return the inner pot to the multicooker and select Sauté-then-Simmer STS® once again.
4. Add the diced onion and sauté for about 2 minutes, or until they begin to soften and turn translucent.
5. Season to taste with salt and pepper, then stir in the sauce.
6. Using a long-handled wooden or heat-safe spoon, mix everything. Cook for another 2-5 minutes, or until all of the flavors have melded together.
7. Turn off the stove. Scoop into dishes and top with fresh cilantro and sesame seeds right away.

29. ZUCCHINI & BLACK BEAN SOUP

SERVINGS: 8-10

PREP TIME: 10 MINUTES

COOK TIME: 30 MINUTES

INGREDIENTS

- 4 small zucchini, cut into half circles
- 10 oz pico de gallo salsa
- 10 oz medium spice salsa
- 48 oz chicken broth (or vegetable)
- 1 sweet yellow onion, chopped
- 1 bell pepper, diced
- 2 tsp cumin
- 1 tbsp chili powder
- salt & pepper, to taste
- small pinch cayenne pepper
- 4 oz tomato paste
- 15 oz can black beans, drained and rinsed
- 2 cups frozen corn
- avocado, fresh cilantro, and radish to garnish

DIRECTIONS

1. In the inner pot of the pressure cooker, combine the zucchini, salsas, broth, onion, bell pepper, cumin, chili powder, salt, pepper, cayenne, and tomato paste.
2. Place the lid on the cooker and select Soup with PP50. Check to see if the steam vent is closed.
3. Cook until the soup achieves pressure, then switch to Keep Warm on the cooker. Change the steam vent to VENTING for a speedy pressure release. Keep an eye out for escaping steam.
4. Open the lid once the pressure has been totally released and the lid safety has been unlocked.
5. Combine the black beans and corn in a mixing bowl. Set the STS® (Sauté-then-Simmer) function on the cooker.
6. Cook for an additional 10 minutes after the soup has reached a slow boil.
7. Switch off the stove. To serve, ladle soup into bowls and garnish with chosen toppings. Enjoy!

30. HOLIDAY POT ROAST

SERVINGS: 5

PREP TIME: 10 MINUTES

COOK TIME: 45 MINUTES

INGREDIENTS

- ⅓ cup kosher salt
- 3 tbsp dry mustard
- 4 tsp coarsely ground black pepper
- 1 ½ tsp garlic powder
- 1 tbsp onion powder
- 2 tsp dried thyme
- 2 tsp dried oregano
- 2 tsp cumin
- 2 tsp celery seeds
- 1 tbsp olive oil
- 1 (4-6 lbs) beef rib roast
- 6 oz small potatoes
- 2 cups baby carrot sticks
- 4 cups beef broth

DIRECTIONS

1. Remove some of the liquid from the roast by blotting it with paper towels. Toss together all of the dry spices and rub them into the roast, making sure to coat the entire piece of meat evenly.
2. Place the meat, beef broth, carrots, and potatoes in the pressure cooker. Press the "Meat" function on your pressure cooker after locking the lid in place.
3. Cook for 35 to 40 minutes at 350°F.
4. Unlock the cover, execute a pressure release, and set aside for 15 minutes before serving, or baste the meat with more sauce and brown it on the grill.

31. SPINACH ARTICHOKE MACARONI AND CHEESE

SERVINGS: 6

PREP TIME: 5 MINUTES

COOK TIME: 30 MINUTES

INGREDIENTS

- 2 tbsp olive oil
- 1 yellow onion, chopped
- 8 large garlic cloves, minced
- 1 can (13.75 oz.) artichoke hearts, drained and roughly chopped
- 16 oz rigatoni, uncooked
- 10 oz baby spinach
- 4 cups vegetable broth
- 2 cups water
- 4 oz cream cheese, room temperature
- ½ cup parmesan cheese, grated
- 1½ cups mozzarella, grated
- pinch of red pepper flakes

DIRECTIONS

1. Add the oil to the cooker and set it to Sauté-Then-Simmer STS®; heat for a few minutes.
2. Add the chopped onion and the oil. Cook for about 2 minutes, stirring regularly with a long-handled wooden or heat-safe spoon until the onions soften.
3. Stir in the garlic and simmer for 1 minute. Cook for another minute after adding the artichoke hearts.
4. Place the pasta in the cooker with 3 cups of broth and 2 cups of water; set aside the remaining cup of veggie stock.
5. Stir thoroughly, making sure that most of the pasta is submerged in the liquids.
6. Tighten the lid and check that the vent is set to Sealing.
7. Continue to cook on Sauté-Then-Simmer STS® mode for another 9 minutes.
8. Switch the steam vent to Venting and turn the cooker off. Keep an eye out for escaping steam.
9. Unlock and remove the cover after it has released. Stir the pasta a few times.
10. Toss the pasta with the remaining stock. If the pasta looks a little watery already, skip this step.
11. Add the spinach and fold it in until it wilts.
12. Finally, add the cream cheese, parmesan, mozzarella, and red pepper flakes, if desired.
13. Stir until the cheeses are completely melted.
14. Garnish with more grated parmesan and freshly cracked black pepper and serve immediately.

32. MOLTEN CHOCOLATE LAVA CAKES

SERVINGS: 3-4 PERSONAL CAKES

PREP TIME: 5 MINUTES

COOK TIME: 10 MINUTES

INGREDIENTS

- 1 stick butter
- 1 cup semi-sweet chocolate chips
- 1 cup powdered sugar
- 3 eggs
- 1 egg yolk
- 1 tbsp vanilla extract
- 6 tbsp flour
- 3-4 roughly 8-oz. glass bowls
- nonstick cooking spray

DIRECTIONS

1. In a large microwave-safe bowl, melt the butter and chocolate chips for 2 minutes. Remove the pan from the heat and whisk with a fork or spatula until everything is fully incorporated.
2. Stir in the powdered sugar until smooth, breaking up any large clumps.
3. Stir in the eggs and egg yolk until thoroughly mixed.
4. Stir in the vanilla and flour until thoroughly mixed.
5. Spray the nonstick cooking spray into each of the glass bowls.
6. Fill roughly two-thirds of the way with batter to make as many as possible.
7. Fill the inner pot of the pressure cooker with 1 cup of water, then add the steam rack.
8. Place one of the bowls on the steam rack, cover, and set the pressure valve to Sealing.
9. Select the Cake setting on the cooker.
10. Cook for 10 minutes before turning off the stove. Turn the pressure valve to Venting for a rapid release. Keep an eye on the steam.
11. When the lid unlocks, carefully open it and remove the cake with oven mitts. Allow to cool slightly before serving.
12. Cook the remaining cakes in the same manner.
13. Place the cooked cakes upside down on a platter when they've cooled for around 5-10 minutes each. To get them out of the bowls, jiggle them a little.
14. Serve plain or with ice cream on top!

33. TURKEY SLOPPY JOES

SERVING SIZE: ABOUT 16 TACOS

PREP TIME: 10 MINUTES

COOK TIME: 25 MINUTES

INGREDIENTS

- 1 lb ground turkey
- 4 cloves garlic, minced
- salt & pepper, to taste
- 1 green bell pepper, chopped
- 2 ribs of celery, chopper
- 1/2 white onion, chopped
- 8-12 slider buns
- FOR THE SAUCE
- 1/2 cup ketchup
- 1 tbsp brown sugar
- 1 tbsp tomato paste
- 2 tbsp yellow mustard
- 2 tbsp Worcestershire sauce
- 1/4 tbsp chili powder
- 1/4 tbsp cayenne pepper powder
- 1/2 cup vegetable broth
- THICKENER
- 1/4 cup water
- 1 tbsp cornstarch

DIRECTIONS

1. Preheat the cooker on STS and cover with the lid while you chop your vegetables and make the sauce.
2. In a small bowl, combine all of the sauce ingredients; leave aside.
3. Add the ground turkey, garlic, and salt & pepper to taste after the inner pot is hot. Cook for about 5 minutes, stirring often with a long wooden spoon until the turkey is done.
4. Once the fat has rendered, remove about half of it and add the celery, peppers, and onion. Cook for another 3 minutes, or until the veggies begin to soften, then add the ketchup sauce and stir briefly.
5. Replace the lid on the cooker and set the temperature to PP50 on the Poultry setting. Allow 7 minutes for the cooker to come to pressure. Whether the cooker has reached pressure or not, turn it off after 7 minutes and execute a rapid pressure release by switching to venting.

6. In a small bowl, whisk together the water and cornstarch while the pressure is released. Open the lid, turn the cooker on, and set the timer for STS after the pressure has been released, then whisk in the cornstarch mixture. Cook for 2 minutes, stirring constantly, until it thickens.

Keep the cooker warm by spooning a few spoonfuls of the sloppy joe mixture onto the slider buns and serving.

34. LEMONY FETTUCCINE WITH BAKED LOBSTER

SERVINGS: 2

PREP TIME: 10 MINUTES

COOK TIME: 1 HOUR 30 MINUTES

INGREDIENTS

- PASTA
- 1 cup + 1 tbsp flour
- 2 eggs
- zest of 1 lemon
- 1 tbsp freshly squeezed lemon juice
- pinch of salt
- olive oil

BAKED LOBSTER

- 2 lobster tails
- 5 garlic cloves, miced
- 1/4 cup Parmesan cheese
- 4 tbsp butter, melted
- 1 tbsp lemon juice
- 1 tsp lemon pepper seasoning

DIRECTIONS

1. Place all of the pasta ingredients in the bread maker, except the olive oil, and select the Raw Dough setting. Allow for a 10-minute leavening period before removing the dough from the bread machine.
2. Knead the dough by hand for another 5 minutes, or until it is smooth. Return the dough to the bread machine and let it rest for 1 hour in the baking cavity.
3. Divide the dough into two equal pieces. Roll the dough to the desired thickness with a pasta machine or by hand.

4. Fold each pasta sheet lengthwise in half and then in half again. Cut the pasta dough into strands that are 1/2 inch wide.

5. Bring 6 cups of water to a boil in a big pot with 1 tsp of salt. Add the pasta to the boiling water and cook until it floats to the surface, indicating that it is done.

6. Drain the water from the pot, then toss the pasta with the olive oil and season with salt and pepper to taste.

7. To prepare the lobster tails, start by cutting down the centre of the top shell toward the tail with kitchen scissors. Separate the meat from the two sides of the shell with a spoon, then raise the meat up and place it over the seam.

8. Combine butter, garlic, lemon juice, and lemon pepper spice in a small bowl. Brush the lobster tails with the garlic butter mixture using a basting brush.

9. Sprinkle Parmesan cheese on top of the lobster tails in the air fryer cooking pan. Set the timer for 15 minutes on HIGH.

10. Place the lobster tails on top of a bed of spaghetti and serve after they are fully cooked.

35. RED BEAN RICE CAKES

SERVINGS: 6-8

PREP TIME: 15 MINUTES

COOK TIME: 30 HOURS

INGREDIENTS

- 1 lb. rice flour
- 1/2 cup vegetable oil
- 1/2 cup sugar
- 4 eggs
- 2 1/2 cup coconut milk
- 1 tbsp baking powder
- 1 (16oz.) can red bean paste
- oil spray

DIRECTIONS

1. In a large mixing basin, whisk together all ingredients except the red bean paste until smooth and no lumps remain in the batter.
2. Gently fold the red bean paste into the batter with spatulas.
3. Coat the pan with oil or nonstick frying spray before pouring in the batter.
4. Cook for 30 minutes on HIGH in the air fryer.
5. Carefully remove the rice cake from the air fryer and let it aside to cool before removing it from the pan.

6. Enjoy by cutting into bite-size pieces.

36. SALMON AIR-FRIED RICE

SERVINGS: 2-3

PREP TIME: 5 MINUTES

COOK TIME: 25 MINUTES

INGREDIENTS

- 1 lb skinless salmon
- 3 cups cooked white rice
- 5 tbsp mayonnaise
- 2 tbsp ketchup
- salt and pepper
- 2 cheddar cheese slices
- olive oil

DIRECTIONS

1. Season each salmon fillet on both sides with salt and pepper.
2. Lightly coat the bottom of your air fryer with cooking spray and arrange the salmon inside without overlapping.
3. Preheat the fryer to HIGH heat and set the timer for 15 minutes to cook the salmon.
4. Remove the fish and place the fillets in a mixing dish when the cycle is finished. Break each fillet completely apart with a fork. The salmon should be flaky enough to perform this without difficulty.
5. Stir in the mayonnaise and ketchup until everything is well combined.
6. Mix the cooked white rice with the leftover cooked salmon oil and fats in the air fryer's cooking pan.
7. Return the salmon mixture to the frying pan and coat the white rice with it. Set the air fryer to HIGH heat and set the timer for 10 minutes after adding the cheddar cheese.
8. When the frying cycle is over, serve right away.

37. POPCORN CHICKEN

SERVINGS: 2-3

PREP TIME: 30 MINUTES

COOK TIME: 8 MINUTES

INGREDIENTS

- 3 boneless skinless chicken thighs cut into bite-sized pieces
- 2 garlic cloves minced
- 2 tbsp soy sauce
- 1 tbsp cooking wine
- 1/2 tsp white pepper powder
- 1/8 tsp black pepper powder
- 1/2 tsp salt
- 1/8 tsp sugar
- ☐4 cups cornflakes, finely crushed
- cooking spray

DIRECTIONS

1. Combine all ingredients (excluding cornflakes) in a medium bowl and marinate for 30 minutes to an hour. Coat the chicken in cornflakes.
2. Lightly spray the bottom of the Air Fryer with cooking spray, then lay the chicken pieces inside without overlapping them.
3. Preheat the Air Fryer to HIGH and set a 5-minute timer. Open the lid and flip the chicken when the cycle is finished. Cook for another 3 minutes on HIGH in the air fryer.
4. Serve the chicken right away while it's still crispy.

38. ARUGULA PROSCIUTTO NAAN PIZZA

SERVINGS: 1

PREP TIME: 2 MINUTES

COOK TIME: 8 MINUTES

INGREDIENTS

- 1 frozen naan bread
- 2 tbsp pesto
- ½ cup shredded mozzarella cheese
- 1 mushroom, sliced
- 1 tsp olive oil
- salt & pepper to taste
- 1 cup baby arugula
- 1 oz thinly sliced prosciutto
- balsamic glaze for topping

DIRECTIONS

1. Evenly spread pesto sauce on naan bread. After that, top with shredded mozzarella cheese. Distribute the mushrooms evenly.
2. Brush your cook pan with a thin layer of olive oil and add the naan pizza.
3. Preheat the air fryer on HIGH for 8 minutes. Allow to cook until the timer goes off, then close the lid.
4. In a large mixing bowl, combine the arugula with the remaining olive oil and season with salt and pepper to taste.
5. Remove the pizza from the air fryer and cut it into triangles; top with arugula salad and prosciutto. Serve by cutting into slices.

39. STUFFED FRENCH TOAST

SERVINGS: 1

PREP TIME: 20 MINUTES

COOK TIME: 12 MINUTES

INGREDIENTS

- 4 slices of bread
- 2 eggs
- 1 cup of milk
- 1 tsp of vanilla
- 1 tbsp of cinnamon
- 2 tbsp cocoa spread
- 2 tbsp strawberries jam

DIRECTIONS

1. To make a sandwich, apply a layer of chocolate spread on two slices of bread and gently press them together. On the other two slices of bread, repeat the process with strawberry jam.
2. Combine the eggs, milk, cinnamon, and vanilla in a large mixing dish. After that, beat until the eggs are broken up and everything is thoroughly combined.
3. Next, dip each sandwich into the mixture, gently flipping to coat both the top and bottom, and set aside for 3-5 minutes to absorb more of the mixture. Place them in a pan to fry.
4. Preheat the air fryer to high heat and set the timer for six minutes. Allow to cook until the timer goes off, then close the lid. Then flip them over and repeat the process for another 3 minutes.
5. Remove from the air fryer and cover with maple syrup or any other desired topping.

40. CUCUMBER PANCAKE

SERVINGS: 2

PREP TIME: 10 MINUTES

COOK TIME: 13 MINUTES

INGREDIENTS

- 2 cups cucumber, shredded
- 1 egg
- ½ cup sweet potato starch
- 1 tsp olive oil
- salt & pepper, to taste
- mayo & hoisin sauce for topping

DIRECTIONS

1. Toss shredded cucumber, egg, and sweet potato starch in a large mixing dish with salt and pepper.
2. Brush your cook pan with a little layer of olive oil and add the cucumber mixer.
3. Preheat the air fryer to 350°F and set the timer for 15 minutes. Allow to cook until the timer goes off, then close the lid.
4. To serve, take it out of the air fryer and cut it into triangle pieces, then cover with mayo and hoisin sauce.

41. SALMON EN PAPILLOTE TWO WAYS

SERVINGS: 2-4

PREP TIME: 20 MINUTES

COOK TIME: 12 MINUTES

INGREDIENTS

- 4 (4oz) salmon fillets
- 1 bulb garlic, minced
- ½ tbsp soy sauce
- 1 tsp sugar
- 1 tsp cooking wine
- ¼ tbsp butter, melt
- 1 tsp lemon juice
- salt & pepper, to taste
- 4 12*18-inch pieces of parchment paper

DIRECTIONS

1. Season salmon fillets with salt and pepper after patting them dry.
2. Combine half of the minced garlic, melted butter, and lemon juice in a small bowl. Mix the remaining half of the mince garlic with the soy sauce, cooking wine, and sugar in a separate small bowl.
3. Fold a sheet of parchment paper in half crosswise and place two salmon fillets on one side. Fold the parchment paper over the salmon and pour the lemon butter mixture in. To seal the salmon inside a parchment paper envelope, fold the edges of the paper over many times all around the open edges. Place the envelopes in the frying pan, sealed.
4. Finish the garlic soy in the final step.
5. Preheat the air fryer to 400°F and set the timer for 12 minutes. Allow to cook until the timer goes off, then close the lid.
6. Remove the paper from the air fryer and cut it open to unleash the aroma. Serve right away.

42. CHEESY CAULIFLOWER BREADSTICKS

SERVINGS: 16

PREP TIME: 25 MINUTES

COOK TIME: 10 MINUTES

INGREDIENTS

- 8.5 oz caulifier rice
- 1 egg
- 1 cup of cheddar jack cheese, shredded
- 1 tbsp Italian seasoning
- salt and pepper, to taste

DIRECTIONS

1. In a large mixing bowl, combine all ingredients and stir until thoroughly combined.
2. Line your air fryer pan with parchment paper so that the paper's edges extend up the side of the pan, making it easier to remove the breadsticks when they're done.
3. Smooth the cauliflower mixture into an even layer with a level top in the prepared air fryer pan.
4. Preheat the air fryer to HIGH and set a 10-minute timer.
5. Place the lid on the pot and cook until the timer beeps.
6. Remove the air fryer basket from the air fryer and set aside to cool for at least 10 minutes. Lift the parchment paper out of the air fryer to remove it.
7. Cut the sheet of cauliflower mixture into 16 breadsticks on a cutting board.
8. Allow to cool completely until it is safe to handle. For dipping, serve with marinara sauce.

The Foodie Physician provided the inspiration for this recipe.

43. APPLE PIE BITES

SERVINGS:8

PREP TIME: 10 MINUTES

COOK TIME: 15 MINUTES

INGREDIENTS

- ¼ cup light brown sugar, packed
- 2 tsp pumpkin pie spice
- 3 tbsp butter, melted
- ⅓ cup pecans, chopped
- 1 small granny smith apple, cored and sliced into 8 slices
- 1 (8-oz) can crescent roll dough

DIRECTIONS

1. Combine the brown sugar and 2 tsp pumpkin pie spice in a small bowl. Remove from the equation.
2. Toss the apple slices in the melted butter and leave aside.
3. On a floured cutting board or work surface, arrange the crescent roll triangles. Distribute the brown sugar mixture evenly among the triangles.
4. Evenly sprinkle chopped pecans over each triangle.
5. On the wide end of each triangle, place an apple slice. Each apple should be wrapped in crescent roll dough. The remaining butter from the apples should be saved.
6. Arrange the packed crescents in the bottom of the pan.
7. Brush the remaining butter over each crescent roll. Add a pinch of pumpkin pie spice if desired.
8. Preheat the air fryer to 350°F and set the timer for 15 minutes. Open the cover after about 10 minutes and rotate the crescents to ensure even browning. Cook for 5 minutes more, or until golden brown.

44. SPICY EGGS & POTATOES

SERVINGS: 6

PREP TIME: 15 MINUTES

COOK TIME: 1 HOUR 10 MINUTES

INGREDIENTS

- 2 tbsp olive oil
- ½ yellow onion, chopped
- 4 cloves garlic, minced
- 3 tsp chili powder
- salt & pepper, to taste
- ½ cup vegetable broth
- 28 oz can diced tomatoes
- 1 cup small diced mini gold potatoes
- 2 cups kale, chopped
- 6 eggs
- 4 oz goat cheese

DIRECTIONS

1. Set the timer for 30 minutes on HIGH in the air fryer.
2. Pour the oil into the pan. Allow to heat for 1-2 minutes with the lid closed.
3. Remove the cover and quickly toss in the onions with a long-handled wooden or heat-safe spoon that won't scratch the pan. Close the lid and cook for 10 minutes, or until they are tender, stirring occasionally.
4. Combine the garlic, salt, two tbsps chili powder, vegetable broth, and tomatoes in a large mixing bowl. Close the lid and cook for the remaining time on the timer, stirring occasionally.
5. When the timer goes off, carefully open the lid and transfer the cooking pan to a heat-safe surface. Scoop up the sauce and purée it in a blender until smooth. Remove from the equation.
6. Return the frying pan to the air fryer without washing it. Preheat the fryer to HIGH and set the timer for 30 minutes.
7. Stir in the potatoes and the remaining 1 tsp of chile powder. Close the top and cook for 15 minutes, or until the outside is golden brown, stirring occasionally.
8. Return the sauce to the pan and stir well. Close the lid and cook for the remaining time on the timer, stirring occasionally with a wooden or heat-resistant spoon.
9. When the timer goes off, open the cover and mix in the kale until everything is well combined.
10. Make small holes in the sauce with a spoon for the eggs. The eggs should be cracked directly into the hot sauce. Set the air fryer to MED and set the timer for 7-8 minutes.
11. Cook until the timer goes off, then cover and set aside for another 5 minutes without turning on the heat. This should result in yolks that are medium-cooked.

12. Remove the lid and sprinkle goat cheese and freshly cracked pepper on top.

45. SWEET POTATO TOTS

SERVINGS: 2-4

PREP TIME: 10 MINUTES

COOK TIME: 1 HOUR 10 MINUTES

INGREDIENTS

- 15 oz can cut sweet potatoes in light syrup
- ½ tsp cumin
- ½ tsp ground coriander
- salt & pepper, to taste
- ¼ cup Panko breadcrumbs
- ¼ cup Italian breadcrumbs
- nonstick olive oil spray

DIRECTIONS

1. Drain the sweet potato liquid from the can. In a food processor, puree the potatoes until smooth. You can use a can of already pureed sweet potatoes if you prefer and can find them.
2. Place the sweet potatoes in a large mixing dish that has been pureed.
3. Combine the remaining ingredients in the bowl with the sweet potatoes and stir until thoroughly combined.
4. Scoop the mixture into balls using a tbsp. Form into tot shapes and set aside; continue to make tots until the mixture is completely gone. There should be roughly 25 tots total.
5. Lightly coat the inside of the pan with nonstick cooking spray. Spray the tops of the tots with the cooking spray before placing them in the pan.
6. Set the timer for 15 minutes on HIGH in the air fryer.
7. When the timer goes off, flip all of the tots over with rubber tongs. Spray the tops of the tots with nonstick spray once more.
1. Set the timer for 15 minutes on HIGH in the air fryer. Remove the air fryer from the heat after the food is done.
8. Top with guacamole, ketchup, or chipotle mayo and serve right away.

46. LEMON PARMESAN BROCCOLI

SERVINGS: 2-4

PREP TIME: 10 MINUTES

COOK TIME: 1 HOUR 10 MINUTES

INGREDIENTS

- 1 to 1½ lbs fresh broccoli
- 4 cloves garlic, sliced
- ¼ cup olive oil
- salt & pepper, to taste
- pinch of red pepper flakes
- 1 lemon, zested
- ¼ cup parmesan cheese, grated

DIRECTIONS

1. Cut the broccoli into florets of roughly the same size.
2. Arrange the broccoli and sliced garlic in the air fryer pan. Season with salt, pepper, and red pepper flakes after drizzling with olive oil.
3. Preheat the air fryer and set the timer for 17 minutes on HIGH.
4. Cover the pot and simmer until the timer beeps. Broccoli florets should be starting to brown at this point.
5. When the broccoli is done, remove the lid and top it with lemon zest and parmesan cheese; gently toss the broccoli to coat it.
6. Serve right away.

47. AIR FRYER CHICKEN PARMESAN

SERVINGS: 6 FILLETS

PREP TIME: 40 MINUTES

COOK TIME: 1 HOUR 10 MINUTES

INGREDIENTS
FOR THE CHICKEN:

- 3 chicken breasts, halved horizontally to make 6 fillets
- 2 eggs
- 2 cloves garlic, minced
- 2 tbsps chopped parsley
- salt and pepper, to taste
- 1 cup Panko breadcrumbs
- ½ cup Italian breadcrumbs
- ½ cup parmesan cheese, grated
- 1 tsp garlic powder
- 1 tsp onion powder

FOR THE SAUCE:

- 1 tbsp olive oil
- 1 yellow onion, chopped
- 3 cloves garlic, minced
- 14 oz. canned tomato sauce
- salt and pepper, to taste
- 1 tbsp Italian seasoning
- 1 tbsp sugar

FOR THE TOPPING:

- about 12 ounces mozzarella cheese, sliced into 12 slices
- ⅓ cup parmesan cheese, grated
- 3 tbsps chopped parsley

DIRECTIONS

1. Whisk together the eggs, garlic, parsley, salt, and pepper in a large shallow dish (such as a casserole dish).
2. Toss the chicken in the egg mixture and toss it over several times to evenly coat each fillet. Cover with plastic wrap and refrigerate while you create the sauce, or for at least 15 minutes if using a readymade sauce.

3. Pour the oil into the air fryer's frying pan. Close the lid and set the timer for 30 minutes on HIGH.
4. After 5 minutes, add the chopped onion to the hot oil.
5. Cook for about 10 minutes, or until transparent, stirring every few minutes with the lid open. Cook for 1 minute, or until the garlic is aromatic.
6. Combine the tomato sauce, salt, pepper, Italian seasoning, and sugar in a mixing bowl. Stir everything together thoroughly.
7. Put the lid on the cooker and set the temperature to MEDIUM. Allow the sauce to cook until the timer beeps, stirring occasionally.
8. Remove the sauce from the pan and place it in a bowl when the timer goes off.
9. Using the cool touch handles, remove the frying pan. Return to the air fryer after rinsing with cold water and thoroughly drying.
10. In a large shallow bowl or pie dish, combine the two types of bread crumbs, Parmesan, garlic powder, and onion powder from the chicken ingredient list. A platter will also work, but it will be a little more messy.
11. Fully cover each of the chicken fillets in the breadcrumb mixture. Place the breaded fillets on a platter and put aside until all of the fish have been breaded.
12. Cook 3 of the chicken fillets in the air fryer and keep the other 3 in the fridge.
13. Make sure the air fryer's temperature is set to MEDIUM. Set the timer for 12 minutes after closing the lid.
14. Flip the chicken pieces over when the timer goes off.
15. Drizzle a generous amount of sauce over each piece, then top with two slices of mozzarella cheese, parmesan, and chopped parsley.
16. Put the lid on the container and set the timer for 8 minutes.
17. Using a rubber spatula, carefully remove the chicken when the timer goes off. Cook and top the remaining 3 chicken fillets as before.
18. Serve immediately, either on their own or with spaghetti.

48. COCONUT CRUSTED FISH TACOS

SERVINGS: ABOUT 16 TACOS

PREP TIME: 10 MINUTES

COOK TIME: 25 MINUTES

INGREDIENTS
FOR THE TACOS:

- 1 cup shredded unsweetened coconut
- ⅓ cup panko bread crumbs
- 1 tbsp garlic powder
- 1 tsp cumin
- pinch cayenne
- juice of 1 lime
- 4 tilapia fillets
- 16 taco sized tortillas
- 1 avocado, diced to garnish
- queso fresco or sour cream, to garnish

FOR THE MANGO SALSA:

- 1 mango, diced
- 1 roma tomato, cored and diced
- ½ small red onion, diced
- ½ red bell pepper, diced
- ½ cucumber, peeled and cut into quarters
- small bunch of cilantro leaves (about 1 cup), chopped
- juice of 1 lime
- 1 tsp apple cider vinegar
- salt and pepper, to taste

DIRECTIONS

1. Combine the coconut, panko, garlic powder, cumin, and cayenne in a shallow dish or plate. Remove from the equation.
2. Squeeze a little lime juice on both sides of two of the tilapia fillets. Dip the fillets into the coconut mixture, making sure they are completely covered and the crust adheres.
3. Place in the air fryer's nonstick pan and close the lid. Set the timer for 10 minutes set the cooker to MED.
4. When the timer goes off after 10 minutes, open the cover and flip the fish fillets over with a spatula. Close the cover again, leave the temperature on MED, and cook for another 7 minutes.

5. Remove the fillets from the cooker when they are done. Bread and cook the remaining two fillets in the same manner.
6. Prepare the mango salsa while the fish is cooking.
7. In a mixing dish, combine the diced mango and sliced veggies.
8. Toss in the cilantro, lime juice, apple cider vinegar, and season to taste with salt and pepper. Mix thoroughly.
9. Assemble the tacos once the fish and salsa are finished: add the fish, salsa, avocado chunks, and cheese to warmed tortillas and serve immediately.

49. FLAKY CINNAMON SUGAR DOUGHNUTS

SERVINGS: 8 DOUGHNUTS + 8 DOUGHNUT HOLES

PREP TIME: 15 MINUTES

COOK TIME: 10 MINUTES PER BATCH

INGREDIENTS

- ⅓ cup sugar
- 1 tsp cinnamon
- ¼ cup brown sugar
- 1 can of 8 flaky layers biscuits
- 5 tbsp butter, melted

DIRECTIONS

1. In a small mixing bowl, whisk together the sugar, cinnamon, and brown sugar with a fork, breaking up any big clumps of brown sugar. Remove from the equation.
2. Take the biscuits out of the can and set them aside. Cut holes in the center of the biscuits with a doughnut cutter. If you don't have a doughnut cutter, make a 1-inch hole in the center with something comparable.
3. Place the doughnuts in the air fryer four at a time. Set the temperature to MEDIUM and the timer to ten minutes.
4. Cook for about 8 minutes with the lid closed, then check for doneness.
5. When the doughnuts are golden brown, turn off the oven and carefully remove them with a rubber spatula. If not, leave them to simmer for another 2 minutes before removing them.
6. Cook the remaining doughnuts in the same manner.
7. To make the holes, put everything in the air fryer at the same time. Set the timer for 8 minutes and remove when done; after 6 minutes, check for doneness.
8. Brush the melted butter over the entire surface of the finished doughnuts.
9. Coat the buttered doughnuts and holes completely in the sugar mixture. Remove any excess by gently shaking it off.

Enjoy while it's still warm!

50. GRILLED CORN TWO WAYS

SERVINGS: 6

PREP TIME: 15 MINUTES

COOK TIME: 30 MINUTES

INGREDIENTS

- 8 corn on the cob
- 2 cups water
- 1/4 cup mayonnaise
- 1/2 cup cotija cheese
- 1 tbsp chili powder
- 1 lime
- 1/4 cup cilantro
- 1/4 cup butter
- 1/4 cup maple syrup

DIRECTIONS

1. Preheat the Gillet to 350 ° Fahrenheit. Place 4 corn on the cob into the grill once it has heated up, then add 1/4 cup of water and close the lid.
2. Cook the corn for 5 minutes before flipping each one 90 °. Remove from fire once all sides have been roasted and continue with the remaining 4 corn on the cob.
3. Spread mayonnaise over 4 corns and top with cheese, chili powder, and cilantro. To taste, squeeze lime juice over the top.
4. Brush the remaining four corns with butter and drizzle with maple syrup.

51. SPINACH STUFFED FLANK STEAK

SERVINGS: 6

PREP TIME: 20 MINUTES

COOK TIME: 1 HOUR 20 MINUTES

INGREDIENTS

- 2 lb beef flank, cut across the grain into 6 pieces
- 2 cups mushrooms, sliced
- 1 cup sweet onion, sliced
- 4 oz. cream cheese, softened
- 2 cups spinach
- 3 tbsp butter
- salt and pepper
- ½ cup beef broth
- 1/4 cup beer
- olive oil

DIRECTIONS

1. Preheat the inner pot on HIGH heat and then add the butter. Allow the butter to melt and distribute evenly around the inner pot's surface.
2. Add the sliced onion and mushrooms and cook until the onions are translucent and the mushrooms have shrunk in size, about 5 minutes. Manually switch the cooker to Keep Warm when it has been properly sautéed.
3. Combine the softened cream cheese and spinach in a mixing bowl.
4. Set aside about 2/3 of the cheese mixture from the inner pot. In the inner saucepan, add the remaining cheese mixture and beef broth.
5. Reduce the heat to MID/MEDIUM and stir until the broth and cheese mixture are thoroughly blended and the consistency of a thick sauce.
6. In the meantime, pat the beef flank slices dry with a paper towel and season them on all sides with salt and pepper.
7. Spread the reserved cream cheese mixture on one side of each steak.
8. Roll the steak tightly to completely encompass the stuffing. Tightly secure the roll with cooking twine or yarn. If you don't have any thread or yarn, simply secure each roll with a toothpick in the middle.
9. Remove the stainless steel pot from the cooker with caution and replace it with the grill pan.
10. Brush the grill pan lightly with olive oil and preheat on HIGH.
11. When the oil is hot, add the steak rolls to the pan and sear them on all sides (about 2-3 minutes on each side).

12. Pour in the beer and reduce to a low heat setting. Cook for 15 minutes, flipping halfway through to keep the beef rolls from adhering to the bottom of the pan.
13. Toss with the remaining cream cheese sauce while still heated.

52. ALOHA BURGERS

SERVINGS: 4

PREP TIME: 25 MINUTES

COOK TIME: 30 MINUTES

INGREDIENTS

- 1 (8-oz.) can pineapple rings
- 2 cups cucumber, sliced
- 1 lb. ground beef
- 1 cup purple onion, chopped
- 1 large tomato, sliced
- 4 slices Swiss cheese
- 4 slices American cheese
- 4 eggs
- 4 brioche burger buns
- 1 tbsp mayonnaise
- 1 tbsp salt

DIRECTIONS

1. Combine chopped onion and salt in a mixing basin and let aside for 20 minutes. Drain after rinsing with water.
2. Combine the ground beef and salted onion in a mixing bowl. Make four patties out of the beef.
3. Preheat grillet to 450°F and arrange meat patties on griddle side and pineapple rings on grill side. Remove pineapple rings from the grill after 2 minutes on each side.
4. Grill hamburger patties for 5 minutes on each side, then top each with 1 slice Swiss cheese and 1 slice American cheese. Cook for an additional 4 minutes, or until the cheese is completely melted.
5. Evenly spread mayonnaise on the brioche buns. To toast the buns, place them on the grill side of your Grillet.
6. Crack your eggs on the griddle side and fry sunny-side up.
7. Layer cucumber, hamburger patties, tomatoes, grilled pineapple, and a sunny-side up egg on the bottom bread. We suggest serving with honey mustard sauce or BBQ sauce.

53. UDON NOODLE SOUP

SERVINGS: 1

PREP TIME: 5 MINUTES

COOK TIME: 10 MINUTES

INGREDIENTS

- 1 pack udon noodles (frozen or fresh)
- 6 cups low sodium chicken stock
- 1 tbsp dry seaweed
- 1 cup spinach
- 5 fish ball
- 1 tsp light soy sauce
- optional toppings:
- hard boil egg
- green onion

DIRECTIONS

1. Fill the stainless steel pot halfway with chicken stock, set your Whatever Pot on High, and come to a boil.
2. Cook for 4 minutes, or until the udon noodles and salmon balls are softened. Remove the noodles from the pot and place them on a plate to cool.
3. Add the seaweed to the pot and cook for another 5 minutes, allowing the taste of the seaweed to permeate the soup. Remove the fish balls and seaweed from the pan and place them on top of the udon noodles.
4. Return the soup to a boil and stir in the spinach. Cook for 30 seconds, then remove from the heat.
5. Toss the noodles with the boiled broth and cooked spinach, then top with a boiled egg and green onion, if preferred.

54. CAULIFLOWER CAKES

SERVINGS: 12 PANCAKES

PREP TIME: 10 MINUTES

COOK TIME: 20 MINUTES

INGREDIENTS

- 16 oz frozen cauliflower rice
- 2 egg
- 3 tbsp green onion, more for garnish
- ½ cup cheddar cheese
- ½ cup bread crumbs
- ½ tsp salt
- ½ tsp garlic powder
- sour cream for garnish
- olive oil

DIRECTIONS

1. Squeeze out all of the liquid from the cauliflower rice before defrosting it. Place in a large mixing basin.
2. Combine the cheese, eggs, green onion, bread crumbs, salt, and garlic powder in a large mixing bowl. Season with salt and pepper to taste.
3. Brush the grill pan with olive oil and preheat it to high heat.
4. Form the cauliflower mixture into patties and fry for 4 minutes on each side, or until golden brown and firm. Remove the pan from the heat.
5. If preferred, top the pancakes with sour cream and additional green onion.

55. CREAMY SHRIMP PASTA

SERVINGS: 3

PREP TIME: 10 MINUTES

COOK TIME: 15 MINUTES

INGREDIENTS

- 2 cups fusilli
- 2 cups water
- 1 tbsp salt
- 1/2 heavy whipping cream
- 2 tbsp olive oil
- 1 cup cherry tomato, halves
- 1/2 cup corn
- 1 lb shrimp shell less.
- 1 tsp paprika
- 1 tsp garlic powder
- 1/2 cup Parmesan cheese, grated
- salt and pepper for taste

DIRECTIONS

1. Preheat the grillet to 450 ° Fahrenheit. In a mixing dish, combine the shrimp, paprika, garlic powder, and olive oil. Place the shrimp on the warmed Grillet in a single layer and cook for 30 seconds on each side, or until the shrimp turn pink. Place the cooked shrimp on a platter and set aside once they are done cooking.
2. Cook for 10 minutes or until the pasta is al dente, adding 2 cups of Fusilli, 2 cups of water, and 1 tbsp salt to the Grillet. Stir together the heavy cream, cherry tomatoes, and corn.
3. Reduce the grillet's temperature to 350 ° Fahrenheit. Allow the Parmesan cheese and shrimp to fully melt in the pot. Enjoy with a pinch of black pepper!

56. SHRIMP TOAST

SERVINGS: 4-8

PREP TIME: 15 MINUTES

COOK TIME: 6 MINUTES

INGREDIENTS

- 2 cup shrimp, peeled and deveined
- 1 large egg white
- 1 tbsp corn starch
- 1 tsp oil
- 4 slices of white bread
- 1 tbsp butter
- salt and pepper to taste
- parsley for garnish

DIRECTIONS

1. Pulse the shrimp, egg whites, corn starch, salt, and pepper in a food processor until smooth.
2. Remove the crusts from the bread and cut it in half.
3. Spread 2 tsps of shrimp paste on each slice of bread evenly.
4. Preheat the grill to 400°F and grease both the grill and the griddle. Add the shrimp toasts 4 at a time to the griddle side, shrimp side down. Place the remaining 4 bread slices on the grill side, bread side down. Toast for another 3 minutes after flipping and changing sides.
5. Sprinkle with parsley and serve immediately.

57. SUMMER SQUASH BOAT

SERVINGS: 4-8

PREP TIME: 35 MINUTES

COOK TIME: 35 MINUTES

INGREDIENTS

- 3 large zucchinis
- 3 yellow squashes
- 1 lb ground beef
- 1 cup onion, chopped
- 1 cup cheddar cheese, shredded
- 2 tbsp ketchup
- 2 tbsp olive oil
- salt and pepper, to taste

DIRECTIONS

1. Remove the ends of each squash and trim them. Scoop off the inner pulp of the zucchini and yellow squash, leaving 1-2 inch broad grooves.
2. Brush each squash with a thin layer of olive oil and finely slice the pulp that has been removed.
3. Preheat the grillet to 350 ° Fahrenheit. When the grill is hot, place the squash face down on it and cook until grill lines appear. Remove the pan from the heat.
4. In a large skillet, combine the beef, zucchini pulp, and onion and simmer until the meat is no longer pink. Remove the pan from the heat and drain any remaining liquids.
5. Reduce the temperature of the grillet to 300°F. Toss the beef mixture with 12 cup cheese, ketchup, salt, and pepper in a mixing bowl.

Fill the squash shells with the beef mixture and return them to the grill. The remaining cheese should be sprinkled on top. Cook for 10 minutes, or until the squash is soft and the cheese is melted, with the lid closed

58. CHICKEN RANCH WRAPS

SERVINGS: ABOUT 8

PREP TIME: 10 MINUTES

COOK TIME: 40 MINUTES

INGREDIENTS

- o lbs precooked chicken, chopped
- 1 tsp cayenne
- salt and pepper, to taste
- ½ cup ranch dressing
- 1 cup mozzarella cheese, shredded
- ¼ cup fresh cilantro, minced
- 4-6 cups shredded lettuce
- 8 taco-sized flour tortillas

DIRECTIONS

1. Preheat the GrilletTM to 350 ° Fahrenheit. Put the cover on and wait for it to heat up.
2. Sprinkle the cayenne pepper, salt, and pepper over the chicken.
3. On a dish, place a tortilla. On the tortilla, layer about a half cup of seasoned chicken, 1-2 tbsps ranch, 2 tbsps cheese, cilantro, and a small handful of shredded lettuce. Fold it in half like a burrito.
4. Continue creating wraps until all of the ingredients have been used.
5. Place two wraps seam-side down into the GrilletTM at a time. Allow 5 minutes on one side before flipping using silicone-tipped tongs or a rubber spatula. Cook for another 5 minutes, or until both sides are crisp and charred.
6. Place the finished wraps on a platter and remove them from the GrilletTM. Continue until all of the wraps have been cooked.

59. CAULIFLOWER QUINOA BURGERS

SERVINGS: 10

PREP TIME: 20 MINUTES

COOK TIME: 40 MINUTES

INGREDIENTS

- 1½ cups cooked quinoa
- 1 head cauliflower
- 4 tbsp olive oil
- 1 tsp cumin
- 1 tsp chili powder
- 1 tsp cayenne powder
- 1 tsp roasted garlic powder
- ¾ cup Italian breadcrumbs
- ¾ cup panko breadcrumbs
- ¾ cup shredded pepper jack cheese
- 3 eggs

TO ASSEMBLE:

- hamburger buns (we recommend pretzel buns or brioche)
- chipotle mayo (½ cup mayonnaise, ½ cup sour cream, juice from 1 lime, 1 tbsp adobo sauce)
- tomato
- red onion
- lettuce

DIRECTIONS

1. Preheat the oven to 400 ° Fahrenheit.
2. Remove the florets from the cauliflower and place them on a baking sheet. Drizzle olive oil over the cauliflower and season with salt and pepper. Remove and stir after 20-30 minutes of baking until browned. Allow the florets to cool before pulsing them in a blender or food processor until they resemble rice. Do not purée the mixture too much.
3. Combine the cauliflower, quinoa, breadcrumbs, cheese, and eggs in a mixing bowl. Make 10 patties with the mixture, adding a bit more breadcrumbs if it appears too wet.
4. Preheat the GrilletTM to 400 ° Fahrenheit. Cook 4 patties at a time until golden brown, about 5 minutes per side. Assemble the burgers by spreading some Chipotle mayo on top and adding other toppings.

60. GRILLED BANANA BOATS

SERVINGS: ABOUT 6

PREP TIME: 5 MINUTES

COOK TIME: 15 MINUTES

INGREDIENTS

- 6 large ripe bananas
- 6 tbsp dark chocolate chips
- 6 tbsp marshmallows
- 2 tbsp chopped walnuts

DIRECTIONS

1. Preheat the grillet to 350 ° Fahrenheit.
2. Make a deep cut lengthwise along the interior curve of each banana with a sharp knife. Make sure you're not cutting all the way through. To make a tiny pocket, push out the corners of the slice you just cut. Form a boat out of a sheet of aluminum foil by crimping and shaping it around each banana.
3. Place 1 tbsp chocolate chips, 1 tbsp marshmallows, and a dusting of chopped walnuts in each pocket. Crimp the corners of each foil boat so that they almost completely cover the banana but have a slit at the top to allow steam to escape.
4. Place three banana boats in the Grillet at a time and cover. Cook for about 8 minutes, or until the marshmallows are fluffy and the chocolate has melted. Remove with tongs with care. Rep with the remaining three bananas.
5. Remove the foil boats from the oven and serve straight from the peel, or peel and serve in a bowl or on a plate. Enjoy with ice cream on top!

61. RICE & BEAN QUESARITO

SERVINGS: ABOUT 6

PREP TIME: 5 MINUTES

COOK TIME: 1 HOUR

INGREDIENTS

- 4 rice cooker cups of cooked white rice (equal to 3 standard U.S. cups)
- 30oz. can black beans, drained and rinsed
- 1 cup chunky salsa
- 12 burrito-sized flour tortillas
- 2 cups Mexican cheese blend, shredded
- ½ cup queso dip
- ½ cup sour cream
- any other add-ins you'd like

DIRECTIONS

1. Preheat the GrilletTM to 350 ° Fahrenheit. Put the cover on and wait for it to heat up.
2. While the GrilletTM is heating up, combine the black beans and salsa with the rice and stir until the salsa is evenly distributed throughout the rice. Remove from the equation.
3. Place a tortilla in the GrilletTM that has been preheated. Cover with a second tortilla, then top with a generous amount of Mexican cheese.
4. Carefully press the tortillas using a spatula. Place the lid on the GrilletTM and cook the quesadilla for around 2 minutes on that side.
5. Carefully open the lid and flip the quesadilla over with a spatula. Replace the lid and cook until the cheese is completely melted and grill marks appear.
6. Take it off the grill and let it aside to cool for a minute or two until you can handle it comfortably.
7. Spread about a quarter cup of the rice and bean mixture down the center of the quesadilla. Toppings: some queso, sour cream, and anything else you like.
8. Fold the quesarito in half and roll it up like a tortilla.
9. Repeat with the remaining tortillas to make 6 quesaritos.

62. GRILLED CORN & BLACK BEAN SALSA

SERVINGS: ABOUT 6

PREP TIME: 5 MINUTES

COOK TIME: 25 MINUTES

INGREDIENTS
FOR THE SALSA:

- 2 ears of corn
- 30 oz black beans, drained and rinsed
- 2 cups cherry tomatoes, halved
- ½ red onion, diced
- ⅓ cup fresh cilantro, roughly chopped
- 2 avocados, cubed

FOR THE DRESSING:

- juice from 4 small limes
- 3 tbsp olive oil
- 1 tsp agave or honey
- 1 tsp garlic powder
- 1 tsp chili powder
- salt and pepper, to taste

DIRECTIONS

1. Preheat the GrilletTM to 400°F. Close the lid and heat for a few minutes.
2. Remove the husks off the corn and lay the two ears on the GrilletTM, then close the cover.
3. Cook for 25 minutes, turning every 5 minutes with rubber-tipped tongs to ensure the kernels cook and receive some grill marks.
4. Once the corn is cooked and colored, remove it from the GrilletTM and turn it off.
5. Allow the corn to cool before removing the kernels from the cob and placing them in a medium mixing dish.
6. Whisk together all of the dressing ingredients in a small bowl; leave aside.
7. Toss the black beans, cherry tomatoes, onion, and cilantro into the bowl with the corn.
8. Toss the vegetables in the dressing. To properly coat the vegetables, give everything a vigorous swirl.
9. Scatter the avocado on top and gently mix the salsa again to integrate it without crushing it.
10. Serve with tortilla chips right away.

63. MOJITO ICED TEA

SERVINGS: 4

PREP TIME: 5 MINUTES

COOK TIME: 15 MINUTES

INGREDIENTS

- 4 cups water
- 2 green tea bags
- 4 sprigs fresh basil leaves, chopped
- 1/4 cup lime juice
- 1 cup white rum or hard alcohol of your choice, if desired

DIRECTIONS

1. Fill the kettle halfway with water and come to a boil.
2. After the water has been brought to a boil, soak the green tea bags for around 10 minutes before removing them. Before discarding the tea bags, squeeze them into the water.
3. Set aside for 20 minutes to allow the tea to cool.
4. In a serving pitcher, combine the chopped basil, rum (if using), and lime juice, then pour in the brewed tea and stir thoroughly.
5. Chill in the refrigerator or serve over ice.

65. RASPBERRY ROSE TEA

SERVINGS: 2-4

PREP TIME: 7 MINUTES

COOK TIME: 10 MINUTES

INGREDIENTS

- 1L milk
- 2 rose tea bags
- 3/4 cup frozen raspberries
- crushed dried rose petals
- honey, to taste

DIRECTIONS

1. Place both tea bags in the pot with the milk.
2. Turn on the Milk Tea mode.

3. Remove the tea bags and add the frozen raspberries after the water has been brought to a boil.
4. Ladle the tea into heat-safe glasses, top with crushed rose petals, and drizzle with honey to taste.

64. MULLED WINE

SERVINGS: 2-4

PREP TIME: 7 MINUTES

COOK TIME: 30 MINUTES

INGREDIENTS

- 1 bottle any dry red wine
- 2 oranges
- 2 apples, sliced
- 1 cinnamon stick
- 12 whole cloves
- 1 star anise
- ½ cup honey

DIRECTIONS

1. Peel the orange and squeeze out as much juice as possible. Set aside the peels for another time.
2. In a kettle, combine all of the ingredients and turn it on. Bring the liquid to a boil and keep it there.
3. After 30 minutes, bring the wine back to a boil.

Garnish with orange peels and additional cinnamon sticks while still warm.

66. RICE COOKER QUICK WHITE RICE

Cook Time10 mins

Servings4 cups

INGREDIENTS

- 2 cups white rice Using the measuring cup provided by your rice cooker.
- 4 cups water filled to Line 2 in the rice cooker

INSTRUCTIONS

1. Rinse and drain the rice before placing it in the rice cooker's inner pot. Fill the pot with water until the water line reaches the Line 2 marker (approximately 4 cups).
2. Place the inner pot in the rice cooker, secure the lid, and set the rice cooker to the RICE setting. Allow 10 minutes for rice to cook.
3. •
4. When the rice cooker is finished cooking, it will automatically switch to "Keep Warm." Serve immediately after opening the saucepan and fluffing the rice with a fork or spatula.

67. RICE COOKER CHILI

Prep Time: 5 mins

Cook Time: 35 mins

Total Time: 40 mins

INGREDIENTS

- 1 Tbsp olive oil
- 1/2 lb. ground beef
- 1/2 Tbsp chili powder
- 1/2 tsp cumin
- 1/8 tsp cayenne pepper
- 1/4 tsp garlic powder
- 1/2 tsp onion powder
- 1 tsp brown sugar
- 1/2 tsp salt
- freshly cracked pepper
- 1 15oz. can diced tomatoes
- 1/2 6oz. can tomato paste
- 1 15oz. can kidney beans
- 3/4 cup water

INSTRUCTIONS

1. In a rice cooker, combine the olive oil and ground beef. Close the lid and choose the "white rice" or "cook" function, depending on your cooker's options. Allow the beef to cook with the lid closed until it is fully browned, stirring and breaking up the meat every couple of minutes (about 5 minutes total). Many rice cookers, including the one I used, will not heat unless the lid is closed, so close it after each stir.
2. Drain the excess fat from the beef once it has thoroughly browned if it has a greater fat content. In the rice cooker, combine the chili powder, cumin, cayenne, garlic powder, onion powder, brown sugar, salt, and pepper with the ground beef, stir to blend, then cover and cook for one minute more.
3. Drain the kidney beans and combine them with the diced tomatoes (and their liquids), tomato paste, and water in the rice cooker. Stir everything together until it's completely smooth.
4. Replace the top, select "white rice" or "cook," and let the chili simmer for another 30 minutes. To keep the chili from sticking to the bottom, stir it occasionally. If your cooker finishes the cook cycle before the 30 minutes are up, just start it over.
5. Taste the chili after 30 minutes of boiling, adjust the seasoning if necessary, and serve with your favorite chili toppings.

NOTES

*Instead of the individual spices, half of a store-bought chili seasoning packet can be used.

68. BEST RICE COOKER RECIPES THAT ARE SURPRISINGLY EASY TO MAKE

Ingredients

- 1 cup rice (uncooked)
- 1 cup water
- 1 potato peeled (use a smaller potato so that it can be fully cooked through)
- 1 cup carrots diced
- 1 cup Chinese style sausage sliced
- 1 cup onions
- 1 cup frozen green peas
- 2 tbsps soy sauce
- 1 tbsp oyster sauce
- 2 tsps oil
- salt to taste

Instructions

1. Gently swirl the rice grains in cold water after rinsing. Then drain the water.
2. Fill the rice cooker halfway with rinsed rice.

3. Place a peeled potato in the center of the rice cooker, then add carrots, sausage, onions, and green peas.
4. Combine the soy sauce, oyster sauce, and oil in a mixing bowl.
5. Pour 1 cup of water into the container and seal the lid.
6. If "white rice" is an option, choose it.
7. When the timer goes off, open the cover and use a spoon to break the potato. Then gently combine everything. (Be careful not to scratch your rice cooker's bottom.)
8. Season to taste with salt. Serve and have fun!

Nutrition

Calories: 473kcal | Carbohydrates: 59g | Protein: 17g | Fat: 18g | Saturated Fat: 6g | Trans Fat: 1g | Cholesterol: 43mg | Sodium: 1036mg | Potassium: 695mg | Fiber: 5g | Sugar: 6g | Vitamin A: 5669IU | Vitamin C: 30mg | Calcium: 58mg | Iron: 2mg

69. FRENCH ONION BROWN RICE: EASY, DELICIOUS & MAKE AHEAD!

INGREDIENTS

- plain brown rice (not instant or quick cooking)
- beef consommé (beef broth can be used but is not as rich)
- Lipton dry onion soup
- 2-3 TB butter, melted (I sometimes use EVOO instead but the taste isn't "buttery")

INSTRUCTIONS

1. Place 3 cups brown rice in the cooker insert for 6 cups brown rice.
2. Combine the beef consommé, onion soup, and melted butter in a mixing bowl. F 3. Fill the rice cooker insert to the #3 line on the interior.
3. Place the insert in the cooker, mix the rice thoroughly, and close the lid.
1. For each hour you wish to wait until the rice is fully cooked, press "delay timer" once. (Press the delay timer four times if you want rice ready in four hours.)

NUTRITION INFORMATION:

YIELD: 8 SERVING SIZE: 1
Amount Per Serving: CALORIES: 122TOTAL FAT: 11gSATURATED FAT: 6gTRANS FAT: 0gUNSATURATED
FAT: 4gCHOLESTEROL: 24mgSODIUM: 246mgCARBOHYDRATES: 5gFIBER: 0gSUGAR: 1gPROTEIN: 2g

70. QUINOA IN A RICE COOKER

Ingredients

- 1 cup Quinoa White, red, black and tricolor quinoa would all work
- 2 cups water or broth chicken stock, vegetable stock would both work
- 1/2 tsp kosher salt
- 1 tbsp vegetable oil olive, coconut and avocado oil would all work

Instructions

1. Wash the quinoa in a medium-mesh strainer under cold running water until it is clear.
2. To prevent sticking, grease the rice cooker insert with a tbsp of vegetable oil. To properly pour the oil in the insert, I use a sheet of paper towel.
3. Combine washed quinoa, beverage of choice, and salt in a mixing bowl. Give it a good shake.
4. Cover the rice cooker and set it to the white rice setting. If your rice cooker doesn't have that feature, simply select "cook."
5. It should take about 25-35 minutes to cook through entirely.
6. To serve, fluff it with a fork after it's done.

71. EASY RICE COOKER OATMEAL WITH APPLES AND CINNAMON

yield: 2 SERVINGS

prep time: 5 MINUTES

cook time: 15 MINUTES

total time: 20 MINUTES

INGREDIENTS

- 1 apple, small diced
- 1 cup old-fashioned oats (or steel-cut oats)
- 1/2 tsp cinnamon
- 1 tbsp brown sugar
- 1 3/4 cups water
- pinch of salt

INSTRUCTIONS

1. In the rice cooker's base, combine the apple, oats, cinnamon, brown sugar, water, and a bit of salt. Cook on the steam/cook or porridge mode (or the rice setting if you have one) with the lid closed.
2. The oatmeal is done when the rice cooker beeps. Allow for a few minutes of resting time before stirring and serving a warm breakfast any day of the week. What a treat!

72. HOW TO COOK RICE IN A RICE COOKER

PREP: 2 MINS

COOK: 30 MINS

TOTAL: 32 MINS

INGREDIENTS

- tap water for rinsing
- 2 c rice short grain, long grain, or medium grain
- 2 c filtered water

INSTRUCTIONS

1. Measure out 2 cup of rice and place it in the rice cooker. I always use the measuring cup that came with my rice maker to measure both rice and water.
2. Run cold water over the rice in the pot to rinse it. To clean the grains, gently stir the rice around with your hands. Once the water begins to change color, pour it out. Repeat the procedure two more times. When you're finished, make sure to drain all of the water.
3. Pour 2 cups of filtered water into the pot after cleaning the rice and removing the rinse water.
4. Place the rice pot back in the rice maker. Make sure your rice cooker is turned on and that you're following the directions in the manual. In addition to a "normal" setting, our rice cooker has a "quick" one. I frequently select "rapid" because it provides me with the same outcomes in a shorter length of time. To avoid losing steam, do not lift the lid while the rice is cooking.
5. After the rice is finished, close the cooker for another 5 minutes.
6. Using a rice paddle, fluff the rice after opening the cover.
7. Arrange rice in bowls and serve.

NOTES

In this recipe, you can use any sort of rice grain you choose. With the same ratio, you can use short grain, medium grain, or long grain. You can use the same proportions if you want extra rice. Two cups of rice, for example, for two cups of water, and so on.

NUTRITION FACTS

Calories: 225kcal | Carbohydrates: 49g | Protein: 4g | Fat: 1g | Saturated
Fat: 1g | Sodium: 7mg | Potassium: 71mg | Fiber: 1g | Sugar: 1g | Calcium: 20mg | Iron: 1mg

73. STRAWBERRY SHORTCAKE

SERVINGS: 9

PREP TIME: 25 MINUTES

COOK TIME: 40 MINUTES

INGREDIENTS

- 2/3 cup sugar
- 1/4 cup butter, melted
- 1 large egg
- 1 tsp vanilla extract
- 1/4 tsp salt
- 1 1/2 cup all-purpose flour
- 2 tsp baking powder
- 1/2 cup whole milk
- 1 cup whipped cream
- 1 1/2 quart fresh strawberries, sliced

DIRECTIONS

1. In a mixing basin, thoroughly combine the sugar and butter.
2. Combine the egg, milk, and vanilla extract in a mixing bowl.
3. In a separate dish, combine the dry ingredients, then stir them into the liquid ingredients.
4. Pour the batter into the inner pot and turn on the Cake setting.
5. Remove the cake from the stove and cool on a wire rack after the cooking cycle has finished.
6. Split the cake in half horizontally and top one half with whipped cream and chopped strawberries. Serve with more whipped cream and strawberries on top of the other half of the cake.

74. HOW TO PREPARE AUTHENTIC SUSHI RICE

SERVINGS: 4-6

PREP TIME: 5 MINUTES

COOK TIME: 50 MINUTES

INGREDIENTS

- 3 cups raw Japanese short-grain rice
- 3 cups water
- 1 piece dried kelp
- 1/3 cup rice vinegar
- 3 tbsp sugar
- 1 1/2 tsp sea salt

DIRECTIONS

1. Drain the rice completely after rinsing it until the water is clear.
2. Gently remove the excess white powdery stuff from the dried kelp. NOTE: It is not necessary to remove all of the powder; the umami flavor will be enhanced.
3. Place the dried kelp on top of the rice and water in the rice cooker.
4. Choose the White Rice option.
5. In a small saucepan, combine rice vinegar, sugar, and salt and bring to a boil over medium-high heat while the rice is cooking. Set aside and allow it cool after whisking until the sugar is completely dissolved.
6. When the rice is done, put it all to a big glass mixing bowl.
7. Pour the vinegar mixture over the rice and toss well to combine.
8. Cover the rice with a paper towel and let it aside to come to room temperature before eating it plain or rolling it into your favorite sushi rolls!

75. CHICKEN TAMALES

SERVINGS: 12

PREP TIME: 90 MINUTES

COOK TIME: 45 MINUTES

INGREDIENTS

- 15 dried corn husks
- 2 cups masa harina
- 1 tsp salt
- 1/2 tsp cumin
- 1/3 tsp baking powder
- 2 cups chicken stock
- 1/4 cup oil
- 1 cup chicken breast, shredded
- 1/4 cup tomatoes, finely diced
- 1/4 cup pico de gallo

DIRECTIONS

1. Fill a big basin halfway with water and add the dried corn husks. Soak the husks for at least 30 minutes, or until they are softened.
2. While the corn husks soak, start making the dough by completely mixing the masa marina, salt, and baking powder with a hand mixer.
3. Slowly drizzle in the oil and chicken stock, continuing to mix on low speed.
4. Increase the mixing speed to Medium and beat for about 10 minutes, or until the dough is frothy, after all ingredients have been mixed.
5. Wrap the dough in a moist paper towel and place it in the refrigerator until ready to use.
6. In the inner pot, place the chicken breast, tomatoes, and pico de gallo to start creating the filling. Heat the ingredients for 20 minutes using the Sauté-then-Simmer® feature.
7. Begin by putting out the corn husk on a level surface to prepare the tamales.
8. Spread about 1/4 cup of the masa dough mixture onto the corn husk, making sure it's equally distributed.
9. Spoon a dollop of chicken mixture into the masa's center.
10. Carefully fold the corn husk in half vertically to completely cover the filling with masa. Fold into a burrito or cylinder shape as needed. Fold both sides down to completely encapsulate the masa in the corn husk. Optional: tie a string across each end to ensure they stay closed while cooking.
11. Fill the inner pot with 1 cup of water, then arrange the tamales inside.
12. Cook for around 30 minutes with the Steam function selected.

13. Toss with salsa, guacamole, and sour cream before serving! If you want to save them for later, keep them refrigerated for up to 3 days or freeze for up to 3 months in a well sealed ziplock bag.

76. PRIME RIB ROAST

SERVINGS: 6

PREP TIME: 3 HOURS

COOK TIME: 8 HOURS 30 MINUTES

INGREDIENTS

- 4 lbs. boneless prime rib
- 2 tbsp salt
- 1 tbsp pepper
- 1 cup butter, softened
- 7 garlic cloves, minced
- 2 tbsp fresh rosemary, finely chopped
- 2 tbsp fresh thyme, finely chopped
- 1 large onion, chopped
- 1 tsp olive oil
- 2 tbsp flour

DIRECTIONS

1. Salt and pepper the prime rib before wrapping it in plastic wrap or tin foil. Place the prime rib in the refrigerator overnight to marinate.
2. Take the prime rib out of the fridge and set it aside to come to room temperature.
3. In a large mixing bowl, blend the butter, garlic, fresh herbs, salt, and pepper until well incorporated.
4. Rub the herb butter mixture all over the prime rib, making sure it is uniformly coated.
5. Using the Sauté-then-Simmer® mode, heat the olive oil in the inner pot. Sauté the onion for 12 minutes, or until tender and golden, once the pan is hot.
6. Place the prime rib in the inner pot with the onions and set the slow cooker to 8 hours on low.
7. Remove the prime rib from the inner pot and lay it on a serving plate after 8 hours.
8. In a small mixing basin, whisk together the water and flour until no lumps remain. To thicken the sauce, add the flour mixture to the sauce that is still in the inner saucepan. Coat the prime rib with the leftover sauce once it has thickened.

77. LOW-CARB CITRUS CHICKEN

SERVINGS: 4

PREP TIME: 10 MINUTES

COOK TIME: 55 MINUTES

INGREDIENTS

- 2 cups Greek yogurt
- juice from 1/2 orange
- 2 tsp minced garlic
- 2 tsp cumin
- 1 tbsp salt
- 1 tsp pepper
- 1 tsp cayenne pepper
- 1 whole (2-3 lb.) chicken, spatchcocked
- 1 tsp olive oil
- 1 small sweet onion, sliced
- 2 mini bell peppers, sliced

DIRECTIONS

1. Dry the chicken thoroughly with a paper towel.
2. Combine Greek yogurt, orange juice, minced garlic, cumin, salt, pepper, and cayenne pepper in a large mixing bowl.
3. Massage the yogurt mixture into the chicken, making sure it is evenly coated on both sides.
4. Wrap the chicken in plastic wrap and set it in the refrigerator overnight to marinate.
5. Take the chicken out of the fridge and let it come to room temperature.
6. Using the White Rice feature on your cooker, preheat olive oil in the inner pot. When the pan is hot, add the onion and bell peppers and cook for 5 minutes, or until they are translucent and softened.
7. Put the chicken in the inner pot and cover it tightly.
8. Allow the cooking cycle to finish, then set the cooker to Keep Warm for 20 minutes.

Serve with veggies, grains, or a side dish of your choice!

78. MARSHMALLOW NOUGAT

SERVINGS: 80-100 PIECES

PREP TIME: 30 MINUTES

COOK TIME: 15 MINUTES

INGREDIENTS

- 12 oz mini marshmallows
- 14 oz crackers, crushed
- 4 oz butter
- 4 oz powdered milk
- 1 1/2 cups honey roasted peanuts, chopped
- 1 1/2 cups dried cranberries

DIRECTIONS

1. In the inner pot, melt the butter using the Sauté-then-Simmer® function.
2. When the butter has melted, add the marshmallows and let them melt as well.
3. Toss in the powdered milk, honey roasted peanuts, and dried cranberries after manually setting the cooker to Keep Warm mode. Turn off the cooker once everything has been completely combined.
4. Fold in the broken crackers, then take the nougat from the inner pot and place it on a parchment-lined baking sheet.
5. Place another sheet of parchment paper on top of the nougat and flatten it out with a rolling pin until it is about 2"-3" thick.
6. Place the nougat on parchment paper to cool for about 1 hour before cutting into little bite-size squares. If desired, dust the squares with extra powdered milk before serving.

79. GREEK YOGURT CAKE

SERVINGS: 8

PREP TIME: 10 MINUTES

COOK TIME: 1 HOUR

INGREDIENTS

- 1 cup plain Greek yogurt
- 3 large eggs
- 1/2 cup vegetable oil
- 3/4 cup sugar
- 1 1/2 cup all-purpose flour
- 1 1/2 tsp baking powder

DIRECTIONS

- Allow the eggs and Greek yogurt to come to room temperature before using. We recommend removing them from the refrigerator two hours before baking.
- Lightly beat the eggs in a medium mixing dish. Mix together the oil, sugar, flour, baking powder, and yogurt until smooth.
- Spray the inside of the inner pot with nonstick cooking spray before pouring in the cake batter. To begin baking, select the White Rice mode on your cooker.
- After the cycle has finished, leave the cake in the cooker for another 30 minutes on Keep Warm mode. To test whether the cake is thoroughly baked, insert a toothpick into the center. Remove the inner pot from the cooker if the toothpick can be removed cleanly.
- Once the cake has cooled, remove it from the inside pot and frost with your favorite frosting!
- Green Deviled Eggs & Ham
- SERVINGS: 6-10
- PREP TIME: 2 MINUTES
- COOK TIME: 9-15 MINUTES
- INGREDIENTS
- 8 eggs
- 2 cups water
- a bowl of iced water
- 4 medium-thick slices of honey baked ham, cut into small pieces
- 3 avocados, peeled and mashed
- 3 tbsp mayonnaise
- 1 tbsp lemon juice
- salt and pepper, to taste
- parsley, for garnish

DIRECTIONS

1. Fill the inner pot with 2 cups of water.
2. Crack the eggs into the steam tray, then place it inside the cooker with the steam tray. Select the Steam function and cook the eggs for around 15 minutes after closing the lid securely. If all 8 eggs do not fit in the tray at the same time, repeat the process until all eggs are hard-boiled.
3. When the cooking cycle is over, immediately place the hard-boiled eggs in a bowl of ice water to stop them from cooking. Allow for 1-2 minutes for the eggs to cool.
4. Split each egg in half after cracking it and removing all of the eggshells. Remove the entire egg yolk and set it aside in a basin.
5. In the same bowl as the yolks, combine the avocado, mayonnaise, lemon juice, salt, and pepper. Mash the items together with a fork or spoon until there are no huge lumps and the texture is smooth.
6. Spoon or pipe the egg yolk mixture into each half of an egg white, then top with little ham bits. Repeat with each egg and, if wanted, sprinkle with parsley.

80. SHRIMP AND GRITS

SERVINGS: 8

PREP TIME: 10 MINUTES

COOK TIME: 1 HOUR

INGREDIENTS
GRITS

- 1/2 cup uncooked old-fashioned grits
- 1 1/3 cups chicken broth
- 1 cup milk
- 2 tbsp butter
- salt and pepper
- 1/3 cup cheddar cheese

SHRIMP

- 8 slices bacon, chopped
- 1 lb. medium peeled shrimp
- 3 garlic cloves, minced
- 1 tsp Cajun seasoning
- 4 green onions, chopped

DIRECTIONS

1. In the inner pot, combine all of the Grits ingredients except the cheese. After mixing thoroughly, turn the cook knob to the lowest setting to begin heating.
2. Cook, stirring periodically, for 15-17 minutes, or until the grits have thickened.
3. Add the cheese and stir until it melts. Manually switch the cooker to Warm mode once the butter has melted.
4. Preheat the Grillet® on a medium heat setting. When the pan is hot, add the bacon and cook until crisp.
5. Remove the bacon from the pan and set it aside. In the grill pan, set aside 4 tsp oil from the bacon.
6. Add the shrimp, garlic, and Cajun seasoning to the pan and cook until the shrimp are pink.
7. Serve with cooked grits and a sprinkle of onions on top.

81. ITALIAN MEATBALL SOUP

SERVINGS: 8

PREP TIME: 15 MINUTES

COOK TIME: 40 HOURS

INGREDIENTS

- 1 tbsp olive oil
- 1 cup yellow onion, diced
- 1 cup carrots, shredded
- 1 cup celery, diced
- 1 cup zucchini, diced
- 3 garlic cloves, minced
- 1 lb. fresh or frozen meatballs
- 1 (16-oz.) can fire-roasted diced tomatoes
- 4 cup low sodium chicken broth
- 1 cup kale leaves
- salt and pepper
- parmesan cheese, for serving

DIRECTIONS

1. In the inner pot, heat the olive oil using the Sauté-then-Simmer® function. Once the inner pot is hot, add the onions, carrots, celery, zucchini, and garlic and sauté until fragrant and soft.
2. Add the frozen meatballs and continue to stir for another 3 minutes.
3. Add the diced tomatoes and chicken broth to the pot and cover to keep the mixture warm. The cooker will move to a low-heat setting.
4. Stir in the kale leaves and season with salt and pepper to taste once the unit has done boiling.

Garnish with fresh parmesan cheese and serve.

82. OLD-FASHIONED EGGNOG

SERVINGS: 2-4

PREP TIME: 7 MINUTES

COOK TIME: 35 MINUTES

INGREDIENTS

- 1 cup heavy cream
- 2 tsp pure vanilla extract
- 2 cinnamon sticks
- ¼ tsp nutmeg
- 4 cups whole milk
- 8 large eggs
- ¾ cup granulated sugar
- pinch of kosher salt

DIRECTIONS

1. In the inner pot, combine heavy cream, vanilla, cinnamon, nutmeg, and 2 cups milk.
2. Cook until little bubbles form around the perimeter of the inner pot, using the Sauté-then-Simmer® setting and leaving the lid off your rice cooker. Turn off the rice cooker after the bubbles appear and set aside for 30 minutes.
3. Separate the egg yolks from the egg whites and set the whites aside in the meantime. With a hand mixer, beat the sugar, salt, and egg yolks until the mixture is thick and pale in color.
4. Strain the spiced cream mixture from the pot of boiling water, then whip 1 cup at a time into the yolk mixture on low speed. Return the mixture to the inner pot once it has been well mixed.
5. Once more, select the Sauté-then-Simmer® feature. Allow the mixture to heat up while regularly swirling it with a long-handled wooden spoon. Remove the mixture from the heat once it begins to adhere to the back of the spoon.
6. Allow to cool before adding the remaining 2 cups of milk.
7. Beat the egg whites with a hand mixer until soft peaks form, then fold into the chilled eggnog.
8. Garnish with nutmeg and a cinnamon stick before serving.

83. RICE COOKER CUPCAKES

SERVINGS: 2

PREP TIME: 5 MINUTES

COOK TIME: 15 MINUTES

INGREDIENTS

- 1 large egg
- 1 tbsp vegetable oil
- 1 tbsp maple syrup
- 3 tbsp plain yogurt
- 1½ tbsp sugar
- ½ cup all-purpose flour
- 1 tsp baking powder
- 1 tsp milk powder
- whipped cream or frosting, for topping

DIRECTIONS

1. Whisk together the egg, vegetable oil, maple syrup, and yogurt in a medium mixing dish. After the butter has been well combined, add the sugar and stir thoroughly.
2. Sift together the flour, milk powder, and baking powder to ensure no clumps, then stir into the egg mixture. Fold the mixture until it resembles a thick batter.
3. Divide the batter evenly among four cupcake liners, then place one in each steam tray. Lower the steam tray into the rice cooker's inner pot.
4. Select the Steam function and bake the cupcakes for about 15 minutes, or until a toothpick inserted in the center comes out clean.
5. Take the cupcakes out of the steam tray and set them aside to cool completely before icing.
6. When completely cold, top with whipped cream or your favorite icing and serve!

84. POMEGRANATE & GINGER PORK TENDERLOIN

SERVINGS: 2-4

PREP TIME: 7 MINUTES

COOK TIME: 30 MINUTES

INGREDIENTS

- 1 lb. pork tenderloin
- 1 tbsp olive oil
- 2 tbsp fresh ginger, chopped
- 2 cloves garlic
- ¼ cup honey
- ¼ cup soy sauce
- 2 tbsp rice vinegar
- 2 tbsp toasted sesame oil
- 1½ cups pomegranate juice
- ⅓ cup pomegranate seeds

DIRECTIONS

1. Pour oil into the inner pot and preheat it using the Sauté function.
2. Place the pork tenderloin in the inner pot once the oil has heated up. Repeat on all sides until the tenderloin has a golden crust.
3. Whisk together all of the remaining ingredients in the inner pot. Season with kosher salt to taste.
4. Select the Steam feature and close the lid. Allow 2 hours for the tenderloin to finish cooking.
5. Slice the tenderloin and put the slices on a big dish once the time has passed or the pork is cooked to your preference. Pour the remaining sauce over the slices, making sure to coat each one completely.
6. Garnish with pomegranate seeds and serve!

85. PUMPKIN PIE PARFAITS

SERVINGS: 2

PREP TIME: 5 MINUTES

COOK TIME: 15 MINUTES

INGREDIENTS

- 1 ½ cups coconut cream
- 2 cups pumpkin butter (chilled)
- 1 cup maple granola
- 1/2 cup pecans (roughly chopped)
- 1/2 tbsp coconut oil
- 1/2 tbsp maple syrup
- 1/2 tbsp brown sugar
- 1 pinch ground cinnamon
- 1 pinch sea salt

DIRECTIONS

1. Place the chopped pecans in the inner pot of your rice cooker and set it to Sauté-then-Simmer®. To keep the pecans from burning, toast them for about 4 minutes, stirring often.
2. Toss the coconut oil, maple syrup, brown sugar, cinnamon, and salt into the inner pot once it has been roasted. Cook for another 1-2 minutes on Sauté-then-Simmer® after stirring to incorporate. Remove the inner pot from the heat and set it aside to cool.
3. Beat the coconut cream in a mixing basin until it reaches a light and frothy consistency.
4. Place 1 tbsp of granola in each of the small serving glasses or bowls. Tap the bottom lightly to let the layers settle, then top with a layer of cold pumpkin butter and coconut whipped cream. Rep until the bowl or glass is completely filled.
5. Garnish with maple cinnamon pecans and serve!

86. CRANBERRY PECAN STUFFING

SERVINGS: 5-8

PREP TIME: 7 MINUTES

COOK TIME: 2 HOURS

INGREDIENTS

- 1 bag cubed stuffing
- 1/2 cup dried cranberries
- 1/2 cup golden raisins
- 1/2 cup chopped pecans
- 3 cup chicken broth
- 1/2 cup butter, melted
- 1 egg
- 1/2 tsp salt
- 1/4 tsp pepper
- 1 tsp ground mustard

DIRECTIONS

1. In the inner saucepan, combine the cubed stuffing, dried cranberries, golden raisins, and pecans.
2. Whisk together the chicken broth, melted butter, and egg in a separate medium mixing dish.
3. Pour the whisking mixture into the inner pot, then fold in the filling gently.
4. Cook for roughly 2 hours or until the centre is completely set, using the Slow Cook function.

87. PUMPKIN BREAD PUDDING

SERVINGS: 6-8

PREP TIME: 10 MINUTES

COOK TIME: 3 HOURS

INGREDIENTS

- 1/2 loaf egg-based bread (such as challah or brioche), cut into cubes
- 1/2 cup toasted pecans, chopped
- 4 eggs
- 1 cup pumpkin filling
- 1 cup half and half
- 1/2 cup brown sugar
- 1/2 cup butter, melted
- 1 tsp vanilla extract
- 1/2 tsp cinnamon
- 1/2 tsp nutmeg
- 1/4 tsp ground ginger
- 1/8 tsp ground cloves
- whipped cream (optional)

DIRECTIONS

1. Place the bread pieces and chopped pecans in the rice cooker's inner pot.
2. Whisk together the eggs, pumpkin filling, half-and-half, brown sugar, melted butter, vanilla, cinnamon, nutmeg, ginger, and cloves in a separate mixing dish before pouring the mixture over the cubed bread. To blend, carefully stir everything together.
3. Put the lid on the slow cooker and turn it on. Cook for approximately 3 hours, or until a toothpick inserted in the center comes out clean.
4. If desired, serve the pudding warm with whipped cream on top.

88. GREEN BEAN CASSEROLE

SERVINGS: 6-8

PREP TIME: 10 MINUTES

COOK TIME:2 HOURS AND 40 MINUTES

INGREDIENTS

- 3 cans cream of mushroom soup
- ½ cup milk
- ⅛ tsp black pepper
- ⅛ tsp onion powder
- 10 cans green beans, drained
- 12 oz fried onions

DIRECTIONS

1. In the inner pot of the rice cooker, whisk together the cream of mushroom soup, milk, black pepper, and onion powder.
2. Stir in half of the fried onions and the drained green beans. Mix all of the ingredients together gently.
3. Place the inner pot in your rice cooker, then set the rice cooker to Slow Cook and cook for around 2½ hours.

When the cook time is up, transfer the finished casserole to a large serving bowl and top with the remaining fried onions.

89. EASY VIETNAMESE PHO

SERVING SIZE: 4

PREP TIME: 15 MINUTES

COOK TIME: 45 MINUTES

INGREDIENTS

- 2 large yellow onions, peel and cut in half
- 1 (4-inch) piece fresh ginger, peel and sliced
- 2 whole cinnamon sticks
- 2 star anise
- 3 cloves
- 2 tsp coriander seeds
- 6 cup low-sodium beef broth
- 1 tbsp soy sauce
- 1 tbsp fish sauce
- 3 medium carrots, peeled and chopped
- 8 oz sirloin, sliced
- 8 oz dried rice noodles
- 1 jalapeno, sliced
- 1 cup bean sprouts, washed
- 1 cup scallions, chopped
- 1 cup cilantro
- sriracha and hoisin sauce for serving

DIRECTIONS

1. Using the saute function on your inner pot, add all of the spices and stir constantly until roasted and fragrant.
2. Combine the broth, soy sauce, fish sauce, carrots, onions, and ginger in a large mixing bowl.
3. When the cycle is over, close the lid and utilize the soup function. Using a strainer, remove the particles from the broth. Remove the sediments and save the broth for later.
4. Fill the inner pot halfway with water and use the saute function to bring the water to a boil. Cook the rice noodles according to the package directions. After draining the noodles, rinse them in cold water. Immediately divide them into four serving basins.
5. Use the reheat feature to reheat the soup.
6. Meanwhile, arrange all of the toppings in a single layer in the heated broth so that they may cook evenly.
7. When the soup has finished reheating, ladle the hot broth into each bowl.
8. If preferred, top the pho with sriracha and hoisin sauce.

90. VEGGIE MAC AND CHEESE

SERVING SIZE: 2

PREP TIME: 15 MINUTES

COOK TIME: 20 MINUTES

INGREDIENTS

- 1 cup sweet potato, peeled and shredded
- 2 cup zucchini, shredded
- 1 cup yellow onion, shredded
- 1 tsp. olive oil
- salt and pepper, to taste
- ½ cup whipping cream
- 1 clove of garlic, minced
- 1 cup macaroni
- 1 cups shredded cheddar cheese
- 4 oz cream cheese
- parsley, for garnish

DIRECTIONS

1. Toss the veggies in the inner pot with the oil, salt, and pepper. To soften veggies, use the STS feature.
2. Pour in all of the cheese, stir often to combine the cheese and the vegetables, and heat until the cheese has completely melted.
3. Pour in the whipped cream and macaroni, then cover.
4. When the cycle is over, remove the lid and season to taste with salt and pepper.
5. Remove the vegetarian mac and cheese from the pan and, if desired, garnish with parsley.

91. BACON MUSHROOM RISOTTO

SERVINGS: 6-8

PREP TIME: 5 MINUTES

COOK TIME: 40 MINUTES

INGREDIENTS

- 2 tsp olive oil
- 2 Portobello mushrooms, sliced into 1-inch pieces
- salt and pepper, to taste
- 2 garlic cloves, minced
- 1¼ cups vegetable broth
- ¾ cups white wine, like chardonnay
- 1 cup Arborio rice
- large pinch of dried basil
- 1/4 cup Parmesan cheese, grated
- 4 strips bacon, cooked crispy and crumbled

DIRECTIONS

1. Heat the olive oil in the inner pot of the cooker on the Sauté-then-Simmer STS® function for a few minutes. Add the mushrooms, salt, and pepper to taste, and simmer, stirring constantly with a long-handled wooden or silicone spoon, until they begin to soften. Cook for 3 minutes after adding the garlic.
2. Combine the vegetable broth and white wine in a mixing bowl. Combine the rice, basil, and a touch of salt and pepper in a mixing bowl. For 12 minutes, use the Steam function.
3. Season with salt and pepper to taste, then add the cheeses. Add the bacon and mix well. Serve in dishes with extra crumbled bacon on top.

92. CLASSIC FLUFFY PANCAKES

SERVING SIZE: 1

PREP TIME: 10 MINUTES

COOK TIME: 20 MINUTES

INGREDIENTS

- 1 1/2 cups all-purpose flour
- 3 1/2 tsp baking powder
- 1 tsp salt
- 1 tbsp sugar
- 1 1/4 cup milk
- 1 egg
- 3 tbsp butter, melted
- 1 tbsp olive oil
- 1 cup fresh strawberry, cubed
- 1/2 cup maple syrup
- Option: whipping cream and powder sugar

DIRECTIONS

1. Sift together the flour, baking powder, salt, and sugar in a large mixing basin. Pour Combine the milk, egg, and melted butter in a mixing bowl and whisk until smooth and no clumps remain.
2. Lightly oil the inner pot of your rice cooker and heat it up using the STS feature. Scoop about 1/4 cup of batter into the inner pot for each pancake. Cook till golden brown on both sides and serve with fresh strawberries and maple syrup.

93. EASTER ONIGIRI - JAPANESE RICE BALL

SERVING SIZE: 6 RICE BALL

PREP TIME: 15 MINUTES

COOK TIME: 1 HOUR 15 MINUTES

INGREDIENTS

- 2 cups white rice
- Salt for taste
- Optional: 1 to 2 sheets of dried seaweed
- Optional: 1 or 2 pieces of Spam
- Optional: 1/4 tsp curry powder
- For the Fillings:
- 3 pieces 1 inch cubed Spam
- 3 Tbsp tuna salad

DIRECTIONS

1. Prepare white rice in your rice cooker according to the manufacturer's instructions.
2. Color half of the cooked rice with curry powder to make it yellow.
3. Wet your hands with water to prevent the rice from sticking to them. After that, smear some salt on your hands.
4. Take a third of a cup of steaming rice in your hand and make sure it is dense and thick.
5. Place 1 tbsp tuna salad on the rice and lightly press the filling into the rice.
6. Place the rice in the palms of your hands. By pressing lightly with both palms, form the rice into a circle. Roll the rice ball a few times in your hands, pressing lightly.
7. Take a third of a cup of curry rice and stuff it with Spam. 3 curry rice balls can be made by reversing the preceding processes.
8. Add sliced dried seaweed and spam to your rice ball for decoration.

94. CORNED BEEF AND CABBAGE

SERVING SIZE: 8

PREP TIME: 10 MINUTES

COOK TIME: 3 HOURS

INGREDIENTS

- 1 pack 3-lb corned beef
- 12 oz pale ale
- 1 yellow onion
- 2 cloves garlic
- 2 dried bay leaves
- 2 tbsp olive oil
- 1 small green cabbage, cut into 8 wedges
- Chopped parsley, for serving

DIRECTIONS

1. In the inner pot, place the corned meat. Bring the beer, onion, garlic, bay leaves, 3 cups 2. water, and spice packet contents to a boil with STS. 3. Simmer with the cover closed. Remove the corned beef from the oven and blot dry with a kitchen towel after the cycle is finished.
3. After washing the inner pot, return it to the stovetop and brown the corned beef and sauté the cabbage with STS.
4. Serve the corned meat thinly sliced with cabbage. parsley, if desired

95. CREAMY SPINACH DIP

SERVING SIZE: 6

PREP TIME: 5 MINUTES

COOK TIME: 25 MINUTES

INGREDIENTS

- 20 oz baby spinach
- 2 tbsp butter
- 1/2 onion, chopped
- 3 cloves garlic, minced
- 1/4 cup heavy whipping cream
- 1/2 cup almond milk
- 4 oz cream cheese
- Salt and pepper for taste

DIRECTIONS

1. Fill the inner pot halfway with water and use STS to bring it to a boil.
2. Cook spinach for 30 seconds in boiling water. Drain and rinse under cold running water. Drain and squeeze off extra water once it's cold enough to handle.
3. After cleaning the inner pot, melt butter with STS. Simmer until the onion is tender, then add the garlic and cook until fragrant.
4. Fill the inner saucepan with almond milk, heavy whipping cream, and cream cheese. Close the cover and continue to cook until the cream cheese has melted. Add salt and pepper to taste.
5. Toss in the spinach and mix well.

96. RICOTTA & PARMESAN PASTA SALAD

SERVINGS: 8

PREP TIME: 10 MINUTES

COOK TIME: 25 MINUTES

INGREDIENTS

- 1 head garlic
- 1 tbsp olive oil
- 16 ounces small shell pasta, uncooked
- 15 ounces ricotta
- salt and pepper, to taste
- 18 ounces cherry tomatoes, sliced in half
- 5 ounces baby spinach
- ⅔ cup parmesan, grated

DIRECTIONS

1. Trim around 12 inches from the top of the garlic head.
2. In a small dish, sprinkle the olive oil over the exposed cloves of the bulb.
3. Place an upside-down plate on top of the bowl. Microwave for 3 minutes on high, in 1 minute increments, until the garlic is tender and fragrant.
4. Using oven mitts, carefully remove the dish from the microwave. Remove from the oven and set aside to cool.
5. Fill the pasta cooker to the MAX line with water while the garlic cools. Allow to come to a boil on the Medium Pasta setting.
6. Stir in the noodles and cook for 7-10 minutes, or until they are al dente.
7. Squeeze the garlic cloves off the head and finely chop them while the pasta is boiling.
8. In a medium mixing bowl, combine the minced garlic, ricotta cheese, and salt and pepper to taste. Remove from the equation.
9. Turn off the stove when the pasta is done. 12 cup pasta water is set aside, then drain the pasta while keeping it in the pot using the lid. Place the pot back in the oven.
10. Stir in the ricotta cheese mixture with the reserved pasta water. Stir until the sauce is smooth.
11. Toss the pasta in the pot with the sauce. Stir until everything is completely blended.
12. Toss in the cherry tomatoes and spinach, followed by the parmesan cheese.
13. Toss everything together until everything is well incorporated and the spinach has wilted little. Serve immediately.

97. CREAM CHEESE MACARONI & CHEESE

SERVINGS: 6-8

PREP TIME: 5 MINUTES

COOK TIME: 45 MINUTES

INGREDIENTS

- 16 ounces elbow macaroni
- 2½ cups half-and-half
- pinch cayenne pepper
- 16 ounces cream cheese, room temperature
- 8 ounces sharp cheddar, shredded
- 3 ounces gruyere, shredded

DIRECTIONS

1. Pour 34% of the water into the inner pot of the Aroma Housewares Co multicooker. Set the rice cooker for 30 minutes on STEAM. Allow to come to a boil with the lid closed.
2. Once the water is boiling, add the pasta. To keep the spaghetti from sticking to the bottom of the Aroma multicooker, bring it back to a boil while stirring often. Cook for about 8 minutes, with the lid open the entire time, until the pasta is al dente.
3. When the pasta is done, carefully ladle out 1 cup of the cooking water into a bowl. Remove from the equation.
4. Remove the inner pot with oven mitts and turn off the Aroma multicooker; drain the pasta and set it aside.
5. Set the multicooker on Sauté-then-Simmer STS® with the inner pot.
6. Stir in the half-and-half and cayenne pepper and bring to a simmer.
7. Cook for 15 minutes, whisking often.
8. Stir in the cream cheese until it is completely melted.
9. Put the rice cooker on Keep Warm mode. Whisk in the cheddar and gruyere until the cheese has completely melted and the sauce has smoothed out.
10. Stir in the cooked macaroni until everything is well combined. If the sauce needs to be thinned, add some of the leftover pasta water.

If preferred, season with salt and pepper. Serve right away.

98. BBQ PULLED PORK

SERVINGS: 12-16

PREP TIME: 5 MINUTES

COOK TIME: 6-7 HOURS

INGREDIENTS

- 2-2.5 lbs boneless pork loin
- ½ yellow onion, sliced
- 2 cloves garlic, minced
- 1 tbsp black pepper
- 1 tbsp salt
- 2 tbsp cayenne, or less to your liking
- 2 tbsp chili powder, or less to your liking
- 8 oz your favorite bottled BBQ sauce, plus more for serving
- ½ cup water

DIRECTIONS

1. Place the pork loin in the inner pot of the multicooker after opening the cover.
2. In the inner saucepan, combine the sliced yellow onion, minced garlic, black pepper, salt, cayenne pepper, chili powder, BBQ sauce, and water, then secure the cover.
3. Turn on the cooker by pressing the START button twice, then select Medium heat by pressing SLOW COOK twice. Press the (+) button until the digital display reads 6 hours to set the amount of slow cook time. Press START once everything is in place. To signal the start of the cooking cycle, the cooker will beep and the display will stop flashing.
4. While cooking, the digital display will count down from the preset time of 6 hours in 1 minute increments. Allow to cook until the timer beeps at the end of the timer.
5. When the multicooker is done, it will beep and switch to KEEP WARM mode.
6. Using two forks and tugging them in opposing directions, open the lid to see if the pork is done. The pork is fully cooked when it shreds easily and no pink remains. If the pork is still tough and/or pink after 4 hours, use the SLOW COOK feature on Medium heat for another 4 hours, checking on it every 2 hours or so.
7. Toss the pulled meat in the sauce after shredding, making sure it is evenly coated.
8. To serve, arrange the pulled pork inside slider buns with extra BBQ sauce on the side if preferred, using tongs.

99. TUSCAN STYLE SALMON

SERVINGS: 4

PREP TIME: 10 MINUTES

COOK TIME: 45 MINUTES

INGREDIENTS

- 8 oz spaghetti, linguini, or fettuccini
- 1 lb fresh salmon, cut into 4 fillets (skin off)
- salt & pepper, to taste
- ¼ tsp, garlic powder
- ¼ cup flour
- 1 tbsp olive oil
- 1 tbsp butter
- ½ cup vegetable stock
- 1 tsp lemon juice
- ¼ cup sun-dried tomatoes
- 1 cup heavy cream
- 1 cup baby spinach, packed

DIRECTIONS

1. Cook the pasta according to package directions in a large saucepan. Drain the water and set it aside.
2. Combine the flour, salt, pepper, and garlic powder in a large mixing bowl.
3. Dredge each salmon piece in flour, making sure it is well covered.
4. Select Sauté-then-Simmer STS® on the cooker. Allow it to heat for 5 minutes with the lid closed. Keep the lid open while adding the oil and butter.
5. Add the fish when the butter has melted. Only cook 2 at a time if necessary.
6. Cook for 3-4 minutes on one side, or until a beautiful crust has formed. Cook for 3-4 minutes on the other side as well. Check to see if the salmon is still raw. Remove the salmon from the inner saucepan and place it on a plate.
7. Add the vegetable stock, lemon juice, and sun dried tomatoes to the cooker while it is still set to STS®. Bring to a low simmer and continue to boil for a few minutes.
8. Stir in the heavy cream and cook for a few minutes more.
9. Fill the inner pot with spinach. Allow for 30 seconds of wilting while stirring, then return all of the fish to the pan, spooning some of the sauce on top.
10. Cook for a few minutes longer, until the salmon is cooked to your preference and the sauce has thickened slightly.
11. Spoon the sauce over the spaghetti and serve.

100. CREAMY CHICKEN NOODLE SOUP

SERVINGS: 8-10

PREP TIME: 10 MINUTES

COOK TIME: 40 MINUTES

INGREDIENTS

- 3 cups chopped cooked chicken, if desired
- 10 ounce can condensed chicken soup
- 48 ounces chicken broth
- 1 cup milk
- 5 stalks celery, chopped
- ¼ white onion, chopped
- 2 carrots, peeled and chopped
- 1 ounce packet ranch dressing mix
- 4 ounces cream cheese, softened
- 1½ cups cheddar cheese, shredded
- 8 ounces angel hair pasta, uncooked and broken in half
- salt & pepper, to taste

DIRECTIONS

1. Combine the chicken (if using), soup, chicken broth, milk, celery, onion, carrots, ranch mix, and cream cheese in the inner pot of your slow cooker. Stir it thoroughly.
2. Cover the cooker and set the timer for 30 minutes on the Steam function.
3. When the cooker begins to count down from 30, the contents have begun to boil. Give it a thorough stir after you've opened the lid.
4. Cook for 20 minutes with the lid open, stirring regularly. Make sure the soup stays at a rolling simmer; if it starts to dry out, gently close the lid but do not lock it. This allows the cover to be cracked and the heat to be maintained without the pot boiling over.
5. Add the broken noodles and cheese when the timer says 10 minutes is up on the cooker. Stir them well and cook for the remainder of the time with the lid open and stirring often to prevent the noodles from sticking together or to the bottom.
6. The noodles will be done cooking and the soup will be ready when the multicooker switches to Keep Warm. To taste, season with salt and pepper.
7. If the soup is too thick, add more stock until it reaches the required consistency. Enjoy by serving in bowls!

101. FRENCH ONION SOUP BOMBS

SERVINGS: 8

PREP TIME: 20 MINUTES

COOK TIME: 1 HOUR

INGREDIENTS

- 1 can flaky biscuit dough (8 biscuits)
- 2 tbsp butter
- 2 medium onions, thinly sliced
- 2 sprigs of thyme
- salt & pepper, to taste
- ¼ cup red wine
- ¼ cup flour
- 2 cloves garlic, minced
- 2 cups vegetable stock
- 1 cup Swiss cheese, shredded
- 8 slices mozzarella
- chopped parsley, to garnish

DIRECTIONS

1. Preheat the oven to 350 ° Fahrenheit.
2. Separate the biscuit dough into two parts. Roll each biscuit into a little ball between your hands to keep it in place.
3. Bake biscuits in DoveWare casserole dish according to package directions, plus a few minutes more to ensure golden browning.
4. Remove the pan from the oven and set aside to cool while you prepare the soup, leaving the oven on. Use readymade dinner rolls if you don't have an oven or want to save time.
5. Turn the cooker on to Sauté-Then-Simmer STS®, close the lid, and heat for a few minutes.
6. Place the butter in the inner pot and melt it.
7. Add the onion and thyme after it has melted, then season with salt and pepper.
8. Cook for about 20 minutes, stirring regularly with a long-handled wooden or heat-safe spoon, until soft and caramelized.
9. Discard the thyme and pour in the wine.
10. Bring to a moderate simmer and stew for a few minutes, or until most of the wine has evaporated.
11. Stir in the flour and garlic and cook, stirring constantly, for 2-3 minutes, or until the garlic is aromatic.
12. Stir in the stock until it is completely mixed. Allow for a few minutes of simmering time until the sauce has thickened.

13. Turn off the stove and set it aside to cool.
14. Hollow out the middle of each roll with a paring knife, creating a small cup for the soup bug, being careful not to cut through the bottom.
15. Spoon some swiss cheese into each of the rolls' holes. Place in a casserole dish and bake for 7 minutes at 350°F until the cheese is melted.
16. Take the rolls out of the oven. Fill each with part of the soup, then top with a slice of mozzarella.
17. Bake for a further 5-7 minutes, or until the cheese is completely melted.
18. Remove from the oven, set aside for 5 minutes to cool before serving, garnished with parsley.

102. SPINACH & GOAT CHEESE STUFFED SPAGHETTI SQUASH

SERVINGS: 4

PREP TIME: 10 MINUTES

COOK TIME: 1 HOUR

INGREDIENTS

- 1 medium spaghetti squash
- 2 tbsp olive oil
- 1 red onion, chopped
- 1 tbsp garlic powder
- 1 tsp oregano
- 1 tsp basil
- 2 cups spinach
- 4 oz goat cheese
- salt and pepper, to taste

DIRECTIONS

1. Preheat the oven to 400 ° Fahrenheit.
2. Thoroughly clean and dry the spaghetti squash. Poke holes in the squash with a fork from stem to base and back on the other side. Microwave for 2 minutes to soften and make cutting simpler.
3. CAREFULLY follow the fork poke holes on a cutting board and cut the squash in half with a knife.
4. Scoop off the seeds and stringy section of the meat using a spoon.
5. Drizzle the olive oil over the spaghetti squash cut side. Cut side down, place both halves in the casserole dish.
6. Preheat oven to 350°F and bake for 35-45 minutes.

7. Start making the filling while the squash is baking by setting the multicooker on Sauté-Then-Simmer STS®. Close the lid and heat for a few minutes.
8. Combine the onion, garlic powder, oregano, and basil in a mixing bowl. Cook until soft, about 5-8 minutes, stirring often with a long-handled wooden or heat-safe spoon.
9. When the onion is cooked, remove the pan from the heat and add the spinach. Stir for 2-3 minutes, or until the spinach is wilted.
10. Add the goat cheese and stir until it is completely melted. Set aside the filling in the pressure cooker.
11. Remove the squash from the oven once it has done cooking and let it cool for about 10 minutes.
12. Turn the spaghetti squash over so the meat side is facing up. Pull the flesh off the skin with a fork until it resembles spaghetti.
13. Place the spaghetti squash in the multicooker and stir to combine. Gently mix with the spinach filling. If desired, season with salt and pepper.
14. Serve by putting the filling back into the skin or scooping it into dishes.

103. LEMON PARMESAN ORZO

SERVINGS: 4

PREP TIME: 5 MINUTES

COOK TIME: 20 MINUTES

INGREDIENTS

- 1½ cups orzo, uncooked
- 1 tbsp olive oil
- 3 cloves garlic, minced
- 1 tsp fresh thyme leaves
- 3 cups vegetable broth
- 1 lemon, zested
- juice from half of the zested lemon
- 1½ cups frozen peas
- 1 cup parmesan, grated
- salt and pepper, to taste

DIRECTIONS

1. Select Sauté-Then-Simmer STS® on your multicooker. Add the oil, seal the top, and cook for a few minutes.
2. Stir in the orzo and toast for about 1 minute, stirring constantly with a long-handled wooden or heat-safe spoon.

3. Stir in the thyme and minced garlic. Cook for a few minutes, stirring constantly, until the garlic is aromatic.
4. Pour in 1 cup of the broth and mix well. Allow to cook until it reaches a boil with the lid open. Add another cup of broth and bring to a boil, then add the final cup and bring to a boil once more.
5. Cover the pot once all of the stock has been added and it has reached a boil. Cook for 14-16 minutes, or until the orzo is soft and the broth has been absorbed to a large extent.
6. Put the cooker on Keep Warm mode.
7. Stir in the lemon zest and juice, as well as the frozen peas. Stir for 3 minutes, or until the peas are thoroughly warmed.

Season with salt and pepper to taste, then add the parmesan. Stir until everything is fully blended, then serve hot.

104. DULCE DE LECHE CHEESECAKE

SERVING SIZE: 6

PREP TIME: 15 MINUTES

COOK TIME: 1 HOUR

INGREDIENTS

- 2 cans (13.4 oz) Dulce de Leche
- 16 oz cream cheese
- 3 large eggs
- 3 tbsp flour
- 1 cup shortbread cookies

DIRECTIONS

1. Put the inner pot in the freezer and leave it there until it is completely frozen.
2. In a medium mixing basin, beat the cream cheese with a handheld mixer for about 4 minutes, or until smooth and creamy. Then, one at a time, add the eggs, beating vigorously after each addition.
3. Continue mixing after adding the flour. Mix in 1 can of dulce de leche well.
4. Take the inner pot out of the freezer and pour the cream cheese filling into the chilled pot. Set your Aroma pressure cooker to "Brown Rice" and close the lid. Allow for 20-30 minutes of cooking time before turning off the oven.
5. Allow 10 minutes for the cheesecake to cool before manually removing the pressure.
6. The middle should jiggle a little! Allow it to chill for another 45 minutes in the freezer in the inner pot.

7. Fill a microwave-safe bowl halfway with Dulce de Leche. Microwave the dulce de leche for 30-45 seconds, or until it is soft and runny. This mixture should be poured on top of the chilled cheesecake.
8. Crumble the shortbread cookies into little bits in a resealable bag. (Alternatively, use a food processor.) On top of the cheesecake, strew cookie crumbs.
9. Chill for 4-6 hours or until firm.

105. PEANUT BUTTER CHOCOLATE SKILLET COOKIE

SERVINGS: 4-6

PREP TIME: 15 MINUTES

COOK TIME: 17 MINUTES

INGREDIENTS

- 1/4 cup butter, softened
- 1/4 cup coconut oil
- 1/2 cup brown sugar
- 1/2 cup sugar
- 2 eggs
- 1 tsp vanilla
- 2 cup all-purpose flour
- 1 tsp baking soda
- 1/2 cup peanut butter
- 1/2 cup chocolate chips
- 1/2 cup almonds
- ice cream, for serving
- melted chocolate, for serving

DIRECTIONS

1. Cream together the softened butter, coconut oil, and sugar with a hand mixer until light and fluffy.
2. Beat in the eggs and vanilla extract until well mixed.
3. Combine the peanut butter, flour, and baking soda in a mixing bowl until the batter resembles dough.
4. Add the chocolate chip and almonds and mix well.
5. Spread the dough evenly in the baking sheet and bake for 17 minutes on HIGH.
6. Allow it cool somewhat before serving with ice cream and melted chocolate drizzled on top.

106. HONEY-GLAZED BALSAMIC CARROTS

SERVINGS: 4-6

PREP TIME: 5 MINUTES

COOK TIME: 30 MINUTES

INGREDIENTS

- 2 lbs. rainbow carrots, peeled
- 1 tbsp olive oil
- 1/4 tsp salt
- 1/4 tsp pepper
- 2 tbsp honey
- 1/4 cup balsamic vinegar
- 1 tbsp butter, melted

DIRECTIONS

1. Drizzle 1 tbsp olive oil over the peeled carrots in the cooking pan. Salt & pepper to taste.
2. Set the timer for 20 minutes on HIGH.
3. Meanwhile, combine the honey, balsamic vinegar, and melted butter in a small basin.
4. After the carrots have been cooked for 20 minutes, pour the balsamic mixture into the frying pan and stir to coat all of the pieces evenly.
5. Cook for a further 10 minutes on HIGH.

If desired, season with more salt and pepper before serving.

107. BAKED BLUEBERRY OATMEAL

SERVINGS: 6-8

PREP TIME: 10 MINUTES

COOK TIME: 25 MINUTES

INGREDIENTS

- 2 cups old-fashioned oats
- 1/4 cup almond flour
- 1 tsp baking powder
- 1/4 tsp baking soda
- 1/2 tsp salt
- 1/4 cup sugar
- 2 tbsp butter, melted
- 2 cup milk
- 1/4 cup blueberry yogurt
- 2 eggs
- 2 cup blueberries

DIRECTIONS

1. In a large mixing bowl, combine the oats, almond flour, baking powder, baking soda, salt, and sugar; set aside.
2. Whisk together the blueberry yogurt, eggs, melted butter, and milk in a separate bowl until well blended.
3. Combine the wet and dry ingredients in a large mixing bowl. Fold the blueberries into the mixture until it has been well absorbed.
4. Pour the contents of the mixing bowl into the frying pan.
5. Cook for 25 minutes on HIGH in the air fryer.
6. Allow 15 minutes for the oats to cool before serving warm with maple syrup and whipped cream, if desired.

108. TWISTED NUTELLA BREAD

SERVINGS: 10

PREP TIME: 15 MINUTES

COOK TIME: 3 HOURS

INGREDIENTS

- 1 cup milk
- 3 tbsp butter, cubed
- 1 tsp salt
- 4 tbsp sugar
- 5 tbsp milk powder
- 3 cups flour
- 1 tsp active dry yeast
- 1 cup Nutella or hazelnut spread

DIRECTIONS

1. Fill the baking cavity with milk, butter, salt, sugar, milk powder, flour, and active dry yeast, then select the Raw Dough option.
2. Transfer the dough to a level, lightly floured work surface and roll out to a 1/2 inch thick rectangle once the cycle is through.
3. Spread the Nutella or hazelnut spread evenly over the rolled-out dough with a spatula, going all the way to the edges of the dough.
4. Roll the dough tightly lengthwise. Place the log seam side down and cut it in half lengthwise.
5. With each half-cut side facing up, screw the two halves together.
6. Remove the bread maker's churning paddle and return the twisted dough to the baking cavity.
7. Choose Ferment as the function and let the cycle run for 1 1/2 hours.
8. Select the Bake function when the Ferment cycle has finished and bake the bread for 1 hour.
9. When the bread is done, remove it from the baking cavity and serve!

109. BACON CHEDDAR SCONES

SERVINGS: 2-4

PREP TIME: 10 MINUTES

COOK TIME: 43 MINUTES

INGREDIENTS

- 1 cup milk
- 3/4 cup butter, softened
- 1 egg
- 5 tsp baking powder
- 1/2 tsp salt
- 1/2 cup sugar
- 3 cups all-purpose flour
- 1/2 cup cheddar
- 1/2 cup cooked bacon, chopped

DIRECTIONS

1. Place all ingredients in the baking cavity of your bread maker, except the bacon and cheese. Set the timer for 23 minutes and select the Raw Dough function.
2. For the last 5 minutes of the Raw Dough function, add the cheese and bacon.
3. Place the dough on a floured board and spread it out to a thickness of about 1/2 inch.
4. Cut the dough into bite-sized pieces, about 1 inch by 1 inch, and set them in the air fryer frying pan.
5. Preheat the air fryer to medium heat and set the timer for 20 minutes.
6. When the pieces are done, remove them from the pan and set them on a serving platter. Serve with butter and jam of your choice.

110. MEAT LOVERS PIZZA

SERVINGS: 2

PREP TIME: 10 MINUTES

COOK TIME: 1 HOUR 54 MINUTES

INGREDIENTS

- 3 cup flour
- 1 cup warm water
- 2 tbsp olive oil
- 1 tsp salt
- 1 tbsp active dry yeast
- 1/2 cup pizza sauce
- 1 1/2 cup mozzarella cheese, shredded
- 1 cup sausage, cut or crumbled into small pieces
- 1 cup grilled chicken breast, cut into bite-sized pieces
- 1 cup meatballs, cut into bite-sized pieces
- 4 pepperoni slices
- 1/2 cup arugula

DIRECTIONS

1. In the bread maker, combine flour, water, olive oil, salt, and yeast, then select the Leaven Dough setting. Transfer the dough to a lightly floured work surface and divide it in half after the cycle is finished.
2. Roll out the dough into a 12-inch circle. Transfer the dough to the air fryer heating surface and evenly pour the pizza sauce across the top.
3. On top of the sauce, spread 1 cup mozzarella cheese.
4. Evenly distribute the sausage, grilled chicken breast, meatballs, and pepperoni slices on top of the cheese. The remaining mozzarella cheese should be sprinkled on top.
5. Preheat the air fryer to HIGH and cook for 16 minutes.

When the pizza is done baking, remove it from the pan and top with fresh arugula.

111. TOMATO AVOCADO MELTS

SERVINGS: 3

PREP TIME: 5 MINUTES

COOK TIME: 4 MINUTES

INGREDIENTS

- 3 slices bread of your choice
- 1½ tbsp mayonnaise
- chili powder, to taste
- 1 Roma tomatoes, sliced
- 1 avocado, sliced
- 6 slices cheese of your choice

DIRECTIONS

1. On one side of each slice of bread, spread around 12 tbsps of mayonnaise.
2. Season with a pinch of chile powder, to taste.
3. Arrange the tomato and avocado pieces on the toast.

4. Add two slices of cheese on top, then place them in the air fryer pan. If necessary, work in batches.
5. Set the timer for 4 minutes on HIGH in the air fryer.
6. Place the lid on the pot and simmer until the timer beeps.
1. Tastes Better From Scratch provided the inspiration for this recipe.

112. GARLIC PARMESAN FRIES

SERVINGS: 1

PREP TIME: 10 MINUTES

COOK TIME: 25 MINUTES

INGREDIENTS

- 1 russet potato, peeled and cut into French fry shaped wedges
- 1 tbsp olive oil
- ½ tbsp garlic powder
- ¼ cup Parmesan cheese, grated salt & pepper, to taste
- nonstick cooking spray
- ½ tbsp parsley, finely chopped

DIRECTIONS

1. Place the potato pieces in a medium bowl after cutting them to the desired size.
2. In a large mixing bowl, combine the oil, garlic powder, cheese, and any salt and pepper, and stir to coat all of the potato pieces equally.
3. Use aluminum foil to line the grill grate so the French fries don't fall through. Using cooking spray, lightly coat the aluminum foil-lined grill grate. Place in the cooking pan's center.
4. Arrange the fries on the grill grate in a non-overlapping pattern (it is OK if they are crowded as long as they do not touch or overlap).
5. Replace the lid. Turn the air fryer to HIGH and set the timer for 20 minutes after plugging it in.
6. After about 10 minutes of cooking, remove the lid. Carefully turn over all of the French fries with silicone tipped tongs that will not harm the cooking pan.
7. Continue to cook for another 10 minutes, or until they're done to your liking.
8. Remove the fries from the air fryer with tongs and place on a plate or in a bowl.
9. Season with salt and parsley while still heated. Allow to cool slightly before serving.

113. AVOCADO & HUMMUS QUESADILLAS

SERVINGS: 8 QUESADILLAS

PREP TIME: 10 MINUTES

COOK TIME: 40 MINUTES

INGREDIENTS

- 8 whole wheat fajita-size tortillas
- 8 ounces roasted red pepper hummus
- 2 tsps cumin
- 2 tbsps cilantro, minced
- 1 avocado, each half cut into 12 slices
- 8 ounces queso fresco

DIRECTIONS

1. Take one of the tortillas and spread about 2 tbsps hummus all over it, leaving a little room around the borders.
2. Season the hummus with cumin and cilantro.
3. Arrange three slices of avocado on one half of the tortilla. You want the slices to be thin; believe me, more isn't always better in this case!
4. Top the avocado with about 2 tbsps queso fresco. To make a half-circle, fold the tortilla in half.
5. Place the quesadilla in the air fryer's cooking pan with the straight edge in the middle.
6. To prepare another quesadilla, repeat steps 1-4, then place in the air fryer with the other so that their two straight edges are facing each other.

7. Put the lid back on. Set the timer for 6 minutes in the air fryer on MED. After the timer beeps, carefully flip the quesadillas over and cook for an additional 6 minutes. Remove the air fryer from the oven.

Continue preparing and heating tortillas until all of the ingredients have been used up and the quesadillas are ready.

114. SUMMER SQUASH & TOMATO BAKE

SERVING SIZE: 6-8

PREP TIME: 5 MINUTES

COOK TIME: 45 MINUTES

INGREDIENTS

- 4 tomatoes, sliced
- 4 zucchini, sliced
- 5 yellow squash, sliced
- 1/4 cup plus 4 tbsps marinara sauce
- 1/4 cup Parmesan cheese, grated (use nutritional yeast or non-dairy cheese for vegan option)
- salt & pepper, to taste

DIRECTIONS

1. Cut small circles out of the tomatoes, zucchini, and yellow squash.
2. Spread 1/4 cup marinara sauce evenly across the bottom of the air fryer pan with a rubber spatula.
3. Arrange the vegetables in a spiral or any pattern you desire by standing them up in a circle around the perimeter and proceeding towards the center.
4. Season with salt and pepper, then top with a dollop of the remaining sauce and a sprinkling of Parmesan cheese.
5. Replace the lid. Connect your air fryer to the outlet, set the temperature to MED, and set the timer for 30 minutes.
6. After the full time has passed, set the timer for another 15 minutes and continue cooking until desired doneness has been reached.
7. When the pan is done, take it from the cooker using the heat-resistant handles and place it on a heat-proof oven mitt or pot holder. Allow a few minutes for it to cool.
8. Using a wooden or silicone spoon that will not scratch the cooking pan, scoop out the vegetables.

115. CRISPY CAULIFLOWER BITES

SERVING SIZE: 2-4

PREP TIME: 20 MINUTES

COOK TIME: 15 MINUTES

INGREDIENTS

- 1 head of cauliflower
- 3 eggs
- 2 tbsps milk
- salt and pepper to taste
- 1 cup Italian seasoned bread crumbs
- 1 cup Panko bread crumbs
- ½ cup grated Parmesan cheese
- nonstick cooking spray

DIRECTIONS

1. Cut the cauliflower into bite-size florets and keep them aside.
2. In a medium-sized mixing bowl, whisk together the eggs, milk, and salt and pepper, then put aside.
3. Combine the two types of bread crumbs with the cheese in a separate bowl.
4. Insert the grill grate into the air fryer's middle.
5. Dip the cauliflower florets in the egg mixture one at a time, then roll in the breadcrumb mixture, shaking off the excess.
6. Place the florets on the grill grate of the air fryer after coating them; if necessary, protect the grate with aluminum foil to prevent the florets from falling through. Depending on the size of your head of cauliflower, you may need to cook it in batches.
7. Lightly spritz the breaded cauliflower with the nonstick spray. This will ensure that they are crispy and golden on the outside. Put the lid back on.
8. Connect the air fryer to the outlet. Set the timer for 15 minutes and turn the dial to HIGH.
9. Cook the cauliflower until the timer goes off.
10. Remove the cauliflower bits with silicone tipped tongs that will not harm the frying pan after opening the lid.
11. Serve with ketchup on the side.

116. SWEET POTATO & BLACK BEAN FLAUTAS

SERVING SIZE: 12 FLAUTAS

PREP TIME: 10 MINUTES

COOK TIME: 30 MINUTES

INGREDIENTS

- 1 large sweet potato
- 15 oz black beans, drained and rinsed
- 1½ cups frozen corn
- ½ sweet yellow onion, diced
- 1 tbsp diced chipotles in adobo
- ½ tsp chili powder
- ½ tsp garlic powder
- ½ tsp cumin
- ¼ tsp cayenne
- 2 tbsps salsa
- 12-15 taco sized corn tortillas
- 1 cup pepper jack cheese, shredded (or non-dairy cheese for vegan option)
- salt and pepper to taste
- nonstick cooking spray

DIRECTIONS

1. Poke a few holes in your sweet potato with a fork. Microwave for 8 minutes, wrapped in a slightly damp paper towel.
2. In a large mixing bowl, combine the black beans, corn, diced onion, chipotles, chili powder, garlic powder, cumin, cayenne, and salsa while the sweet potato cooks.
3. Cut the sweet potato in half and fluff the inside with a fork when it's done. Combine the sweet potato flesh with the black bean and corn mixture and stir completely. To taste, season with salt and pepper.
4. Wrap each tortilla in a damp paper towel and microwave for 30 seconds in small batches of 3 or 4. The idea is to steam the tortillas to make them easy to roll without breaking.
5. Spray the nonstick spray on one side of the tortilla and flip it over. Fill the center with a line of veggie filling. Add a layer of cheese on top.
6. Make a roll with the tortilla. To keep it closed, secure it with a few toothpicks. In the air fryer, place the rolled flauta on the grill grate.
7. Continue until the grill grate is completely full, about 4 flautas.
8. Lightly mist the flautas' tops with nonstick spray. Put the lid back on.
1. Set the timer for 20 minutes on HIGH in the air fryer.

9. After about 17 minutes, check the flautas to see if they are done and crispy to your preference. If preferred, cook for a further 3 minutes.
10. Remove the flautas from the air fryer with silicone tongs. Remove the toothpicks with care.
11. Continue with steps 4–11 until all of the flautas are cooked. Fresh cilantro, sour cream, and guacamole are optional garnishes.

117. GWEN'S BREAKFAST TACOS

SERVINGS: 5 TACOS

PREP TIME: 10 MINUTES

COOK TIME: 10 MINUTES

INGREDIENTS

- tortillas of choice, flour or corn
- 1/2 white onion, diced
- 1 large potato, diced
- 1 cup red and yellow bell peppers, diced
- 5 eggs, beaten
- 1 cup cheddar cheese, shredded
- cilantro, for garnish
- lime, to taste
- 1 avocado
- salt and pepper, to taste
- olive oil

DIRECTIONS

1. Preheat the grill pan by coating the bottom with oil and allowing it to heat up.
2. Once the oven is warmed, add the diced potatoes and season to taste with salt and pepper.
3. Cook for 10-12 minutes, or until the potatoes are crispy, then add the diced onions. TIP: REFRAIN FROM STIRRING THE POTATOES WHILE COOKING TO GET PERFECTLY CRISPED POTATOES.
4. Stir in the diced bell peppers when the onions have become translucent.
5. Remove the grill pan from the base and replace it with the stainless steel pot after the peppers have softened.
6. In a stainless steel pot, combine the beaten eggs and shredded cheese and cook over high heat until the eggs are totally set.
7. Toss the potato mixture and scrambled eggs onto each tortilla, then top with avocado slices, cilantro, and lime, if preferred.

118. BACON-WRAPPED HOT DOGS

SERVINGS: 4

PREP TIME: 20 MINUTES

COOK TIME: 20 MINUTES

INGREDIENTS

- 6 kosher hot dogs
- 6 strips of bacon
- 6 hot dog buns
- 2 cups frozen corn
- 2 cups sweet onion, finely chopped
- 2 tbsp butter
- 2 tbsp parsley, chopped
- salt and pepper, to taste

DIRECTIONS

1. Secure each hot dog with a toothpick after wrapping a strip of bacon around it.
2. Preheat your Grillet to 450°F and grill the hot dogs for 1 minute on each side.
3. Arrange all of the hot dogs on one side of the Grillet, then tilt the pan slightly to gather the bacon fat on the empty side. Reduce the heat to 350°F and stir in the diced sweet onion and 12 tbsps butter to the bacon fat. Sauté until golden and translucent, about 5 minutes.
4. Remove the bacon-wrapped hot dogs and onions from the grill once they've finished cooking.
5. Wipe the excess oil from the grill pan with a paper towel before adding the remaining butter and frozen corn. As needed, stir until the corn has just started to color. To taste, season with salt and pepper.
6. Remove the corn from the Grillet and combine with the chopped parsley.
7. Layer grilled onions and/or corn on top of the bacon-wrapped hot dogs in the buns, if preferred.

119. CLASSIC AMERICAN BREAKFAST

SERVINGS: 2

PREP TIME: 5 MINUTES

COOK TIME: 15 HOUR

INGREDIENTS

- 2 large eggs
- 4 slices of bacon
- 4 breakfast sausages
- 2 cups shredded hash browns
- 1 tsp olive oil

DIRECTIONS

1. Preheat the grillet to 400 ° Fahrenheit. Place hash browns in a heated pan with a thin layer of olive oil. With a spatula, flatten the potatoes into a consistent thickness around the pan. Once the bottom is crispy, cut it into four halves and turn. Cook until the crispiness is to your liking.
2. Reduce the heat to 350°F, crack the egg into the pan, and cook for 3 minutes, or until the whites are mostly set. Near the yolks, there should be some still-runny whites.
3. Transfer the griddle pan to the oven and preheat to 350°F. Cook for 7 to 10 minutes after laying out the bacon and sausage. Every 2 minutes, flip the bacon and sausage until golden and crispy.
4. Place the bacon and sausages on a dish lined with paper towels using tongs. Serve with hash browns and eggs.

120. BEER-BASTED BABY BACK RIBS WITH MUSHROOMS

SERVINGS: 2-4

PREP TIME: 20 MINUTES

COOK TIME: 1 HOUR

INGREDIENTS

- 1 rack of pork baby back ribs
- 1 tbsp salt
- 2 tsp garlic powder
- 2 tsp onion powder
- 2 tsp black pepper
- 1 tsp cayenne pepper
- 3 tbsp dark brown sugar
- 12 oz. dark beer
- 16 oz. mushroom

DIRECTIONS

1. Cut the ribs in half or as small as possible in order to put them into a large basin. Combine all of the spices and 6 oz dark beer in a large mixing basin. Rub the ribs with the beer spice mixture. Allow them to sit in the refrigerator overnight, covered.
2. Preheat the grillet to 450 ° Fahrenheit. Remove the ribs from the basin, pat them dry, and store the remaining beer mixture for another time.
3. Arrange the ribs in the grill pan and cook for 5 minutes on each side, or until the ribs have lovely grill marks.
4. Pour in all of the leftover mixture, cover, and preheat the grill to 300°F.
5. Remove the ribs from the grill after 40 minutes or when the internal temperature reaches 195°F.

Preheat the grill to 400°F and mix in the mushrooms with the remaining 6 oz dark beer. Cook until the mushrooms are softened, then serve!

121. TRI-TIP TACOS WITH GRILLED PINEAPPLE SALSA

SERVINGS: 4

PREP TIME: 25 MINUTES

COOK TIME: 45 MINUTES

INGREDIENTS

- 1 tablespoon ground coffee
- 2 tsp brown sugar
- 2 tablespoon salt
- 2 tablespoon pepper
- 2 lb tri-tip
- 2 cups of tomato, diced
- 6 fresh pineapple rings
- ½ cup onion, chopped
- ☐ ¼ cup fresh cilantro, chopped
- 3 tablespoon lime juice
- 1 bag corn tortillas
- guacamole

DIRECTIONS

1. In a small mixing bowl, combine the ground coffee, salt, pepper, and brown sugar. Season the tri-tip all over with the spice and gently press it into the meat. Place the beef in a storage bag and place it in the refrigerator overnight (or at least 6 hours). Place the tri-tip on a platter and set aside to come to room temperature before grilling.
2. Preheat the grillet to 450 ° Fahrenheit. Grill the pineapple rings for 2 minutes on each side before chopping them up.
3. Combine the pineapple, tomato, onion, and cilantro in a large mixing basin. Stir in the lime juice until everything is well combined.
4. Place the tri-tip on the Grillet and cook at 450°F for 5 minutes per side. Reduce the heat to 350°F, cover, and cook for 10 minutes on each side.
5. Place the tri-tip on a cutting board and set aside for 15 minutes to rest.
6. Heat corn tortillas on the Grillet at 350°F until heated while the tri-tip is resting.
7. Slice the tri-tip and fill each tortilla with the proper amount of meat. Top with guacamole and grilled pineapple salsa.

122. TUNA MELT

SERVINGS: 2

PREP TIME: 15 MINUTES

COOK TIME: 12 MINUTES

INGREDIENTS

- 4 slices Brioche bread
- 1 6-oz can tuna
- 2 tbsp mayonnaise
- 1 tbsp green onion, chopped
- 2 slices smoked gouda cheese
- 2 slices sharp cheddar cheese
- salt and pepper to taste

DIRECTIONS

1. Preheat the grillet to 300 ° Fahrenheit. Combine mayonnaise, drained tuna, and green onion in a large mixing basin. Break up the tuna into flakes with a fork. Salt & pepper to taste.
2. Spread tuna mixture on one slice of bread, then top with 1 slice sharp cheddar cheese, 1 slice smoked gouda cheese, and another slice of bread. Place the remaining ingredients on Grillet and repeat with the other ingredients. Grill for 6 minutes on each side.

123. S'MORES MINI PIE

SERVINGS: 4-8

PREP TIME: 15 MINUTES

COOK TIME: 5 MINUTES

INGREDIENTS

- 1 pie crust dough
- 12 milk chocolate segments
- 1 cup graham cracker crumbs
- 20 mini marshmallows

DIRECTIONS

1. Cut the pie crust dough into eight rounds by rolling it out (about 3 inches each).
2. In the middle of the dough circle, sprinkle one tbsp of graham cracker crumbs.
3. Add a chocolate square and 5 small marshmallows.

4. Moisten the dough's edges. Fold the dough over the s'mores toppings and firmly press it down.
5. Next, fold the edges up and press them into a cushion form.
6. Preheat the Grillet at 350 ° Fahrenheit. Begin by cooking one side of the small s'mores pies for two minutes.
7. Cook the bottoms of the small pies for two minutes after flipping them over.
8. Finally, set the Grillet to Warm for one minute more.
9. To serve, top with marshmallows and chocolate after removing them from the grill.

124. APPLE GINGER CIDER

SERVINGS: 4

PREP TIME: 5 MINUTES

COOK TIME: 14 MINUTES

INGREDIENTS

- 4 cups unfiltered apple juice
- 4 cup water
- 2 ginger tea bags, unsweetened
- ☐ 2 tsp cinnamon stick

DIRECTIONS

1. Fill your kettle halfway with water and bring to a boil. Open the top after the boiling cycle is finished and add the ginger tea bag inside. Allow for a 7-minute steeping period.
2. Combine the ginger tea and apple juice in a heat-safe mug or cup and stir with a cinnamon stick.
3. Serve immediately!

125. BUTTERFLY PEA LEMONADE

SERVINGS: 4

PREP TIME: 5 MINUTES

COOK TIME: 14 MINUTES

INGREDIENTS

- 5 cups water
- ½ cup sugar
- ☐ ½ cup dry butterfly pea flower
- 1 cup freshly squeezed lemon juice

DIRECTIONS

1. Fill the kettle halfway with water and sugar, then bring to a boil.
2. After the cycle has completed, open the lid and add the dried butterfly pea blossom. Allow for a 10-minute steeping period.
3. Remove the flowers from the liquid with a strainer.
4. Fill the cup with 1 tsp lemon juice. Serve over ice with extra dried butterfly pea tea.

125. HIBISCUS TEA

SERVINGS: 4

PREP TIME: 5 MINUTES

COOK TIME: 14 MINUTES

INGREDIENTS

- 4 cups water
- ½ cup sugar
- ☐ ½ cup dry hibiscus

DIRECTIONS

1. Fill the kettle halfway with water and sugar, then bring it to a boil.
2. After the cycle is complete, remove the cover and add the dry hibiscus. Allow for a 10-minute steeping period.
3. Remove the hibiscus from the liquid by straining it.
4. Serve cooled after pouring over ice.

The end

Made in the USA
Thornton, CO
12/09/24 14:58:26

d11e57b4-1f42-437a-bdbc-09bb00e1d18eR01